LONG AGO, FAR AWAY

The Burma Diaries
of
Doris Sarah Easton

COMPILED BY

M. Sylvia Morris

MINERVA PRESS
MONTREUX LONDON WASHINGTON

LONG AGO, FAR AWAY
THE BURMA DIARIES OF DORIS SARAH EASTON

ISBN 1 85863 048 7

First published 1994 by

MINERVA PRESS
2, Old Brompton Road
London SW7 3DQ

Printed in Great Britain by
B.W.D. Ltd., Northolt, Middlesex.

LONG AGO, FAR AWAY

The Burma Diaries
of
Doris Sarah Easton

CONTENTS

CHAPTER I

THE CALL TO MANDALAY

From the diary of Doris Sarah Easton, May 14 1915: "Post as head-teacher at St Mary's school, Mandalay - chaplain wants lady with degree, keen, energetic and sympathetic - experience not necessary."

Mother kept diaries for over fifty years. I do not know when she began. The earliest we now possess dates from November 1904 when she was fifteen and at boarding-school in Harrogate: the last ends in April 1958, a few days before her death. Memory recalls her sitting on the sofa or at her bureau, usually on a Sunday, writing up her account of the week's events if she had not already completed it. We would tease her by pretending to look over her shoulder to read the entries, only to have the book indignantly snapped shut against us. For the diaries were "Strictly Private", the one exception being the journals which were sent from Burma to her family between 1915 and 1919 in place of a weekly letter.

Doris Sarah Easton was born on October 12th 1889 in Cleckheaton at the heart of the Yorkshire textile industry, "the dark satanic mills" and tall chimneys of the industrial revolution. Her childhood memories were of the "knocker" waking the workers in the dark and the sound of clogs as the shawled women made their way to the factories. Her father, the Reverend E. W. Easton, was vicar of St. Luke's, Cleckheaton. It was his first incumbency, later to be followed by others in the diocese of Wakefield, at Warley and Ripponden, until as an old man he moved back to Herefordshire where he had lived when a boy. His wife, Sarah Woolley, came from Somerset. The daughter of a "gentleman farmer", she had a sense of social distinction which in some measure she imparted to her children, though in them - and perhaps in her - it was tempered by the rough and tumble of Yorkshire parish life as well as a liking for people and an enjoyment of the ridiculous. Mrs. Easton was a little older than her husband and over forty when she married him. Nevertheless she bore him four children, Gertrude (born 1884) Mildred (1885) Hubert (1887) and Doris. Hubert died tragically when he was three, but the girls survived and maintained a close relationship throughout their lives. They were good-looking, intelligent and gifted. Gertrude was, I suppose, the most academic in her interests; she read History at Oxford and taught for many years at Barnsley High School. Mildred trained at Athol Crescent, Edinburgh; she, like her younger sister, had inherited her father's musical talents as well as being artistic and an excellent cook. Doris, having failed in an attempt to win a scholarship to Girton, went to Westfield College, London; where she was happy and successful, taking a "first" in Classics.

Of course the girls knew they must earn sufficient to be independent of their parents, for the Eastons were not well-off. The money for their daughters' education had partly, I believe, been supplied by the Crosslands, Quakers who were friends of the family; partly by living a very simple, almost austere life, and by taking lodgers to supplement my grandfather's stipend. However, like most middle-class families of the period, they kept a resident maid, Martha West, who came to them at the age of fifteen when Gertrude was born, and remained with them and their children after them for more than fifty years. She was always known, even to later generations, as Nurse.

At Westfield, Doris Easton came under the influence of the fervent evangelism of the Mistress, Constance Maynard, and her strong Temperance principles. As she had been brought up in a teetotal and "low" church home, Westfield merely confirmed in her views to which she was already inclined. Yet although the early pages of the Burma diaries give the impression of a kind of stubborn narrowness, she was too intelligent to be rigid in her opinions. Much less extreme then some of her contemporaries, and incidentally than Miss Maynard herself, she enjoyed both the theatre and the early cinema, the bioscope. Nor was she a fundamentalist in her attitude to the Bible. Nevertheless the earnest faith and missionary spirit of staff and students of Westfield made a deep impression on her, particularly, I suspect, the personality of one of the tutors, Eleanor Macdougal, who was to become the first principal of Madras College for Women. She was also affected to some extent by the emotionalism which afflicted women's colleges of the period, the intense personal relationships - the kisses, the tears and passion. In those days of more formal manners, even the exchange of Christian names marked a significant point in a friendship and had to be requested ritually. A girl "proposed" or "popped" the question to another. All this strikes us as absurd, even distasteful. It is difficult in reading my mother's account of her student years to avoid an uneasy sense of a faintly morbid sentimentality which was certainly foreign to her nature as I knew her.

Doris Sarah Easton took her finals in 1911 and fulfilled her ambition of getting to Cambridge by a year at Cambridge Training College under Miss Wood. In 1912 she accepted a post as assistant mistress at the Girls' High School in Warwick, intending to gain experience and then offer herself for work in the mission field. She did not want to wait too long, for her mother was now in her late sixties and Doris believed it would be her duty to care for her parents in their old age. Of her sisters, Gertrude was neither robust nor stable: years later the mysterious lameness and semi-paralysis from which she intermittently suffered was diagnosed as multiple sclerosis. Mildred was anxious to marry and start a family of her own: though no man was yet in sight, she was very attractive, warm-hearted and practical: it seemed unlikely she would have to wait long. Doris was certainly a feminist of her period. She supported the suffragettes though she did not approve of the violence of some of their demonstrations: she believed firmly in higher education and careers for women, deploring the idea that marriage was the only possible goal of a lady's existence. Yet her loving, faithful heart could reconcile this with a belief in the duty of children to look after their parents even if it should entail sacrificing their own careers. She accepted, too, that marriage must put an end to other ambitions. Perhaps for that reason, marriage did not form part of her plan for her life. She was going to go out, under one of the missionary societies, to a heathen country, work there for five years or so, spreading the gospel and educating perhaps very poor and primitive people; then return to England to make a home for her parents and take up school-teaching again. Probably she did not formulate it quite as clearly as I have suggested, but something like that was in her mind.

It did not turn out as she had expected. Doris Easton loved teaching and was quickly absorbed in her work at Warwick. A change in headmistresses, which came at the end of her second year, may have helped to shift her from a pleasant and useful rut. By this time the Great War had begun. The optimism which had predicted that it would all be over by Christmas is certainly not reflected in the diaries for October to December 1914: "Turkey has joined in the war," she writes on October 31st, "on the side of Germany. I am afraid it will all prolong it" and she records the sinking of British cruisers and the fall of Antwerp, as well as other disasters. Nevertheless she was not deterred from her intention to serve as a missionary. I have indeed wondered whether the prevalent emphasis on self-sacrifice may not have sharpened her determination.

On November 8th, 1914, Westfield held a farewell celebration for Eleanor Macdougal who was going to America before taking up her post at the Madras College. Doris had an opportunity to talk to Miss Macdougal. "She asked me if I was going out and we talked about that... She asked if I wanted to go. I asked if she did. She does not want to, but says it has to be done and she will be interested." In the following February Doris spent a week-end at Cambridge Training College. Here again the subject of missionary work was discussed, largely because she was now not happy about the way the new headmistress was running the school. The principal listened sympathetically to her troubles, and then "she asked me if I felt inclined to leave, so then with much hesitation I told her about going abroad." Miss Wood offered to write to the Church Missionary Society and enquire if educated people were wanted. "I said I did not know if I was orthodox enough, but she thought they would be sympathetic about that." Miss Wood did write to the C.M.S. However Canon Waller, with whom she corresponded, was doubtful and later it emerged that the society, with a deficit of £1,400, could not afford to send out new missionaries. Meanwhile Doris had broken the news of her plans to her family. "After supper I told Mother I thought it was about time I saw about being a missionary. It seemed to come as rather a blow. I think she almost thought I had given up the idea. She said she could not refuse to give me up."

This was in April. She had not yet lost all hope of being accepted by the C.M.S. Then on Friday May 14th 1915 came what she describes as "a perfect thunderbolt" in a letter from Miss Wood: "post as head-teacher at St Mary's school, Mandalay - chaplain wants a lady with degree, keen energetic and sympathetic - experience *not* necessary - £10 a month and board and lodging, to go to Rangoon in October, study method 2 months and take over charge in January

1916. I felt perfectly miserable." Next day she heard finally from the C.M.S. that there was no chance of her being accepted for training at present; she was advised to stay on in Warwick for another year and apply again.

If Doris Easton hoped that something would indicate that St Mary's Mandalay was not the post for her, she was to be disappointed. Her own mother was willing for her to apply, in fact saw advantages in her going immediately as she feared that if her daughter was to wait for a year, train, then work for five years with the C.M.S. she would never see her again. The head of her school, too, was encouraging and thought she might well be the right person for the post. "She seemed to think it would be wise to apply and let the matter be taken out of my hands." So the application and a testimonial were sent off on May 27th to the Miss Hetty Lea who had approached Miss Wood. An interview was arranged for Thursday June 3rd.

Then came another blow - a letter from Miss Lister, whose brother was the chaplain at Mandalay, offering her the post. "I had expected peace at any rate until after (the interview)". The whole story of the appointment is remarkably complicated. It seems that Mr Lister had wanted his sister, then teaching in Beverley near Hull, to join him in Burma and take over the headship of the girls' section of the new school he was proposing to found.

However, she was unwilling to take the post. Instead she wrote to the principal of Westfield, now Miss de Selincourt in place of Miss Maynard, to enquire if she could recommend anyone. At that point a letter arrived at Westfield from Doris Easton saying that Miss Wood of Cambridge Training College had sent her particulars of a post in Mandalay. Accordingly Miss de Selincourt forwarded Miss Easton's name and details of her qualifications and experience. By chance Miss Lister had been at college with one of the Warwick staff, to whom she now applied for information. On the strength of what she was told, she wrote offering the post, by-passing Hetty Lea who, without his sister's knowledge, had been asked by Mr Lister to find a suitable candidate. Miss Easton tried to gain a little more time by suggesting that the offer should be withdrawn until she had been interviewed. At first Miss Lister agreed. But as Doris was setting out for the interview a telegram arrived saying that it was not necessary, so even this respite was denied. As she comments, "I seem to have been enmeshed."

Nothing she heard made the prospect of Mandalay very attractive. Mission work in Burma, as far as the Church of England was concerned, came under the auspices of the S.P.G. (Society for the Propagation of the Gospel), and the S.P.G. was "high". Nor was what she was told about the Listers themselves particularly encouraging. Miss Pyke, one of the Warwick staff, had taught with Miss Lister in Beverley. "She thinks them rather a mad unpractical family - the father a clergyman near Cheltenham very low - this daughter very high and does not seem to get on well with the brother and less well with the wife who was a girl here and knew Miss Monte. She thinks from what the sister says that the brother is rather pig-headed and interfering. Felt rather down." In spite of misgivings she accepted the post on June 19th, only to face a barrage of discouragement from the Westfield staff. When she visited the college on June 19th, "Miss Richardson put her case that all the business arrangements were unsatisfactory etc. Miss de S. strongly agreed and was very much against my going - absolutely unreasonable to have to pay passage and sign 5 years agreement. I should have no one to look after me, no arrangements or allowances for holidays, no one responsible if invalided home for life, no pension, I ought to be assistant first and learn from others' experience etc, etc." Miss Easton was not to be budged. "When Miss de S. left the room to say good-bye to (another student) I told Miss R. I thought I ought not to give it up, so when Miss de S. returned she held my hand and told her I felt I had a concern to go." Later Miss de Selincourt suggested that she might be insisting upon going because she did not want to, falling into the snare of imagining that the uncongenial and difficult must be God's will for her. Though ready to consider this, Doris Easton remained firm in her intention.

In the prevailing quagmire of muddle, this intention was about all that did remain firm, though doubtless with more inward qualms than the diary records. To gain first hand information was very difficult. The prospectus the chaplain had compiled revealed nothing about the schools size and curriculum. Miss Lister was more informative, but had not, of course, actually been there. An interview at the S.P.G. headquarters in London added to the confusion. The two ladies who saw her advised her to have everything in black and white "as the

Bishop of Rangoon is so unbusinesslike." She was told that the school had not been started under the auspices of the Society, which could take no responsibility if it failed. Yet the medical examination which followed the interview - with a "Mephistopheles looking man - yellow-pointed beard, bad teeth" - was apparently arranged by the S.P.G. Later, on July 6th, she saw the Society's Bishop Knight who was kind but could not really be very helpful as he knew little. "Bishop Knight appeared younger than I expected... We sat and talked about 20 minutes. He said he thought Mr Lister had been very unbusinesslike and it would have been much better to have it a proper Diocesan school or under the Bishop and he would try to get me proper arrangements. He asked me if I were doing this for the kingdom or for professional advancement. He knew practically nothing about the school and could not answer my questions, so I asked him hardly any. After about twenty minutes, he fetched his things and we got a taxi and walked to Cannon Street and walked up and down the platform. It was difficult and uncomfortable to hear what he said amid the screeching trains. He had seen Miss Openshaw (who was to be second mistress at the school) and liked her very much but very young, only 21 or 22 and inexperienced. (Miss Lister said she had taught a good many years.)... He said the only thing was to pray that an obstacle might be raised up if I were not meant to go." These discouraging interviews were followed on August 7th by a long letter from Mr Lister. "He had heard from his sister that I had accepted the post though he had not received my letter." He asserted confidently that the S.P.G. would provide passage and outfit money, a statement in which Doris rightly put no trust. In fact Bishop Fyffe of Rangoon lent the money. Who was to be responsible for repayment was left characteristically unclear.

Nor was the first meeting with Miss Openshaw entirely reassuring. This took place on August 10th in Ripponden where the Eastons now lived. "Met Miss Openshaw by the 12.16 train as I had invited her to lunch and tea. She is short and smallish, dressed quite nicely though in rather cheap things. Not common but rather attractive. Speaks slowly as if she had some slight difficulty in bringing out her words which gives the effect of a slightly foreign accent. I think I can understand why Bishop Knight liked her so much. She is the sort of girl whom men feel they must protect and take care of. Mother was wonderfully attracted to her at first, but did not like her so much afterwards. I do not know whether she will be much support." Janie Openshaw was Froebel trained. Besides being Miss Easton's deputy, she was to take charge of the kindergarten department of the school. She lived in Bury. The return visit was made on September 11th. "Miss Openshaw... met me and took me to her home. Her father is a sort of typical Lancashire man, talks fairly broad, very proud of his town, does not like or pretends not to like his daughter's going - says she thinks she has a "mission for the Lord." The mother seemed rather a nice gentle woman. The other sister showed her birth more than J. but seemed quite nice."

Other acquaintances with experience on the mission field told her tales, some of which she found "interesting but appalling." One was Miss Nixon who had been head of a C.M.S. school in Columbo, had broken down several times, and had finally been obliged to give up. St Mary's, Mandalay, was to be a school for Eurasian children. Miss Nixon informed her, "Eurasian in Ceylon has quite a different meaning from India. There it is a respectable word, but in Ceylon always means the illegitimate children of white people and natives. She would not take them because she could not mix them with others... numbers of government officials wrote asking her to take their children, but she always refused. There is a tendency to self-abuse in boarding schools in the East. Sometimes one girl will teach all the others. Miss N. had small girls of 5 who would push up hair pins etc etc....

That side of things is very much emphasised. When a girl begins to have periods she has to be shut up in her room where no man can see her and her family have a coming of age ceremony and send round cards to all friends and pass round evidence that this has actually taken place! I suppose it is a kind of advertisement that the girl is of marriageable age." On top of all this, though the concern shown by the staff of Westfield was warm and kindly, it cannot have been altogether encouraging, implying as it did that she had made a mistake.

It must have been a time of considerable strain and anxiety. And there was always the war in Europe and the Middle East which showed no signs of coming to an end. The diary, like most private diaries, is primarily concerned with the small unworldshaking trivia of individual life, yet there is enough about battles, rumours, and disasters to reflect the growing dismay in Britain.

"Antwerp has fallen and it was considered almost impregnable." (Oct. 10, 1914).

"The Germans have sunk a submarine off Lowestoft". (Nov. 4, 1914)

"I did not know the Germans had been trying to shell Yarmouth. It had been kept quiet, but the townspeople heard and saw the shells, only fortunately the Germans thought they were near inland because the buoys which mark dangerous sands had been put 3 miles out to sea and this misled the Germans and their shells did not reach." (Nov. 21st, 1914)

"The Germans have sunk a pre-Dreadnought of ours with a crew of 750 in the channel" (Jan. 1st, 1915).

"Monte stayed in Plymouth 2 nights - it was like a city of the dead, so dark and quiet. She was there when the Formidable went down." (Jan. 17, 1915)

"There has been a North Sea battle and the English have sunk a German cruiser, Blucher, which with the other ships was attempting to raid our coast." (Jan. 25, 1915).

"Missed the 8.26... In the waiting room there was a woman with a baby girl 9 weeks, youngest of 12. She was in distress. She had 3 boys soldiers, one at the front and they had lost trace of him for a long time and she had written 3 or 4 times a week and had sent out loaves and spent 4/- on telegrams etc. and he had received none and had written saying he thought it hard she did not write and they were so hungry and would be glad of a piece of dry bread. He was in Belgium." (March 31st, 1915).

"There has been a zeppelin raid over Ipswich. (April 30th 1915).

"The Lusitania has been torpedoed by German submarines, coming from America, about 1,500 lives lost." (May 7th 1915)

"There has been a zeppelin raid on London" (June 2nd 1915).

With such haphazard, disquieting items of information the record continues. From a purely selfish point of view the news of U-boat activity, since she was soon to sail through the Mediterranean and Suez, must have intensified her apprehension. The Lusitania was a civilian ship: that had not saved her.

The summer of 1915 sped past. It was taken up first with the normal frantic activity of school and then by all the preparations for Burma: vaccinations, inoculations, visits to friends and relations to say goodbye, buying equipment and clothes, receiving presents, not all as practical as the sewing-machine from Miss Firth, Mrs Easton's current lodger, or the mosquito curtains which one of the parishioners gave. Clothes included Indian gauze vests from Lewis's in Oxford Street and a grey alpaca costume procured in Halifax, a gift from her parents. Several selections from Tagore figure among the books, jostling with works of devotion, biblical history and many small items which convey strongly the sense of the by-standers that Doris Easton was setting out on an expedition into the unknown - a travelling-cushion, a life-saving jacket, a mattress, a folding work-basket and pockets for the cabin, a sun-shade, a locked canvas bag, a spirit iron and a cashbox. Even the sillier gifts such as doilies, bottles of scent and afternoon tea-cloths must have been consoling, declaring as they did the affection of the givers. But what is singularly lacking is any precise preparation for Burma, any evidence of reading about the country, its history, its religion.

Perhaps the closest she got to acquiring some understanding of people who came from different cultural backgrounds was in Scotland where, in August 1915, she spent a fortnight near Bleasdale, not far from Mallaig. Here her sister, Mildred, was helping to keep house for an extraordinarily international group of male students - Singalese, Indian, Chinese, West Indian, Swedish, Belgian. Some of them, the diary affirms, rather nervously, had "passionate animal natures" and, twice, when Mildred was in a room alone, one of them "threw his arms round her and held her tight and kissed her." In spite of such hazards, the sisters clearly enjoyed their time in Ardnambuith, rowing, fishing, walking, bathing, picnicking and, in the evenings, playing cards or such parlour games as charades or "I love my love with an A." Some of Doris's nervousness melted away, she began to forget colour of skin and difference of background in the interest of shared experiences and the exchanges of talk. All the same when she and Minor, an engineering student from South India, went into Prince Charlie's cave, she comments, "Fortunately Minor is a gentleman. I would not have liked to be alone in the dark with some of these students." It was from Minor that she learnt a little about Hinduism. "He says idols are used as symbols for the ignorant of the power of God etc." Of course, if she had gone abroad under one of the missionary societies, she would have had a period of training and presumably would have learnt something of the country, in which she was to serve, its traditions and culture. Lacking such support, she did her best to glean what scraps she could.

But whatever she lacked in the way of a precise contract, knowledge of the country to which she was travelling, the support of friends or acquaintances when she reached it, Miss Doris Sarah Easton, with a first class degree in Classics, three years' teaching experience and her twenty-sixth birthday behind her, lacked neither courage nor constancy nor a lively appetite for new experiences. She booked her passage on the "Ava", a steamship of the Henderson line, which was due to sail from Liverpool on Nov. 5th 1915 and, trembling but determined, said goodbye to all she loved and set off on the four week voyage to Rangoon.

The story of that journey is best told in her own words.

At this point I should, perhaps, explain the principles which have governed my presentation of the letter diaries, sent home weekly. These documents, which are now in the Indian Office Section of the British Library, are very lengthy. I have reproduced only about 1/3 rd of the whole. They are not polished considered accounts of life in Burma, but written under the pressure of a very heavy work-load with all the roughness and sometimes inaccuracy such a context invites. Names of places and people are at times inconsistent, altering as her knowledge changes. I have deliberately kept most of the errors, though where the punctuation is so light as to obscure the sense or there are obvious slips, I have made amendments.

This method seems to me to preserve more of the flavour of the original manuscripts than careful editing could achieve.

CHAPTER II

PASSAGE TO BURMA. NOVEMBER 1915

Statistics of SS Ava of the Henderson line.
Length 410 feet. Breadth 22 feet. Depth 30 feet 9 inches.
Number of passengers - 80. Officers and Engineers - 21.
Ship's servants - 16. Seamen and firemen - 58.
Cargo capacity - 34,050 cubic feet.
Fresh water 10,690 gallons. Tonnage 7,555 tons.

Fri. Nov. 5th 1915

We left by the 11 o'clock train... Mother, Mildred and Dad came with me. At Liverpool where we arrived about 1.20 we got a cab across the ferry to Mortar Mill Quay. We unloaded there and left my baggage to be taken in, then we walked to the ship to look at it, the Ava... An officer showed us my berth - only Miss Openshaw and I in the cabin altho' 3 berths. The officer asked if I had my passport and as I had not received it he said I must go to Lamport and Holts at Liver Buildings. Fortunately my passport had arrived that morning... Soon after 5 o'clock we took a tram and ferried across and arrived at the ship between 5.30 and 6 pm. Miss Openshaw and cousin and sister were there and an aunt and two friends. We spoke and then separated into our groups and waited in that huge dark shed, dimly lit by lamps and filled with cargo. It was unspeakable. At last, sometime after 6 pm, we went on board, a policeman looking at our passports. Unpacked some things, went in to dinner. There seemed very few passengers, respectable and quiet, but not high class. I wrote home as the ship was not starting that evening.

Friday Nov. 5th (and Sat 6th)

We went to bed about 9.15. I changed my bed from the top to the porthole side. I was bitterly cold in bed... The stewardess brought us tea, a piece of toast and an apple about 7 am. While we were dressing, a steward came with tickets telling us where we had to sit for breakfast. We were put at different tables. I was at the Captain's table. I don't know whether that is an honour, but the two ladies seated next to him are about the 2 most high-class looking. I was put between 2 of the most gentlemanly men. One, elderly, has been in Burma 17 or 18 years, possibly a military man or civil servant. The other next me is young and I discovered by dint of numerous and very tactful questions (à la Gertrude) that he was at Trinity College, Cambridge 4 years, took a classical Tripos part 1 and then a moral science course and is going out to Burma as a magistrate of some sort.

We walked about after breakfast and sat on deck for a time... then went to the music room which is the one and only warm place on the ship besides the dining-room... It was most tedious being on board 18 hours before the boat really started. It finally began to move about lunch time and went on slowly to the mouth of the Mersey... I was very glad indeed to have the gaiters, they helped keep my feet warm. During the day we sighted an English air-ship hovering about.

After dinner we has a little music in the music room. I played the violin, but the lady who was trying to play my accompaniment could not play at all...

Sun. Nov. 7th

We were in sight of the coast of Ireland and found that we had to make this course because of Admiralty's orders. I found out that the gentleman sitting next to me is Major Owen. After breakfast we were standing on the deck and the captain came and had a long talk with us. He has rather a nice face, capable and humorous. He is Scotch as are most of the officers...

It was a tedious day, meals the only variation. People don't dress much for the evening. The first night Miss O and I were about the only 2 with low necks.

Mon. Nov. 8th

Mildred seemed to think it would be so easy to get hot water but really it is very difficult. One has to bath between 5 am and 8 am, then when one tries to go to the bath there are numbers of Indian seamen swilling the decks and paddling about it whom you have to pass. Then another Indian has to get the water for you. Apparently it is never hot in the taps, and he can't speak English very well so it is difficult to make him understand. However he fills the bath very full and a tiny foot-bath as well (I don't know what the latter is for). We did get our baths in the end. Of course it is salt water and will not lather.

After breakfast I spent about 2 hours in the music room listening to the Honourable Mrs Frost who is most interesting and has lovely eyes, altho' she does powder and has some false hair. She seems to be of very good family and move in high society and know dukes and lords. She was an army sister in the Boer war and had charge of a hospital in Mons which was shelled and another hospital where the king was taken after his fall and held his hand when he was X-rayed or something... She says, of course, that the English are wonderful, and splendidly equipped and we have never been short of shell and all the talk about it in the papers is only to bluff the Germans. She showed us very interesting presents from soldiers she had nursed, e.g. a bullet taken from a man's brain which he had mounted in gold. She had various decorations, one of them the Royal Red Cross which she had received for conveying the wounded away from Mons. She had four brothers killed - one day rows of dead were lying outside the hospital waiting for burial and, as she was passing by, she brushed the blanket off the face of one accidentally and, looking back, recognised her own brother...

It was a wet dull day. We did not sight any land. We were out to sea about opposite the Bay of Biscay...

Tues. Nov. 9th

It was a glorious sunny morning... At 11 the officers fired a gun at a barrel in practice for shooting submarines. After that I played skittles on the Tower deck with eleven other people...

(1) The "aristocracy" of the party consist of Major and Mrs Owen, Mrs Underwood (whose husband is in the Indian police), an American and his wife, Mr and Mrs Macguire, the Honourable Mrs Frost.

(2) Slightly less aristocratic: Mrs Roberts (possibly an officer's wife) and two children and Mrs Allen and one child and the Boy who sits next to me, Mr and Mrs Conder.

(3) The Lower middle classes - a number of Scotch[1] young - type of banker's clerks, quite nice, well-behaved (some with rather obvious false teeth) Ken Shepherd, Mr and Mrs Crawford (very Scotch), Mrs Ashcroft and 2 boys (she spends as much time as possible talking to the ship's officers) Mrs Denny and Guy, Miss Birch (going out to be married).

We did not sight land all day. Really we should have been coasting along the coast of Spain and have seen Cape Finisterre, but the admiralty's orders were to keep far out...

After dinner J. 0. wanted to go out to the gang of young men and one or two girls who like to have games and larks. The worst of it is the aristocracy are the elderly or married...

Wed. Nov. 10th

We could see the coast of Portugal. I sat on desk and read. Then played skittles. We passed Cape St. Vincent about lunch time. We

---

My mother persists in this incorrect usage. Later she must have learnt better for she taught me that the noun is Scot, the adjective Scottish and that Scotch is Whiskey.

were quite close and could see steep red and grey cliffs and the lighthouse very plainly.

Afternoon: It rained and grew very gloomy. The time does pass slowly... The Honourable took us into her cabin and showed us most lovely night gowns she had with insertion and silk etc...

During the day we passed 2 hospital ships with red crosses on them. I sat in the cabin and read. J. 0. played "Blind Man's Buff" with some of the others in the corridors. After dinner Mrs Frost got up some charades which were rather fun... After that we had some music. The doctor played my accompaniments and managed quite well. He is an old man, Scotch of course, with a nice, kind face.

Thurs. Nov. 11th

I woke up about 5 am and looked out. It was quite dark, but I saw we were close to Gibraltar, so I woke J. 0. and we went along the corridor. We could see the lights of Africa on one side and on the other the rock and lights. Before I awoke a torpedo boat had come up and asked who we were and what cargo we carried etc. Various searchlights were playing and we could see the phosphoric lights on the water. After breakfast I could see very faintly on our right the mountains of Africa and very clearly on the left magnificent Spanish mountains. We kept the latter in view all the afternoon. Lovely snow clad peaks rose above the grey misty slopes. The sun was very hot...

Afternoon: Read. I did fancy work... I saw a shoal of porpoises jumping in and out of the water during the afternoon.

After dinner we had a most strenuous game of Blind Man's Buff in the corridor. Of course the decks have to be in darkness, so we can't play there.

Friday Nov. 12th

We... passed Algiers with its white houses, red-roofed. The sun was scorching and we had the awning on the upper deck; the air was soft and fresh... We saw 2 destroyers during the day, a British one quite close and a French one in the distance...

After dinner wrote letters in the Music room and listened to the conversation of some of the married Elite who were playing Patience.

Sat. Nov. 13th

...The Chief Engineer took us into the engine room. We went down flights and flights of steps right below the level of the water and saw the huge engines and furnaces and walked right along the shaft of the propeller to the stern of the vessel. We also saw the refrigerator for making ice and the electricity engine and the machine for making fresh water out of salt etc etc. It was very wonderful...

After dinner we had some music and recitations. The "masses" (except one or two) would not come. The cleavage between them and the "aristocracy" is rather marked sometimes and the Honourable Mrs Frost does not mend matters.

She sweeps into dinner in very low and gorgeous dresses, and one night wore a coronet and sometimes appears to be fascinating these young men by being charming to them and talking about her relations and friends in high society, but she tells them that she knows people in Burma whom she would not know in London! Yet there is something very nice and charming about her. I think she means to be kind...

Sunday Nov. 14th

...We passed Malta about lunch time...

The Captain does not let us play skittles etc on Sunday, for which I am glad, but he won't take a service as some Captains do and there is no chaplain on this ship.

After dinner: Wrote letters in my cabin... I found the "Masses" were singing hymns in the dining room, so I went and joined them - it was very nice.

That is one thing about most Scotch youths - they do have some respect for Sunday.

Tues. Nov. 16th

Played skittles for nearly 2 hours. The sun was scorching, but there is a nice cool breeze. They say this is about like the cold season in Mandalay. Major Owen very often entertains me at dinner with gruesome stories of the insects I shall meet, the food I shall eat, and the heat I shall have to endure etc etc. After lunch the old doctor wanted me to come and play the violin while he accompanied me... then the Captain came so I played for him to sing. Then I carried Elizabeth (baby) up and down while Mrs Frost talked to me... I began the conversation because the other night she told J. 0. that she did not think she ought to play lively games with the "Masses" and that her father and mother would not like it... I pointed out to Mrs Frost that I did not think J. 0. and I could cut ourselves off entirely from the young people.

Wednesday Nov. 17th

Afternoon: We could see Port Said houses in the distance... We saw what seemed to be a battleship or cruiser, then a pilot ship came up and the pilot in a white suit and topee came on board and conducted us towards the line of houses on the flat coast near Port Said. We went a long way into the harbour and then anchored and then a crowd of strange men came on board, hotel officials, men selling newspapers etc. Some were Egyptians and some Arabs. Some had coats like ladies' and wide white skirts. Many of them wore fezzes. Some had English costume. After dinner we got our letters, 10 for me but none from home. I was very disappointed though I had tried not to count on it. We sat on deck - the moon and the lights on the harbour were lovely, but it made one very homesick. It is far worse than being at sea.

Thursday Nov. 18th

We heard that 5 steamers had been torpedoed in the Mediterranean between Malta and Port Said. It seemed wonderful that we should have gone the same course and utterly escaped. Directly after breakfast J. 0. and I set off in a boat with Mrs Frost. The man, a fine looking Arab, wanted 1/- each, but we would not give more (than) 7d and when we arrived at the landing-stage we found it ought to have been 4d... It was interesting to row past big battleships and steamers. We saw a hydroplane skim along the water past us and then ascend... We had to show our passports at the Custom house. Then we went into the city... We met a Franciscan monk, an Italian, and asked him to direct us to the mosque, he did not know but sent 2 little school boys with us. On the way we passed the Egyptian Civil hospital and saw some British wounded soldiers outside, so the Honourable would go in to see the sisters, and they took us over the hospital which has been taken over by the government... There were several New Zealand nurses besides French ones. On the stairs we met an Arab carrying a hawk (?) which he was going to kill, so the Honourable gave him something and said she would take it and tame it... I had the pleasure of carrying it the rest of the time after we left the hospital. We stayed there about 1½ hours as Mrs F. has so much to say to the nurses. Her father was Lord Glasgow and he was Governor of New Zealand and she was born there. Her uncle is the Marquis of Ailsa.

Our poor little Arabs were still waiting. They took us to the Mosque and we had to put on big straw slippers over our shoes. It was a nice clean building with passages of the Koran written up on the walls and a kind of narrow throne with a passage up to it for the priest. Various Arabs were on the floor, kneeling and telling their beads. He (the guide) took us also into an outside place where there was water for people to wash their feet and a kind of swimming bath and into a room where the Priest was sitting and his small daughter, a sweet little girl, was on the floor, scribbling in the book. We left 1/- for the Mosque and came through the temple again.

Our guide wanted to know what time the ship started, so we hurried off as Mrs F. was afraid he might shut us up and make us give all our money in order to get to the ship in time... We had taken a carriage at the Hospital and after we had seen the mosque we drove through the Arab quarters. The streets were fairly narrow with high houses of several storeys and verandahs - no chimneys so the roofs look rather flat. Some of the streets were very dirty. The shops are mostly open in front like a Penny Bazaar... We did some shopping. The men in the streets are a perfect nuisance, they pester you to buy postcards etc and ask fabulous prices. You have to beat them down... My hawk caused much amusement. One man ran up with a live chicken and asked me to buy that too. Mrs F. bought us each a little charm of a cradle with a sphinx on it and a baby Moses inside. I think the Arab must have taken a fancy to her. He came with us and carried a parcel to the Custom house and would not take a tip. We got a boat again and arrived back about 2 pm...

Some of the New Zealand nurses came to tea on board about 3.30. They said there had been skirmishing on the Canal the last few days and 2 officers had been killed and New Zealand soldiers had been posted there. We carried a gun as far as Port Said and left it there.

When the cargo was being disembarked, one man was found trying to steal something and was taken to the police station... The Arab policemen look rather nice. Those on land wear white suits and white helmets with flappers. The port policemen wear sailor suits with red on them and red fezzes.

We set sail about 5.30...

Friday Nov. 19th

We went on deck soon after 7.30 to see the canal. We had tied up 4 or 5 hours in the night, Major Owen said, because they are fearing an attack like the one in March and if we had gone during the night we might have been exposed to a fusillade. The nurses said 43,000 New Zealand troops had come or were coming to the Canal... At intervals we came to small camps of soldiers - often Indian soldiers with one or two English officers... Some of the British soldiers we saw in a camp said they were Lancashire and asked if there were any Lancashire lasses. We saw camels by some of the camps. We also saw various battleships and transport ships, one crowded with New Zealanders.

After a time we passed through the Great Bitter Salt Lake which was a very wide expanse of water. We reached Suez about 1.30... We waited about an hour but the mail did not come... When we entered the Gulf of Suez we had fairly high hills on the Egyptian side and low sandy ones on the Arabian side which grew a lovely salmon pink as the sun set...

Mrs Ashcroft left us at Port Said with her two boys, also Mrs Roberts and Dora and Barbara and her nurse and some of the young men. One meets some queer people. Mrs Ashcroft was dreadful. She spent nearly all her time with the young men, both officers and others, and would stand with her arms around them... The last night, Mrs Frost told me, there was a dreadful scene. She went ashore with a number of men and came back dead drunk, and would not stay in her cabin, but lay on deck shrieking... Her brother is said to be a clergyman and has given her some Communion linen with I.H.S. on it which she uses as afternoon tea-cloths... Then the doctor is a very queer man. At Port Said he insisted on taking Miss Birch, who is going out to be married, into a shop saying he would give her a present and made the shopman bring out the most expensive things and also cheap ones in case she preferred to have a number of the latter instead and then said he had to go somewhere else to buy some collars at another shop and went off and left her alone there and so she was obliged to buy something for herself after the man had got all his things out. However the Chief Steward insisted... on giving the bill to the doctor...

After the sun set, the hills stood out with sharp clear outlines against the pale yellow sky and a single star, "The star of the East", shone above...

Sat. Nov. 20th

We entered the Red Sea about 5 am... The heat is very trying when one is going to bed and getting up...

Sat. Nov. 20th

I found the heat pretty bad, tho' there was a good strong breeze, but of course, the breeze is warm... I am afraid I am a bad subject because I am fat. They all seem to think Mandalay about the hottest place in Burma... After tea I played the violin a little with the doctor and then I played some hymns on the piano. We had a most uncomfortable dinner. The doctor sits at the end of our table now because all the people at his table left at Port Said. Well, he was most offensive and whispered remarks about the people on the table to his next door neighbours... the other end of the table sat in moody silence while the captain grew furious... He (the doctor) whispered remarks to Mr Paton about Lady Jane (the name he has given to Mrs Frost) which she heard, and talked about people "putting on side". I had to struggle hard to keep my face straight... When I had finished my dinner the strain was growing so wearisome that I got up and went out as we often do. People imagined the doctor had said something offensive and the Captain came on deck in a great fury and asked what that "beast" had been saying to me. He said he had been drunk 5 or 6 days...

Mon. Nov. 22nd

...We saw no land all day. The Captain who is a great tease said in fun that he wished it would get rough so that he could see whether I should be ill or not. We had done the Ava's record voyage, the distance quicker than she had ever done before. It is Captain Forson's first voyage as Captain... It grew very rough in the night, but I did not feel it in the morning.

Tues. Nov. 23rd

I felt rather giddy while getting up, but at breakfast time I was feeling very well and triumphant at being able to come in and show the captain that I was all right. Several of the ladies did not appear. The sun was shining brightly and the waves were glorious... One wave came and wetted the hawk and the cat took that opportunity to bounce upon it and kill it. But the black cat itself (called Jean) also fell overboard during the day and was drowned and Mrs Underwood remarked that it had gone to apologise to the hawk.... Was beginning to feel a little queer again, so I took some Mothersill and lay down and was all right... We passed some islands called the Twelve

Apostles during the day and another island where the Chindwin ran aground: and a very nice lighthouse.

Wed. Nov. 24th

We passed Aden in the distance about 12 o'clock and so were out of the Red Sea... After dinner I played the piano for the captain and then Mr Kerr to sing. The latter sings exceedingly well and seems a nice man in many ways only he was one of those foolish about Mrs Ashcroft.

That disgraceful scene made a rift worse than ever between the two parties for a time and the young men grew defiant and drank more than at the beginning of the voyage. Now, however, the "aristocracy" are drawing them in more and skittles are a great help as everyone plays...

The Captain seems to get rather sick of the conversation of some of the "Aristocrats". The ladies so often seem to talk about dress and the doings of the other members of society. He remarked to me that he was thankful he had not been born into society.

Thurs. Nov. 25th

...Afternoon: I tried to read, but it is so difficult because people always seem to come and interrupt. The Captain came and spent nearly all the time till tea, talking about the stars, etc.

Friday Nov. 26th

...We had left the Gulf of Aden and were in the Indian Ocean. We passed two rocky islands called The Brothers and then later on we could see the coast of Socotra in the distance.

Sat. Nov. 27th

Another rough day... everyone thought J. 0. and me very wonderful for keeping up. As a matter of fact we did not feel very lively but went into all meals...

After dinner... Mrs Frost asked if I would play Patience... with the Captain while she finished her cigarette. I could not very well refuse so I went, but she left us alone for more than an hour... I can't help feeling angry with her, especially as some of the young men told me in fun that she had been settling my future and saying that I should return home in a year and she would give me away at the wedding... I only discovered 2 or 3 days ago that the Captain was keen on me. I thought he was more attracted to J. 0. and I believe he was to start with. She is so young-looking and bonny... I have to try to avoid him, but it is very difficult on a ship, and I feel sure the eyes of the elite are on me.

Sun. Nov. 28th

I played the organ for about an hour for the Captain and J. 0. and some of the young men to sing hymns...

Afternoon: lay down and read and felt very miserable... We went to bed quite early but for some reason I could not get to sleep.

Monday Nov. 29th

...I was very sleepy all the morning - a hot, wet, gloomy day... After tea we played Patience and the Captain came and joined us. We played Nap also, not for money, of course - the Captain knows I would not as he wanted to teach me Bridge and I explained why I would not learn...

A day or two ago I saw my first flying fish. They were very small and looked rather like swallows flying above the water.

Tues. Nov. 30th

...There was a simply wonderful sunset, the best we have had. The sky was very fiery at the horizon and above that there was a huge bank of clouds of different shades of grey piled up into great ragged peaks. One enormous cloud was a great cruciform shape, very black with its edges lined with gold and orange. Above the grey clouds there was a blue sky flecked with gold and grey clouds which later turned a crimson colour.

As it was St Andrew's day we had a Scotch dinner, dishes with the most extraordinary names e.g. Bubbly Jock (Turkey) Stot's Saut wobble (tongue) Haggis etc etc. After dinner... Mr Kerr and Mr MacFarlaine came and asked me to walk with them... They are both in the Burma Oil Company. It is a pity they are so fond of Scotch whisky. After they left me I sat outside and talked to Mrs Paton and Mrs Underwood...

Presently the Captain and J. 0. came up and sat down and talked. Mrs Frost was sitting there too reading, so in fun Mrs Underwood asked the Captain what he had done to make her so quiet. At that point Mrs Frost roused herself up and began to insult him right and left for no reason at all. She said he had bored her in the extreme at dinner... she was sick of his Scotch voice etc. She said it all in such an insulting tone and the Captain was growing furious so I took J. 0. into the music room... We decided to try to fetch the Captain to sing. So I began playing the accompaniment of one of his songs and J. 0. went and asked him to come in and I kept him singing all the evening till bed-time...

Wed. Dec. 1st

...Mrs Frost confided in me how sorry she was about the evening before and how of course she had not meant it and she thought the Captain a charming little man. She said for the third time that she wanted me to go and stay at her house in the holidays, but I don't want to go. What on earth should I do at the house of a lady who drinks (I don't mean in excess) and smokes and rides and shoots etc. Sat on deck and read. A little before dinner the Captain came and sat down by me. He seemed rather down... He also let off steam a little about Mrs Frost and said he considered her a vulgar woman.

Dec. 2nd

We were passing along the south of Ceylon when we got up... There was rather a sickly spicy smell coming from the island. It was very pretty - low hills thickly wooded with coconut trees close to the water and mountains rising behind. We could see the white houses and red roof of Galle very clearly. There were numbers of little fishing smacks and catamarans...

Mrs Frost began her old tactics again at lunch of making remarks to and about the Captain and calling out... to me at the other side and end of the table, "Don't you think so, Miss Easton?"

I thought she had abandoned her matrimonial projects for me, but apparently it is not so...

After dinner when J. 0. and I went on deck, Mr MacFarlaine intercepted us and asked us to walk about. He was joking and telling us how the match between the Captain and me is quite settled, only there are other competitors on board who will not let the Captain have it all his own way. Then Mrs Frost came and asked me to go and play Patience with the Captain... I had to go in the end as it would have looked so strange for me to refuse...

Mrs Frost is pleased to admire that oriental dress of Mildred's that I wear, also the way I do my hair (the Captain also admires the latter according to J. 0. and thinks it quite unique!!)

Mrs Frost is a big woman, distinguished looking. She looks very nice in evening dress when she wears a good deal of false hair which matches her own perfectly. She is... frank and candid about her hair and comes into dinner and asks the Captain if it is coming off or tells stories of an occasion when she wore false eyelashes and one fell off into the soup at dinner and she had to spend the whole evening with only one on.

Friday. Dec. 3rd

We had skittles. Mr Kerr was rather a nuisance. He sat by me and did some of my fancy-work - the white cushion cover... He is a a great tease and I get rather tired of fencing with him. He and some of the others last Sunday sang the hymn "Only an armour-bearer", when they were by themselves and then asked me later if I knew it. The words come in it "Surely the Captain will remember me". Now they are for ever humming or whistling it.

Sat. Dec. 4th

We were able to get our boxes from the hold so I began to pack away things. To my horror when I took my violin from under my bed it was sopping wet and the wood all warped and ungummed at the bottom... Mr Kerr said he would take it to the shop in Rangoon and they would do it with special gum. I suppose I had better let Mr Kerr take it tho' I don't like putting myself under any obligation to him...

There was a very heavy swell, about the worst we have had. I felt all right till I had been poring over my box packing a long time and then I was rather done up.

Sunday Dec. 5th

The Captain took me down to listen to the Wireless Operator who was sending messages to the Chindwin which left Burma a day or two (ago). The Chindwin told us that a cyclone was reported near the Andaman Islands. This must be the cause of the heavy swell we have had which is most extraordinary at this time of year.

Afternoon: Talked to the Captain. He was reading my Westfield magazine, so I told him about it. (People are rather fond of picking up my books and reading. Mr Kerr carried off the one Miss de Selincourt and Miss Richardson gave me. I hope it may do him good!)... I was talking about packing, so the Captain said, "Don't bother to do it at all, but book your passage back". He said it as if he was serious, but I don't know what he was driving at...

Evening: I came on deck and saw J. 0. walking about with Mr Kerr and Mr MacFarlaine, so I went into the Music Room - there was no one there - and began reading. Then Mr Kerr came in and asked if I would not take a walk and I thought it rather ungracious to refuse, so I went. He is an extraordinary man, I never know when he is serious and when he is romancing. He told me the Honourable had told him of her plan to make a match between the Captain and me, and he said he should step in... He was quite nice and talked quite sensibly about the life in Burma, but I never believe all he says... When we went to bed J. 0. told me that Mr Kerr had said that the young men thought Miss Easton a dear and that he had been thinking himself of "popping the question" that night.

Monday Dec. 6th

...The first sight of Burma was rather uninteresting, muddy water and low lying coast, but as we went up the river (Irrawaddy) we passed one or two pretty native villages with small wooden houses and tropical vegetation. Packed. About 6 pm owing to the fault of the Pilot who had come aboard we ran aground on a sandbank in the river... The Captain... was fearfully worried about our being aground, tho' of course it was not his fault. He felt it had spoilt his first trip as Captain and of course the ship might be damaged. We talked to him for some time and then went to bed. About 12.45 am as the tide rose they got the ship off the bank and we were able to go on.

Tuesday Dec. 7th

Got up about 6 am. We were close in to the wharf, tho' not yet at the landing place. The Steward came to tell us to take our passports on board to show the officer. We also had to give in a big declaration paper of the contents of our luggage to a Customs officer who came on board. We had to wait to land till a steamer had moved from the wharf, but friends and relations were able to come on board by steam launches. Mr Frost was a very nice-looking man - tall with an amused expression on his face. We had breakfast at 8 am. Mr Lister arrived during it - he is a most good looking man - most beautiful eyes and very pleasant and attractive manners, quite young and rather boyish looking. He brought with him a "boy" for us - a Burman. One always takes one's servants here when travelling. Our boy is a man with wife and family, but they are all called "boys".

We finished packing and waited about on deck. It was a trying time. We were very sorry to leave - it is like saying goodbye to the last piece of England.

CHAPTER III

A DIFFERENT WORLD - BURMA 1915

Tuesday Dec. 7th

"The loneliness and strangeness are something appalling."

The "Ava" had been a little self-contained world which, for all the irritations, had provided a kind of security for the two young women now tipped out into an alien environment of new faces, unfamiliar customs, and bewildering difference.

Tuesday Dec. 7th

We disembarked somewhere about 10 am and got into the Bishop's motor. Our boy took the luggage in a gharry, a kind of box for 3 people on wheels, corresponding to a cab... We drove to Bishop's Court and were welcomed by the Bishop and 2 or 3 clergymen. We were put in the same bedroom - a huge room with 2 beds and a kind of dressing-room attached and a bathroom. It is perfectly wretched that there are no lavatories in Burma or India. What happens is that each bedroom has a little room attached called a bathroom with a small tin bath in it and a commode. I hate it - a man called a sweeper sweeps the floors of rooms and empties the commode. People at home think Europeans here keep a great many servants, but you can't help it, because one man will only do one particular piece of work and no other. No other servant would consent to do the sweeper's work.

The meals are normally as follows. Early breakfast generally in your room - tea and toast - any hour. Proper breakfast somewhere between 10 and 12 - fish, meat, curry and rice, fruit etc - tea about 4 - Dinner 8 or 9. We had breakfast after we reached the Bishop's house and unpacked a little and set off again between 11.30 and 12 to see after our luggage. The motor broke down just before we got to the Ava, so we walked the last little piece and went on board to find the Captain... Then we motored to the Irrawaddy Flotilla Co. and put all our heavy luggage on board a river boat. They are quite nice boats - it is the most expensive way of travelling and very luxurious. Of course the 3rd Class where the Burmans go is horrid, one could not travel 3rd possibly...

Then we motored to a big shop and bought topees - 4 rupees 8 annas each - quite nice. We met Mr and Mrs Condor outside and oh! it was a treat to see a familiar face. Then we went back to Bishop's Court about 5 pm, swallowed some tea and motored to the Diocesan Girls' School to see a Kindergarten entertainment... By this time I was utterly tired out and miserable. The loneliness and strangeness are something appalling.... I was introduced to Miss Coback Clark, the headmistress, and to Miss Laughlin, the head of the S.P.G. school. Both are elderly and slightly formidable... Some lady carried off Janie to her house to talk about the Girls' Friendly Society and I went back alone with the Bishop and changed my dress and sat in our room feeling at the last gasp. We had dinner at 8.15... After dinner we sat in the drawing-room a little, while the gentlemen smoked, then came to bed. We had a bed each with a mosquito curtain. The house is very large and roomy and has a fine drawing-room but not very home like.

Wed. Dec. 8th

We had breakfast in bed about 8. Then got up and motored with Mr Lister to St. Mary's S.P.G. school. They have beautiful buildings and even a few lavatories as they are on a water connection... We got back to Bishop's Court about 10.45 and had breakfast. Then we set off again in the motor and drove out to Kemmandine to see St. Mary's Normal and Practising school which is under Miss Laughlin...

Just before we arrived at Kemmandine our motor punctured and we had to telephone to the Cathedral organist to bring a tyre. When it was mended we set off again to St. Michael's, the S.P.G. boys' school... but we were too tired to care about going over the school... We had another puncture outside Kemmandine station, so we had to take a gharry and leave the motor and the driver behind. It is the cold weather, but the sun is scorching, hotter than it ever is in England. When we got in we sent off the organist with another tyre and after some tiffin (fruit and barley water) we rested and packed. We had tea about 4 pm and then the Bishop took us two into his room and talked a little about the school and offered some prayers in the chapel and then we went off in the motor to the station. Somehow the Bishop strikes one as being rather ineffectual, tho' he is very nice...

We found Mrs Denny and Guy on the station and Major and Mrs Owen all going by the same train... The train was packed. Mr Lister had got us 2nd class tickets for half fare, 9 rupees instead of 18, a concession allowed to missionaries, but there was no room so he put us in a first class with another lady... I was unspeakably relieved to find there was a lavatory attached to the compartment as in English trains. The compartment had 4 berths.

Mr L. was really exceedingly kind and nice. You can't help liking him. He let us ask as many questions as we wanted and pointed out things of interest. The country was flat and uninteresting, part of the time large fields of paddy (rice) and part of the time scrub jungle (i.e. uncultivated country with low brushwood).

Somewhere about 7.30 we got out at a station and had a very nice dinner in the Refreshment room... Meanwhile our boy had made up our beds. Mr Lister had brought us pillows and blankets and he had to lend us his soap and towel as we had none. Apparently one is always expected to bring one's own bedding. Mr Lister forgot to tell us. I slept on a top berth, it was not very comfortable and it was rather cold; however I slept a fair amount. Our boy brought us tea and bread and butter at one of the stations about 7.15 and after we had dressed Mr L. came and sat with us. About 9 o'clock we got out at one of the stations and had a 4 or 5 course breakfast. The Owens and Mr Denny were there too.

The country was most interesting - mountains of about 5,000 feet rising sharply from the plain. There are no gradual slopes leading up to them. If only they had snow they would be lovely, but there are no snow mountains here. We saw big water buffaloes which are used as draught animals. The goats are very strange. I did not recognise them. They have great drooping ears like a spaniel's. The cows very often have humps on their backs... It is almost impossible to distinguish a Burmese man from a Burmese woman. Both wear long black hair twisted up on top. Both have a kind of white jacket and a long coloured skirt. The only difference is that a man wears a coloured handkerchief round his head and a woman wears nothing on her head. The small children are often quite naked. The only way to distinguish a nun from a priest is that a priest wears a deep orange-coloured garment and a nun a pale one. There are a great many Indians about; they do most of the work - the Burmans are too lazy and light-hearted. I think the Indians more attractive - they are less like Chinese - but they are said to be worse thieves than Burmans. The latter do not care much about money.

Thurs. Dec. 9th

We reached Mandalay about 1.30 pm. Mrs Lister met us. We neither of us cared for her at first. She seemed rather abrupt and slangy. We went up to the Parsonage in a gharry.

We have to sleep in the same room again. The house struck us as rather shabby and untidy, but I think that is what all the houses here seem to be, partly owing to the fact that the walls are bare wood and the floors wood with just a mat or two. There seems so little privacy. There are verandahs, of course, and one has windows and doors wide open all the time, perhaps a curtain across the door in the passage. There are no bells; from any part of the house you just shout "Boy" when you want anything and he appears.

We both of us felt absolutely wretched and miserable and wished we could have gone and lived in the school straight away. We had a meal and then sat in our room till tea-time... The baby is called Guy and is three months and rather fat - not at all pretty. He has a very nice little Burmese ayah who is very fond of him. After tea we went out for a short walk with Mrs Lister and saw the church which is really very nice. We liked her better. She is distinctly pretty when she is animated. She and her husband are both rather lively and merry and absolutely full of energy. But they have had a time with the school...

Mr Argyll Saxby, the headmaster of the boys came into dinner. He is an extraordinary man - Scotch, the son of a novelist, educated at George Watson college, Edinburgh, had to begin teaching young, because his father died, has taught in various schools in India and elsewhere, has been on a ranch in Canada, manager of a theatre or theatrical company for a time, plays the organ, piano and sings, is a scout master in chief for Burma or something of the sort, wrote a book and was made an F.R.G.S. (Fellow of the Royal Geographical Society) in consequence, is very keen on education and anxious to start a teacher's association here etc etc. He is a little man, not at all good looking or attractive, but rather amusing and I think he has plenty of common sense.

Friday Dec. 10th

We had early breakfast in bed at 7 am and when we were dressed walked with Mrs Lister to the school, which is in the old fort, a huge space of ground enclosed by a wall and beautiful moat. The school is about 1½ miles from here. The girls' part consists of 2 shabby old bungalows (with upstairs). The accommodation, however, was better than I expected. I thought probably several classes would be in the same room, they are not. Each form is in a room by itself and the children have single desks and there are some blackboards. The dormitories, of course, look very bare - no furniture except beds and one or two old looking-glasses. I think it is wonderful what the Listers have accomplished. The school apparently has a great reputation already and a large percentage of the children passed in the government exams which have just taken place. Of course to us the lavatory accommodation seems dreadful - a dormitory with perhaps 20 children and only one bath room with about one bath, one commode and a few tin basins, but I suppose they are used to this sort of thing at home. There are rough wooden sheds outside for the day children. The Eurasian teachers look quite nice and the children are quite attractive, but some of them must come from very poor homes.

We then went to the boys' bungalow a couple of hundred yards away and Mrs Saxby took us over and talked a long time. I think their bungalow is nicer than the girls'. Of course, there are not many boys, somewhere about 30; they have a very nice and very large dormitory which seems to hold them all. At the other bungalows there are about 100 children (girls and little boys). There is no room for J. 0. and me at present as there are so many more children than expected, but we are going to have a large room each and a verandah room at the top of one of the girls' bungalows, and bamboo classrooms will have to be built on downstairs to make up for the loss of room. After tea I talked to Mr Saxby about time-tables etc. He says that Mr Lister has had the school on the brain and has continually rung him up about trifles at all hours, so that he has been rather done up and thinks he will not be able to hold out unless things are better.

Mrs Lister took us to the Club which is also in the Fort. We were introduced to various ladies and drank chocolate and watched badminton... Major and Mrs Owen were there and it was very nice to see familiar faces - they are staying here a few days before going on to Bhamo where he will be a deputy Commissioner...

Mr L. says... practically all the English people here are godless and only come to the church when they can't find anything else to do. I suppose it is very difficult not to be spoilt. It is quite impossible however poor you are to have less than three servants - a cook, a boy and a water carrier (you see there is no water laid on in houses). Then you must have a sweeper, though you can share him with someone else, and if you have a baby you must have an ayah. Then most English people do no walking at all and ride everywhere. The Listers are an exception - they bicycle everywhere... I quite see that it would have been utterly impossible for me to do without a bicycle. J. 0. will have to buy one and learn to ride it...

The Listers are rather a loveable couple, but I think rather young and carried away by their enthusiasm and apt to think they know better than their elders...

Sat. Dec. 11th

...After tea we walked with Mrs Lister to the Fort again. The Fort is a square space 1¼ miles each way with a wall all round it, and a lovely widc moat outside. It is almost like a park inside. Numbers of trees and grass and little pools and white roads and bungalows. The school is inside it and the club and the barracks and dwelling houses. It has a good many advantages over the rest of the town. There is Artesian water so that one can drink unboiled water fairly safely and it does not get so choked with dust as the town outside. The old Burmese palace is in it where the Burmese king used to live. When we were entering the Fort the sun was setting and sky and water were a gorgeous deep orange colour... What I have seen of Mandalay is really very pretty. Mrs Owen calls it a dream city...

We went down to the Club and were introduced to various ladies. They don't attract me at all with their smoking and bridge-playing and gambling and drinking, but I expect we shall find in time that some of them are nice...

We had a game of Badminton with Miss Dunkley, the S.P.G. worker who... I think looks very nice. I expect she and Miss Patch feel rather out of it at the Club, but they go so as not to cut themselves off entirely from other English people.

Sun. Dec. 12th

Church at 7.30. Holy Communion and short sermon... There is no proper morning service because it is so hot that people would not come, so this takes its place, and the school children come to it... Mr L. of course is quite "High" and wears a queer monk-like kind of garment which I have not seen before.

After church Mrs Lister stayed behind to play the organ. She is taking the organist's place and salary and giving the money to the school. We came home and looked after the baby so that Gawlah, the ayah, could go to the Burmese church...

I wore my grey costume to church and black velour hat. A velour or felt is the next best protection against the sun to a topee. (I forgot to say that in Rangoon on Wednesday morning we went to see the great golden Pagoda. It is a sort of cone shaped solid building covered with gold leaf and all round at the base are rather gaudy looking shrines ornamented with gold leaf and coloured glass with images of Buddha inside. There was an enormous image of Buddha reclining. A long flight of steps leads up to the Pagoda on each side of which are numerous shops).

Mon. Dec. 13th

J. 0. and I left about 8.30 am to go up to school. We arrived there at 9 am just in time for Prayers which Miss Backhurst took. She is rather a pretty looking Eurasian girl.

The lessons were pretty bad. In Scripture Miss Walker read a few lines from the "Peep of Day" and then stopped in the middle of a sentence and expected the children to add the last 2 or 3 words... Education in Burma seems to be appalling... These children of 9 or 10... spend hours and hours on transcription, copy books and a reading book which is far too difficult for them as regards subject matter. They get so tired and bored... After breakfast I talked to Miss Backhurst until 1 o'clock, then... inspected the outside lavatories - there is only one for boys and one for girls - they are just rough kind of shelters with one commode in each and a wooden frame with holes in it which should have tins underneath but there were none. It was disgusting and there were several small boys playing about by one. I went and fetched J. 0. from the kindergarten and made her look at them; and then Mrs Pell (the matron) came out and fetched in Billy and Willy. I could not make them understand. They are about 3 years old and are boarders. Their mother is Burmese but wishes them to be brought up as English. They can't understand English, so it is very awkward. They were supposed to be asleep, but had crept downstairs... We came home in one of the buses which bring the children to and from school. There are two buses and a special train run for them... We went to the Club... but I felt very depressed. The people at the Club depress me, they seem so worldly...!

Wed. Dec. 15th

School - Standard III and IV; Miss Kinsman. She seems quite business like and painstaking. She is rather a dark Eurasian and rather Burmese in appearance... Our books and pictures arrived in the afternoon. They came in a bullock waggon. One of Mr Saxby's boys came as interpreter to the Burmese drivers.

We had to wait at 3.30 because the mules for one of the buses had run away and the other bus had to make two journeys. When we arrived, Miss Patch, the S.P.G. worker and a governess from the Lucases were there for tea. I think Miss Patch seems very nice...

J. 0. and I went for a walk with Mr and Mrs L... It was a lovely moonlight night... we wore neither hats nor coats. I had on my striped cotton voile dress and was perfectly warm, so you can imagine what Mandalay cold weather is like... Of course Mr L and I talked school all the time.

Then we came upon a curious Burmese scene - a kind of fair. There was a rough stage where a Burmese play was to be acted. There was a wooden construction with an acrobat on the top and stalls with people selling ingredients for curry etc etc. Some of the sellers had no stalls, but an oil lamp hung on a pole near which they sat with their things on the ground. These affairs go on till day-break and people bring their beds and food.

Thurs. Dec. 16th

...I watched Miss Backhurst teach standards VI and VII. I think she is quite good. There was a good deal of excitement at 11.30 because there is a single railway line between the two bungalows which is used occasionally and a regiment of Punjabees marched up to the school to get into their railway carriages. They were accompanied by the Pioneer band of Madrasees who play very well and by a whole company of friends and relations dressed in white turbans who had come to say goodbye to them as they were leaving for the front. There were 2 English Officers and an English lady seeing them off... After dinner J. put on Scotch costume and danced the reel and hornpipe for us. She looked about 14.

Fri. Dec. 17th

...Mr L. opened my book box for me so I unpacked... We put the story books for school on a shelf in a classroom, but I am very much afraid of the rats getting at them. I went over to the boys' bungalow in the afternoon to enquire from Mr Saxby when next term began. I found that he had dismissed his boys and was reclining on a bed in the dormitory smoking. I said goodbye to the girls at 3.30 and asked the mistresses to come for a 'mistresses' meeting on Jan. 11th as school re-opens on the 12th.

Sat. Dec. 18th

We went to the Bazaar which means the Native shops. There are a number of buildings with stalls inside like a market and also there are shops along the streets with open fronts. These native shops seem to sell everything, only you don't know which one to go to, and have to look round till you find the thing you want as you probably won't know the Burmese word for it. Then you have to bargain somewhat tho' it is not as bad as Port Said. There are English shops as well, but they are much more expensive... Some quite rich Burmese women have stalls just for the fun of haggling and having someone to talk to. It seems the proper thing for a man to have his hair cut in the street, seated in the middle of the pavement.

A small boy followed us all the way from shop to shop with a pannier hung over his shoulders, so that he could carry our parcels for us...

Mandalay is rather a strange mixture. Part of it is very Burmese and part quite like England. In the vicarage garden one can quite easily imagine oneself at home - there are squirrels jumping about and quite English looking trees.

Mrs L. told me all about her husband's illness and the strain they have had this year with that, and the school and Guy's coming... She is still rather worried about her husband because he won't take rest or recreation... I had thought before that the Listers were splendid in their way, in the energy and enthusiasm they put into their work etc etc, but that they were not really very spiritually minded or praying people. However I think that perhaps I was wrong... Mrs L. was telling me how singularly blessed the school had been and how her husband had felt owing to things that had happened that he would be defying God if he did not start it.

I think Mrs L. likes Janie very much. She thinks her such a particularly unaffected girl, with no nonsense about her. I think she is very nice, but I sometimes wish she were a little older in mind. She is so young for her age.

Sun. Dec. 19th

...Service at 7.30. Read in my room. The publicity is very trying. One can hardly ever get alone anywhere or anytime and even if (which practically never happens) I do get the bedroom to myself I know quite well that people can look through the curtains and see I am there, or servants can come stealing in with their bare feet. I consider it rather a trial having a "boy" messing round every day at any hour and interfering with your clothes and things. Ours seems quite nice but I don't altogether like it. I am now badly mosquito bitten. My hands and legs are in a horrid state... (I have just discovered that Mr L. is 30 and Mrs L. is 24).

Mon. Dec. 20th

...Most of the morning and afternoon I spent in studying catalogues of suitable books for the school. After tea J. and I went for a walk by the moat. The reflection of the red wall of the fort and the red turrets on it was beautiful and the setting sun made the mountains in the distance a purple colour.

After dinner we went to a pwe, that is a sort of Burmese fair which begins about 10 pm and goes on till day-break. By the shrine of Buddha there were tables crowded with iced cakes and fruit, offerings given by people and afterwards distributed to beggars. By the stage, where a marionette show was going on, were numbers of rough wooden bedsteads with canopies over them where Burmans were sleeping or watching the stage. There were also people selling food and small fires with Indian corn being roasted on them.

A friend of Mr Lister's got us seats and we watched the marionettes. They were very clever, there was a very nice horse which galloped and shook its head. After the preliminary dances, there was a kind of play acted by the marionettes about a king and his son etc, etc, but the development was so slow that we grew very bored and sleepy and came home about 11 pm.

Tues. Dec. 21st

Worked. After tea J. 0. and I went to the S.P.G. Girls' school to see the end of term entertainment which Miss Patch and Miss Dunkley were conducting... Miss Patch is really a nurse, but the S.P.G. made her teach. Now, however, Miss Dunkley has charge of the school and Miss Patch has more time to give to her nursing. She does a good deal of maternity work. There were a number of Burmans there sitting on carpets on the floor and various fat Burmese babies - their Mothers carry them on their hips. I tried to make one or two smile, but could not succeed... they are most of them very serious. Mrs L. says after a baby is born, the mother and I think the child too is partly roasted to get rid of evil spirits and that in consequence you seldom see an old Burmese woman - they don't live to old age.

Thurs. Dec. 23rd

Mr Saxby had dinner with us. About 9.30 the matron of the hospital arrived in a tum-tum (a 2-wheeled trap) to go to the Parsee theatre... The matron drove the pony herself and her Indian servant and I rode behind and J. in front. We had to pay 2 rupees each for first class seats at the theatre. We sat right in the front and were the only English people there to begin with. Later on the Civil Surgeon, Colonel Penny, came and a friend and 2 other gentlemen. The matron is very much in love with the Colonel so must have been happy as he sat next to her.

There were Burmans sitting behind us and a gallery at the back and stalls down the side of the room, with oranges, tea or coffee, cakes etc... The company was doing "Cymbeline" in Hindustani. In the middle we were given gratis oranges and chocolate. The Burmans had tea and cake etc.

Sat. Dec. 25th

We went to service at 8 am. Holy Communion with short address... There were a fair number of English people at church for a wonder. It seems very sad that it should be the Eurasians who are the keen Church people here and really the pillars of the church...

Mon. Dec. 27th

...About breakfast time Mr L. was taken ill with violent pains - a return of his old trouble - gravel in the kidneys. The Civil Surgeon came but after he had left the pain grew so violent that we had to send up for the assistant surgeon to inject morphia...

Thurs. Dec. 30th

...After tea Mrs L. and I went off on our cycles and left cards at the houses of the English people in the Fort. Dressed for the dance. Mr L. decided not to go because of his health... Mr Saxby had kindly undertaken to come for J's and my sake so that he could introduce us to some men.

The dance was in the Volunteer Hall. It was in aid of the Blue Cross fund. We arrived between 9 and 9.30 but as there were only Eurasians there, we waited in the ladies' room as Mrs L. said it would not do for us to dance with Eurasians as the English people would probably cut us in consequence... There were very few men Mrs L. could introduce us to as she has not been to the club much the past year and the people of the stations have so much changed... However, Mr Saxby was very good and danced with us in turn and the soldiers did not mind coming up and asking us... Mr Lister had asked Captain Willcox, the adjutant, to introduce us to people but he did not come in for a long time. Mr Saxby said he had a bad cold and we think he had been drinking rather too much. Finally he came up by himself... Mr Saxby had teased us and said Captain Willcox had heard all about us from one of the passengers on the Ava, so I enquired into it and found that he had met Mrs McGuire on the river. He asked me if I had come across Mrs Frost and said that she was not an Honourable at all, but had been lady's maid or something to Lady Minto. He thinks she is mad and almost obsessed by the idea that she is a Lord's daughter. She had told a girl whom Captain W. knew... that she was Lord Roseberry's daughter. I can't help being amused, but angry when I think how she has fooled all the passengers and those nurses and people we saw at Port Said. I suppose she gives it out at Yenan-Yong, where she lives, that she is an Honourable.

Fri. Dec. 31st

...After dinner, J. and I had an interesting theological discussion with Mr L. while Mrs L. went on making a new dress for the Lieutenant Governor's visit. Went to church at 11.30 for a Watch Night service. There were a good number of Eurasians there. When we came back Mr Lister gave me the school log book to sign my name in as an indication that I had taken over charge and we drank to the health of the school. The others drank it in sherry and I in water. The Listers aren't teetotallers, tho' of course they don't regularly take anything. I suppose Mr Lister noticed that I didn't take anything at their dinner-party as he asked me straight out if I was a teetotaller and fetched me water at which I was very much relieved as some people don't like your drinking toasts in water. They consider it unlucky.

Sat. Jan. 1st 1916

Mr Saxby came to tea... He is an extraordinary man. His mother is sister to the Duke of Argyll, but she only married a doctor and he died young leaving them badly off, so Mr S. had to begin earning his living quite young. He is very versatile - writes books and plays and music, plays the organ and piano and is said to sing very well (I have not heard him yet). He has been on a ranch in Canada and to one of the American Universities. He has been in Cyprus, Syria etc etc on the stage. In his youth he had numbers of "girls" but the one to whom he was seriously engaged was burnt in a theatre. He has lost £1500 of his savings through the war.

Mrs L. and J. and I went up to the hospital to call on the matron... It is such a pity that she spoils herself with this infatuation for the Civil Surgeon and that too although she knows he has 5 or 6 Burmese children. (Really one wonders whether there are any moral men here apart from the clergy.)

Tues. Jan. 4th

We went to the boys' bungalow and found Mr Lister and Mr Saxby sitting smoking, looking very nice in their khaki uniforms (Mr S. is a lieutenant) but rather bored.

I am so afraid Mr S. will leave the school either because he will go to the front or because he is so worried about the school and can't get another man to help him with the teaching and supervision.

After tea... we went up to the Club and watched... Badminton. It is horrid being there and not knowing people and having no one who takes any interest in you.

Wed. Jan. 5th

We heard that The Persia, a P&O boat, had been sunk with numbers of passengers and thousands of mail bags. In a few weeks' time we shall not receive any letters, as they will all have gone down.

Thurs. Jan. 6th

Mr L. heard that Miss Parsons whom we had taken for granted to be coming to teach Drawing throughout the school and take the 1st form had never received his letter 3 weeks ago and so had taken another post. A day or two before, the master who had promised to come to the boys' school wired to say he could not come, so now we are 2 short... We came to the conclusion that J. must do with only one helper in the K. G. instead of two and the second one must go and teach at the boys' school while Mrs Lister came and taught Form I at the girls. She said she could not cycle backwards and forwards again as she had when Mr L. was ill and she, Gawlah and Guy must come and live in our rooms. J. and I were very depressed at the thought. We knew we should get no quiet for work if she came as she is such a restless person and also we did not want to go on sharing a bedroom. We are tired of having nowhere to ourselves.

Fri. Jan. 7th

...We stayed at school till about 1.45 and then walked back in the blazing sun and lay down till it was time to dress for the Lieutenant Governor's garden party. I wore my blue silk dress and my white hat. We drove in a gharry to Government house which is in the Fort, really on the wall. We walked through the hall and through 2 lines of Military police into the garden which is close to the moat. There is nothing much in the garden but the situation is lovely because the moat and the mountains in the distance are so pretty.

There were Burmans together in one part - a number of princesses and descendants of the Royal House, I think, sitting round in a ring and English people in another part and Eurasians in another. It was rather a stupid affair. The L. G. with his aide de Camp walked round and spoke to different people and we sat round and had tea. We two should have been rather stranded had it not been for Mr Saxby as Mr and Mrs Lister were going about talking to people. However, he stayed with us a good part of the time, so it was not so bad. Also we were able to have 2 ices each.

The dresses of the ladies were not particularly exciting. Of course a good number of them had black tulle or silk hats, so I am rather glad mine is white, except that a black one would look nicer with my blue dress. However I don't suppose I shall have much opportunity for wearing my nicest things as the English people, except for the missionaries, are not likely to take much notice of us.

We drove home in a gharry about 6.30. Mr and Mrs L. were going to the L. G's to dinner, so we were alone.

Sat. Jan. 8th

Mr L. heard that neither of the mistresses he was communicating with could come, so it was practically certain that Mrs L. would have to teach. We had tea with Mr S. on the verandah. Somehow we got into discussion on different religions and different views of life. He does not seem to believe much in missions, chiefly I should think because he has met unsatisfactory and lazy missionaries in India and also because native Christians are often unsatisfactory... Mr L. came up presently and told us he had succeeded in getting one teacher for 3 months, so we were very relieved.

CHAPTER IV

ST. MARY'S, MANDALAY

> "Friday Dec. 31st 1915... Went to church at 11.30 for a Watch Night service. There were good numbers of Eurasians there. When we came back Mr Lister gave me the school log book to sign my name in as an indication that I had taken over charge and we drank to the health of the school. The others drank it in sherry, I in water..."

And so on January 1st, 1916, Doris Easton officially took charge of the girls' division of St. Mary's school with its seven or eight teachers, its constantly changing matrons and servants, its day-girls largely dependent on the uncertain mule-buses to take them to and from school each day and the sometimes unhappy and neglected girls and small boys, toddlers even, who were boarders. There is a rather charming picture of one of the Burmese matrons giving these little ones their meals. "I took the children for dinner and watched the ayah feed the three babies who can't speak English but only Burmese. Two of them are only 3 years old. She had a plateful of rice and gravy and knelt on the ground and put a spoonfull in their mouths in turn out of the same spoon." Others were older but had difficult home backgrounds. The Parrs, for instance, were wards of the school and might not go either to their father or their mother for holidays, so special arrangements had to be made for them. To Miss Easton the behaviour of some of the children appeared almost insane. "A Mrs Montgomery arrived with her daughter, Muriel aged 8. When the gharry was about to go, the child yelled and screamed. Between us we managed to get her into the dormitory. She kicked and screamed and scratched my hand and made it bleed. I could not have held her long, but Mr Lister shut the doors on us and left us while her mother drove off. I thought the child was mad. However she quieted down and I made her show me her toys and then took her over to play with the other children. Her mother says she has a false roof to her mouth which falls at intervals and then she has a fever, but nothing is to be done about it. I could not follow the explanation..."

Problems with the staff began almost immediately. By Burmese standards, the teachers were highly-trained, but Miss Easton was not much impressed. Some of them were competent and willing; but to begin with she was taken aback by standards so different from those to which she was accustomed. Far from sharing her idealism, most of the mistresses were content to be little more than "child-minders", correcting work when they should have been teaching, never volunteering for any task they were not compelled to do.

Only three members of the teaching-staff emerge from the pages of the diary as distinct characters. First there was Miss Backhurst who to begin with seemed to Miss Easton rather officious in her anxiety to please, offering earnestly quite "incongruous flowers" for the Christmas decoration of the church. In fact she was a loyal colleague and a good teacher, very pretty and well-spoken - even if she begged off taking all the drill time-tabled for her because her voice was not strong enough. Talented and attractive, she was a little too frivolous for her high-minded head mistress who records of an entertainment: "Miss Backhurst is such a superior girl, speaks in such a pleasant cultured voice and sings beautifully and yet she took the leading part in some of these silly sea-side songs where the girl speaks to all the men on the promenade. It was not exactly vulgar, only it is a pity for girls to be brought up in this atmosphere where they are taught that the one thing in life for a girl is to put on pretty clothes and attract men." Yet Miss Backhurst endeavoured earnestly to do what was required of her, even to playing netball with the boarders, and she was genuinely kind. When she did become engaged, the diary comments: "to an Eurasian I am glad to say. I was so afraid she would not be satisfied with anyone but an Englishman in high society as she is so pretty and attractive and has had so many admirers."

Miss Carruthers was a very different type: "pleasant, elderly and rather delicate looking," she quickly became something of a trial. "She is so timid and rather fussy and I think fancies we ought to be using slates and hardly thinks it wise for a mistress to take any form beside her own." Although they found her "old maidish and melancholy," Janie and Doris tried hard to be kind: "We asked Miss Carruthers in to dinner with us as she complains so much of being lonely in the evenings. Poor thing - she is always dwelling on the past. She confided to J. that she had lost money and had said something bitter about someone who had been kind to her and it still worries her and keeps her awake. She is always groaning to herself and saying 'my God' under her breath and although it is very pathetic I always want to laugh when she does it." Miss Carruthers was inclined to rather tedious descriptions of her "Object" lessons - a device for focussing a class's attention by producing some tangible object and drawing from it as much useful instruction as possible. For the boredom inflicted, Miss Easton took a gentle revenge when some of Mr Saxby's boys gave her a particularly large lizard, very much alive. She suggested Miss Carruthers might like it for an object lesson. The response is not recorded.

Miss Carruthers provoked by her constant moaning about matters which could not be put right. Miss Porter presented a different problem. She was a student teacher, probably only about 18, and she and the young Burmese Matron, Ma Ay Yin, encouraged the older boys to have "crushes" on them. Worse, Miss Porter was discovered to be leaving the school compound in the evening and not returning till after midnight, a breach of the rules which stated that the mistresses had to be in by 9 pm unless they had special permission! On one occasion, when Ma Ay Yin was taking some of the girls to the circus, "We went over... to see that all was all right and found that Ma Ay Yin was upstairs getting ready to start. One of the big boys from the other school was waiting about, nominally to give back some ointment to Ma Ay Yin and one child was in the compound in her combinations (she does not possess any nightgowns) drinking water and Miss Porter was still out... We sent the boy back, he is not at all a desirable character." Next day Miss Porter insisted she was strolling about the compound in the moonlight. In fact she was meeting a married man who eventually turned out his Burmese wife in her favour.

The staff for whom Miss Easton felt so earnestly responsible may not have been easy to cope with; matrons and servants were worse. Mrs Pell took offence when she was told her son might no longer share a bedroom with her but must sleep with the boys. She left a day or two after the new headmistress took charge of the school. Ma Ay Yin not only "carried on" with the boys; she encouraged the girls in bad habits. "She sleeps in the same bed as some of the big girls here and keeps them talking till 11 o'clock and gives them monkey-nuts and smokes with them in the bathroom." Mrs Wright, who succeeded Mrs Pell, neglected her work, particularly that of checking beds and heads for "creatures" and seeing that the children washed themselves. Instead she spent much of her energy in nagging the servants and quarrelling with them so that some who were otherwise satisfactory gave notice. Her complaints began almost immediately she arrived. "Feb. 18th Mrs Wright came up in tribulation because the paniwalla (water carrier) and sweeper had been fighting and wanted to kill one another. Sweeper sweeps out the cows' stable for the paniwalla and the latter ought in return to fetch water for the sweeper, but now refuses. The paniwalla put all his cooking utensils in the sweeper's house and pretended the sweeper had stolen them." The servants were not slow to involve Miss Easton in their quarrels with Mrs Wright: Ma Mi complained that she had been called a thief: her husband, Maung San Pu, indignantly showed her the curry which Mrs Wright refused to eat. When the new headmistress took her troubles to Mr Lister it was gallingly apparent that he regarded them as molehills not mountains.

As the heat - and tempers - grew fiercer, it became increasingly difficult to maintain a balance. There was dust and wind to contend with as well as temperatures which by March soared to 100 degrees Fahrenheit even in the cooler parts of the houses. "...In our rooms many of the windows have not proper fastenings and they and the windows bang backwards and forwards and it is very hot and stuffy to shut them all up, yet papers and things fly about if we don't." Hair became sticky with sweat and Doris discovered hers was coming out badly. At night perspiration trickled down her legs and she developed prickly heat, an irritating rash on fingers and feet. It is little wonder that an exasperated sharpness creeps into the diaries. "Miss Carruthers spends nearly all the time I am with her complaining about things wrong here, I know there are heaps of things wrong, but I am not in a position to right them because Mr Lister keeps them in his own hands and if he did not I should not have time to see to them. Only it is very harassing not being able to have things I want."

Harassing that first term certainly was. Before its end, Mr Saxby, who for all his quick-tempered oddity was a kind and supportive colleague, left his badly-paid headship for a commission in the Indian army reserve. It looked as if the boys' section of the school would have to be given up as it was unlikely anyone would come for so little money. There were rumours that the owner of the bungalows in which the school was housed was going to sell them over their heads. Mr Lister, ill and weary of arguments with the bishop, was threatening to leave Mandalay. The government grant which had been hoped for did not materialise, yet still the complicated official registers, demanding an analysis of the different tribes and races from which one parent of each child came, had to be completed and the children's examination results forwarded for scrutiny. The success of the school, its fitness to qualify for government aid, was assessed on these - with the obvious temptation. Teachers did not arrive or were unable to teach to the level required. Janie and Doris struggled to fill in gaps - and not only in teaching: in balancing the books - fees were collected monthly direct from the children by form-teachers; in counting the laundry since the Burmese matron could not read or write English; in putting carbolic soap on infested heads; going through boarders' clothes to see which needed mending; buying garments in the bazaar for badly provided boarders, one of the older girls accompanying them to act as interpreter (in fact doing many of the tasks which a competent matron should have been able to undertake); going for walks with the children, playing the piano for them, devising games for them, reading to them, comforting the homesick, while hardly less homesick themselves. Outside plague was raging among the Burmese: children and staff were inoculated with the inevitable tears and faintness. The dreary discomfort of the dirty, shabby bungalows, the torment of mosquito bites waking them in the night and making legs bleed, the food which had to be cheap and was often unappetising, all this combined to depress spirits which badly needed to be lifted up. Miss Easton, struggling as well to teach 35 lessons a week, remarked wryly; "I seem to be head-mistress, form-mistress, matron and nurse-maid rolled into one."

The impression the diaries give of the life of the two young women is of overwork and a suffocating isolation. Yet the part of Mandalay in which the school was situated was perhaps the most attractive in what was described as "a dream city". King Mindon's "Golden City", the last seat of Burmese royalty, had been founded in 1857 in fulfilment of a Buddhist prophecy that on the 2,400th anniversary of the founding of the Buddhist religion a city enshrining Gautama's teaching would be built at the foot of Mandalay hill. Mindon fashioned for himself a great palace at the centre of a foursquare park, surrounded by red brick walls and a moat, with twelve gates, three to a side, each marked with a sign of the zodiac. To this he shifted his government in 1861, dismantling and taking with him most of his previous palace. After Mindon's death, King Thibaw succeeded him, but yielded the city to the British in 1885 at the end of the third Anglo-Burmese war. He himself with his queen was driven into exile and, by 1886, Upper as well as Lower Burma had become part of Victoria's Indian Empire. King Mindon's palace was re-named Fort Dufferin: it is usually referred to in the diaries as "the Fort." The royal palace, later to be totally destroyed in fighting between Japanese and the allies in 1945, still stood in 1915, proud but uninhabited at the centre, used on state occasions and housing a museum.

But the beauty which surrounded the two young English women could not compensate for the lack of companionship and social life. There was, of course, the European Club but the two quickly found that, although admitted, they did not really belong. Miss Easton with her strong views on alcohol and gambling did not take to the style of life she found there and was, perhaps, rather too ready to bristle at imagined slights. "Mrs Aplin, the Commissioner's wife, also came up and introduced herself which was rather a marvel as she is not given to being friendly." Later she was forced to admit that Mrs Aplin, if something too fond of playing the great lady, was also very kind; to begin with her attitude to the English ladies was over-critical and she knew it. Meanwhile she had to be content with the companionship offered by missionaries, particularly Miss Patch and Miss Dunkley who were S.P.G. workers. Miss Dunkley ran a school for Burmese girls. Miss Patch, who helped her, had been trained in nursing which she much preferred to teaching. Both were good friends and very helpful, but were they perhaps a little too easy, too ordinary to satisfy Miss Easton's social aspirations? She remarks wistfully that she is unlikely to have a chance "for wearing my nicest things as English people, except for the missionaries, are not likely to take much notice of us."

Part of the reason - or so they thought - for their isolation was their involvement with Eurasians. It was not considered correct for English ladies of breeding to associate with them as Janie and Doris discovered when they went to a dance in the Volunteer Hall, less exclusive than the Club which would only admit Europeans. The

Listers did not approve of even Mr Saxby who was a Volunteer Officer taking part in Volunteer Hall activities for they feared he would "lose caste". Yet it was a "Club" Captain Willcox and Mr Saxby decided to open that offered Doris and Janie their best chance of recreation. Its founders were very anxious for the two young teachers as "ladies of refinement and breeding" to join, and the two themselves were not indifferent to the lure of a tennis-court. "We shall have such a hard time, if we don't have some amusement", the diary comments wistfully. Besides their work was among Eurasians. Surely their play should be too? But would the men in the Club become too familiar? And what of the Listers with their fear of offending English people, by doing anything which would be considered "infra digne". "But I don't see that it matters very much when English Society here is so rotten and snobbish and when English people will always look on us (with a few exceptions) as rather peculiar for teaching Eurasians at all. It is a social question with perhaps the added difficulty that it is generally rather "fast" English people who mix with Eurasians. But Mr Saxby thinks that I as headmistress can mix with all classes... I should be so glad to have some tennis and we shan't get any at all otherwise." Such scruples seem now a little ridiculous. It is difficult for us to appreciate the delicate circumspection with which single ladies of marriageable age were required to tread in the early part of this century.

In spite of her complaints, Miss Easton did get invited out and made a few contacts with people other than missionaries. There was, of course, strict protocol and a system of "calling" to be adhered to. "After tea Mrs L. and I went out calling. What happens is this. Every new-comer drops cards at the houses of each of the other English people. People have a box for cards at their gates and you put cards in it, but don't ask to see them." In due course some of these visits were returned and even followed up by invitations, though in January she wrote, "Mildred talks of my being inundated with invitations, but we have not been invited to a single house in our nearly 2 months stay." However, in February, dinner with Miss Patch is mentioned and in March she and Janie had tea with Mrs Grossett, "She is a kindly sort of lady... husband an executive engineer. It was really a treat to have tea in a nicely-furnished room with a punkah going and making a cool breeze..."

Another acquaintance was Colonel Penny, the Civil Surgeon who attended Mr Lister, with whom the Matron of the hospital was so desperately in love... "although she knows he has 5 or 6 Burmese children." Later the Waths are mentioned and the Mackintoshes and various others, but few, except for missionaries and clergy figure regularly in the pages of the diary.

What is very noticeable in the Mandalay diaries is how little contact they had with the Burmese themselves, apart from the servants in the compound. Of Burmese life and customs they saw scarcely more than the casual tourist of today, perhaps even less. Doris records a visit to the Bazaar and the smell of the notorious ngapi, the paste made from rotten and fermenting fish. She saw the preparations for the funeral of a Buddhist "priest" as she quite inaccurately calls a monk. (There is no priestly office in Buddhism yet, curiously, my mother made this mistake long after she should have known better.) She records the great paper constructions, the stalls and booths and bands playing and the pongyis in their yellow robes "carrying the coffin and shaking it up and down and tossing it about so that evil spirits could not follow it." Twice she saw a Burmese "pwe" - a street entertainment involving dancing, music and marionettes which went on all night until daybreak. Janie and Doris were particularly taken with "a very nice horse which galloped and shook its head." Marionette plays were, on the whole, esteemed more highly than live plays and they told very long and complicated stories, too long for the English women who came away after an hour or so of watching. The plots were either drawn from legendary Burmese history or were religious in origin, recounting birth stories of the Buddha and of his life in former re-incarnations. Live actors might feel it an irreverence to take the part of the Lord Buddha: such an inhibition did not apply to the use of puppets, who could also portray more convincingly mythological creatures, monsters and heavenly beings with powers of flight. The puppet horse which my mother admired probably represented the starry creature who bought order from chaos. Certainly little wooden horses almost identical to the one she took home from Burma are still a commonplace of pagoda stalls.

Mandalay hill, then as now, was a focal point for excursions. The first time, when Miss Easton walked the boarders there on Sunday after church, she noticed the monastery (pongyi-kyaung) with its "seven or eight red porticoes where people came to offer food for the priests" and the weird Burmese pictures of kings and snakes and dancers and elephants. She did not on this occasion climb the steps, past all the little stalls, to where the impressive golden figure of Gautama, the Buddha, stands with arm outstretched, pointing to the city of Mandalay, for she was growing concerned lest some of the smaller children would not be able to manage the walk back.

The isolation from the Burmese was not, I think, in any way deliberate. Doris and Janie were inevitably cut off by the gruelling demands of their work among Eurasians, by their ignorance of language and culture, by their position as members of a ruling foreign power. When she went to the Post Office and joined a crowd of Burmese waiting for attention, Doris found she must expect to be treated very differently from the natives. "The man left them and came and asked me what I wanted and took me to sit down in the inside while I waited. Another attendant also came to look after me so I had two!" Flattering as this might be, such courteous distinction between Burmese and Europeans did not make for integration. Even in worship the two cultures did not normally meet: there was an English Church and a Burmese church. From time to time there was a joint service in Christchurch, the Burmese church, but even here a physical distinction was maintained. There were pews at the back for Europeans; the Burmese sat on mats at the front; convenience became a separation. And language, of course, was a barrier. The service was conducted simultaneously in two languages - once three, Burmese, English, and Tamil - and the sermon translated sentence by sentence. The only place where the two teachers met Burmese on anything like an equal footing was in a newly-formed Teachers' Association. Even here there were problems. The English of the Burmese members was difficult to follow, making any talks they gave tedious to listen to, and they themselves did not always understand their European colleagues.

The two young women were isolated in so many ways: from their country and its war - mail was at least a month out of date when it arrived; from much of the European as well as the Burmese life of Mandalay - as unmarried girls they could not move freely unchaperoned in the society of the period even apart from any stigma occasioned by their work among Eurasians; from some of the pleasures they might have enjoyed, because of the expense and difficulty of transport. They relied mainly upon bicycles whose punctures on the thorn-strewn tracks occurred with monotonous and irritating frequency, or upon horse-drawn gharries which were cheap but did not operate much beyond the bounds of the city, or, occasionally, upon trams. From any real understanding of the country to which they had come with such good intentions, they were cut off by their ignorance of its language, culture and religion. My mother was certainly aware of this ignorance and wanted to repair it, but she had little time and found few people with the will or ability to enlighten her.

She was not happy. Although the letter-diaries do not often mention her feelings, for she did not want to make her family anxious, her loneliness and frustration come at times to the surface - as when Mr Saxby, who was unfailingly kind and of whom she was genuinely fond, heard that he had been appointed as an officer in the Punjabis. "He says he is going to drop the Listers because they have been telling lies about his commission... It seems rather pathetic when Mr Saxby and Mr Lister were really great friends when we first came. I expect Mr Saxby will drop us too and we shall be lonelier than ever."

The friction between Mr Lister and Mr Saxby she felt keenly. She must also have realised that those who had opposed the setting up of yet another mission school in Mandalay had sense on their side. The Methodists and the American Baptists ran schools, so did the S.P.G. and there was a Roman Catholic Convent for Eurasian girls, while government schools catered for educational if not religious needs. The sole justification for Mr Lister's enterprise was that there was no Anglican school specifically for Eurasians. His first headmistress might fairly have questioned whether that was justification enough.

Her life, of course, was not entirely one of troubled dreariness. Janie might be rather "young in mind", but she was a loyal companion with whom it was possible to laugh and have fun and indulge in lighthearted successes, like securing a second ice cream at the Lieutenant Governor's garden party. There was beauty to be appreciated when there was time to notice it; glowing sunsets reflected in the moat; the startling brilliance of the moonlight; flowers the children picked for her, some blue and some "white and woolly". Then, though the mules were maddeningly stubborn and the white ants a menace, destroying the story-books specially bought out from England, the animals were a source of interest and amusement - squirrels pattering over the bungalows; the family of flop-eared goats which tried to take up residence under the stairs; the bullocks that blundered into the dormitories; above all the little house-lizards which darted up the walls, doing a useful work in catching some of the numerous "creepie crawlies".

There was also work. Miss Easton, it is true, must sometimes have wondered whether it was worth the sacrifice she had made. In her opinion she was not a "real" missionary: the children were, nominally at any rate, Christians already and teaching them was only different from teaching the Warwick children in that they were more frequently socially-deprived and "very devoid of brains", a limitation accentuated by language problems. Yet they were her children. Perhaps only dutifully and conscientiously at first, she studied their needs and gave them the security so many of them lacked. And they rewarded her with an affection which revealed itself in the odd little gifts they brought her: a gecko, a baby squirrel, a scorpion with its sting cut off, serpents' eggs. The boys in particular warmed her heart by their open admiration and the welcome they gave her when she crossed the compound to their part of the school. On one occasion Mr Saxby asked her to bring over some girls to dance as he wanted to teach the boys to behave like gentlemen. "It was great fun. The boys could hardly dance at all, but we danced with them and tried to teach them. We were dancing on a dusty stone floor, so it was rather hard work and we got very hot and thirsty, but they fetched in cups of water for us." On the whole she found the boys livelier than the girls, but the girls, too, responded to her care for them and she perhaps began to warm to them. Muriel, the child she thought almost insane when she first met her, "cried a little" when her mother came to fetch her home. "She is a nice little girl"

Nevertheless it was with heartfelt relief that she wrote on Friday March 31st 1916... "Breaking up prayers about 11.15. I was thankful to see the last of the term."

CHAPTER V

HOT-WEATHER BREAK 1916

April and May brought the hot-weather holiday, the longest in the year. Mrs Lister, baby Guy, Doris and Janie with three servants set off for Maymyo where Mr Lister was to join them later. Maymyo was named for Colonel May, an officer in the Bengal infantry who was stationed there in 1887, and it had become for the British a favourite retreat from the dusty heat of the plains, for it stands at an elevation of some 3,000 feet, in the Shan foothills, and, in its pleasantly temperate climate, many fruits and vegetables familiar to Europeans can be grown. In 1916 it was crowded with English people who could not travel home because of the war as well as the usual annual holiday-makers - government servants, missionaries, and so on.

The diary provides a vivid impression of the place and the recreation it offered - yet it seems that Miss Easton grew restless and unhappy to such an extent that the prospect of a second month there became unbearable. No reason for this is given. But there is a hint of her disillusionment even with missionaries. Mr Garrod, who worked in Mandalay, is "the one missionary I have met... who really devotes himself heart and soul to his work". One senses, too, her feeling of being stifled by people, of needing and not being able to obtain solitude. Was she also in a kind of panic, seeing the years ahead, wondering whether her work would be endurable, let alone valuable, fearing that she might have mistaken her vocation? She would not, of course, spell this out for her family. The diary conceals as well as reveals.

Monday April 3rd. 1916

Packed... Mr Lister came up in the afternoon and said we should not be able to go till Tuesday because one of the fathers had written to say he could not fetch his children till then. I was rather annoyed, but I found he did not really mean we should have to stay, but I think he said it to show that he thought it was really my business to stop, only as a favour he was inconveniencing himself and having the children to stop with him... He has made all the arrangements about the children going home... He ought to insist that the parents fetch them at once - it means keeping on servants, meals etc for the sake of 2 or 3 children...

He also said he was going to Rangoon on Thursday to ask the Bishop about being transferred from Mandalay. He then went to the boys' school and J. was so annoyed at his implying that it was my business to stop on during the holidays to look after boarders that she went over to the other school and had a long talk with him. I advised her not to go as I felt that the question needed consideration... I fancy they had rather a heated discussion...

We had a dreadful time at the last getting off. We had sent for a bullock cart to take our luggage, but it was not allowed into the fort, so then we had to get two gharries. Then the Parrs had to come with us as they also were going to Maymyo and it took some time to collect their luggage from the other 2 schools. Finally J. and I had to cycle down to the station, as the bicycles would not go on the gharries.

We were going to sleep on the train, but the luggage had to be down about 8 o'clock to be weighed and excessed. One gharry arrived down in time for Mr Lister to see to it before the office closed, but the other was too late, so the luggage had just to be put on the platform to wait for the morning... Mr Lister said we must stop on the platform and watch the luggage. We stayed... till about 9.30 feeling very bored as we heard we could not get on the train till 11.30. Then the lugulay (servant) came, so we went back to the school on a gharry (the school is about 2 miles from the station) and got together our small luggage and appealed to Mrs Wright for food and she made us some coffee and found 2 eggs, so we felt considerably better.

We went down again in another gharry between 10.30 and 11 o'clock with the 3 Parrs. Mrs L's cook, Po Kha, was there and helped us. We had to go to the Station-master to let us into the train. He was also kind enough to take the luggage, which had not been booked, into his room to be safe. We put the Parrs into a 2nd Cl. carriage and we went into a first and the lugulay made up our beds.

We undressed properly, but I only got an hour or two sleep. I managed to put up a mosquito net.

Tuesday April 4th

I got dressed about 4 am - it was still very dark - and went along the platform to get the rest of the luggage. It was a great business. To begin with there were no coolies to fetch if from the Station-master's office. Then Po Kha and the lugulay fetched it but the man would not charge for it till I showed the tickets and Mrs Lister had them. So I had to wait about on the platform till she arrived in a gharry with Gawlah and Guy about 5.15. Finally we got everything in. The train was due to leave at 5.39.

We got some chota at a station a little further on. At some of the stations they wait ages which is very wearing.

We had one excitement in that Guy fell off the seat. It was a dreadful moment, but mercifully he did not hurt himself much.

The journey became more interesting when we left the plain and began ascending the hills. We zig-zagged along the sides of the hills and had nice views, but they are not really beautiful because the colouring is uninteresting. Everything is so parched and brown. A few trees dotted about here and there are bright green, but many of them are leafless or dried up. There is no spring here. Some trees never lose all their leaves at once, others suddenly burst into leaf at the beginning of the hot weather and I suppose many will come out suddenly when the rains begin.

When we got to the top of the hills the country grew prettier. There were numbers of really green trees and one or two brooks. We arrived at Maymyo more than an hour late at 10.45 or 11 instead of 9.30. Then we had to wait about ¾ hr on the platform to see our luggage loaded on a bullock cart and put in a gharry. We cycled up to the house. We have taken a partly furnished house for which we have to pay 60 R. the first month and 50 the second. Of course we were most fortunate to secure it as Maymyo is absolutely packed. So few English people are going home this year because of the submarines, that they all flock here. One generally has to give 100 or 150 Rs a month for a house and sometimes the landowners won't let them for less than 6 months. Ours is a kind of a little wooden shanty, built on piles, no downstairs, but upstairs a little sort of recess where Guy and Gawlah sleep. Mrs Lister has had half her bed-room curtained off for a dining-room and we two share the other room. We brought 3 servants - Mrs Lister's cook and boy and a school lugulay and we are getting a sweeper and panniwalla here. This sounds very grand, but I don't fancy we could have done anything cheaper... Of course it is very expensive. This two month holiday will cost £15 to £20 I am afraid.

We brought mats and rugs and curtains and crockery and one or two camp beds with us.

The air of Maymyo felt deliciously cool and fresh after Mandalay, tho' of course the sun is scorching hot. It is about 3,400 feet high, on a big plateau. If one expects a proper hill station, it is disappointing because there are no hills near, but only little wooded hills in the distance, something like the ones at Hereford. The country itself is very like the South of England eg. Bournemouth. Maymyo itself is rather like a London suburb. There are very nice houses and only a small native quarter. It all seems delightful after Mandalay and one realises how oppressive it is to live in a town where everything is swathed in dust and where one hardly ever sees a nice clean looking house.

...It was really very chilly after dinner, but it was very nice to have to sleep under 2 or 3 blankets.

Wed. April 5th

...After tea I had a long talk with Mrs Lister about her husband... She... said she thought he expected other people to sacrifice themselves too much. She seems to think he is determined to leave Mandalay.

We went up to Miss Cook's (a teacher at St. Michael's S.P.G. school in Maymyo) at 5.30 and she walked with us to church for service at 6.30.

I was very worried in Church by prickly heat on my feet... It... comes along the sides and on the soles, and burns and itches in a very exasperating way.

Thursday April 6th

It poured with rain during the night... A cloudy day with only intermittent sunshine seems quite a treat after four months of cloudless weather. We went into some of the shops, both English and native. I bought some stuff to make a skirt for my bathing dress because Mrs Lister says people here are stupid and consider it indecent to bathe in an ordinary dress... After tea we went for a walk, then to the Club. The Club here is very swell. We sat out and looked at the papers and the people.

Friday April 7th

...We heard the cuckoo from the top of the hill. J. had never heard it before. It seems funny to come to Burma to hear it...

There was a heavy thunder-storm after dinner. The rain came down in torrents and as we have an iron roof it made a good deal of noise. The lightning was very vivid - sheet lightning which lit up everything brilliantly.

Sat. April 8th

...It was a glorious morning, so fresh and green after the rain... After tea we cycled to the Blandfords' to get some fresh butter. They are ordering some for us every day from the dairy... Usually out here one has to eat tinned butter which is not very nice, but at Maymyo we get this delicious dairy butter for about the same price (a rupee (1s 4d) a pound).

Sunday April 9th

...Mr Lister has had a dreadful struggle over our bungalows. One of the six notorious villains of Mandalay tried to buy one of the houses so that he could charge an exorbitant rent... Fortunately Mr Lister got wind of what he was after and rushed off and borrowed the money and got the deeds signed and forestalled the man by half an hour or so.

Monday April 10th

We had chota at 7.30, then cycled to Mrs Sparks. Her husband has something to do with Railways and she is staying at the Railway Rest House. Mrs Sparks and we went for a lovely walk in the Jungle. "Jungle" does not necessarily mean dense forest, but just country as opposed to town. People talk about a "jungly" boy, meaning a countrified boy with no town manners. We walked 3 or 4 miles to a natural reservoir. We actually gathered a few buttercups and saw a snake which glided away very fast. We got back to the Rest House between 11 and 11.30 for... a very nice breakfast - porridge, fish and salad, stewed beef and tomatoes, curry and rice, fruit and coffee...

Tuesday April 11th

...Mrs L. and J. went to the station and I began struggling with Burmese, but they were not long so I did not get much done...

At dinner we had a bomb-shell. Mrs Lister had a letter from Mr Lister saying that Mr Saxby was coming back to school. Something had gone wrong about his commission and a telegram had come cancelling it. They knew no more... We are exceedingly sorry for Mr S. He must feel it terribly, but if he really does come back, it sounds like a godsend for the school...

Wed. April 12th

Mrs Lister and I cycled 2 or 3 miles to bathe in a pool in the jungle... It was very rough cycling and we had to go down some rather steep paths. The pool was glorious. It was called Laughing Water. It is pretty deep and one has to swim practically all the time. I dived several times from the side. The pool is shaded a good deal by trees, otherwise the sun would have been scorching. It looks so funny to see someone walking about in a bathing-dress and topee...

Thursday April 13th

...After tea we went a very pretty walk through the jungle to a Shan village. The Shans are quite different from the Burmans, they have a language and customs of their own. We passed a very pretty reedy marsh and gathered a little honeysuckle. There were magnificent bamboos by the village...

Mrs Lister had a letter saying that Mr Saxby is coming up with a tent to stay with us as he wants to get away from Mandalay... When Mr Lister and Miss Dunkley join us there will be six people attached to this house besides Guy and Gawlah, so we shall be somewhat squashed.

Friday April 14th

...After tea we went to the station to meet Mr Saxby at 5.15. He still has had no explanation of the telegram. It merely said, "The Indian Government cancels the appointment of Argyll-Saxby." He says if it had been for disgrace, he would have had the option of resigning or being court-martialled... He tells us that trouble is expected in Afghanistan which may be serious. The Turks who have escaped from Mesopotamia have stirred up the Afghans...

Mr Saxby brought up all his camp outfit and put his tent under our house as it is built on piles.

Saturday April 15th

...Went to the Club swimming baths... Of course it is mixed bathing to which I have never really been used, but I did not really mind as they are gentlemen and behave nicely... Mr Saxby does not like mixed bathing, so he did not come with us...

Sunday April 23rd (Easter Sunday)

...6.45 am non-choral Communion. There were no hymns at all for which I was sorry... It is a pity Mr Garrad has such an unpleasant way of taking the Service. I should think he is the one missionary I have met among the men at Mandalay who really devotes himself heart and soul to his work...

Mr Saxby and I had chota Hazrai after we came in - he told me he is trying to find a place to camp out a mile or so away...

Monday April 24th

We had decided to go for a day's picnic with the Rangoon missionaries, so we had a bullock cart to take the food and 2 servants and some of the others went in a gharry and we cycled to Laughing Water. When we got into the Jungle I walked with Miss Henderson... She told me that they are hoping to get a Christian College for women in Burma, as the Government is hoping to start a Burmese university... We had a very nice day by the pool. There were 8 of us... We bathed twice and kept our stockings off most of the day and some of us had our hair down. One or two had no bathing dresses, so we had to share, giving up parts of ours. Miss Sumner wore her combinations and was washing them out afterwards and the stream swept them away... Some Territorials came along in the afternoon and other people so it seemed quite like an Easter Monday. Picnics here are rather luxurious. Servants do all the work... After dinner... we began a discussion on missions and religion with Mr Saxby which became so exciting that we did not stop till 10.30.

Tuesday April 25th

...I ... went for a cycle ride and a little way into the jungle where I sat down. It gets rather tiring being in such a small house where one can never get really away from other people...

Wed. April 26th

Mr L. is coming up from Mandalay for a month's holiday.

Thursday April 27th

...Mr Saxby departed with his tent and belongings to camp out in the jungle about two miles off. He is taking one of our landlady's sons to stay with him a night or two... We went to the club and watched the tennis for some time and then looked at papers. We bowed to a few people, but it is rather dull as they don't come up and speak.

Sat. April 29th

...J. and I went off on our cycles after tea to try and find where Mr Saxby and the boy were camping... Mr Saxby had explained to us exactly where they were going but we could find no trace of them at all... We passed a tree on the way absolutely enveloped in a gauze of spider's webs... Mr Lister is still very poorly and Mrs Lister is rather down...

Sometimes I don't know how I shall endure another month here. I almost think Mandalay is preferable. At any rate, there, there is work to fill up one's thoughts...

Sunday April 30th

...Mr Lister has begun dysentery again and is staying in bed. The weather has become very hot in the middle of the day...

Wed. May 3rd

Mrs Lister is charging us 60 rupees a month for board and lodging (ie. £1 a week) which is very moderate for here... We have to pay our lugulay 8 rupees as well and of course for 2 months it will be pretty expensive together with the railway fare. I am afraid it will cost considerably over £10...

Friday May 5th

J. and I went off in a gharry at 7.30 to call Miss Sumner and Miss Elliott as we were going for a picnic. We went to the G.F.S. to fetch Miss Drewitt. We dismissed the gharry and put our food on a bullock-cart and walked ourselves. We walked about 6 miles. We intended to climb a hill called One-Tree Hill which is conspicuous for its one solitary tree from all sides of Maymyo. At one point we saw a buffalo and had to make a circuit to avoid it, because buffaloes hate white people and run at them and of course they can gore to death. They don't dislike natives at all. We got separated from the bullock-cart as it went along a different track, and, as we had told it to wait by the reservoir, after we had climbed a hill not very far from One-Tree Hill, we had to scramble down to the water to reach the cart instead of going on. The cart had our food and we were too tired to go on without it, so we gave up the idea of climbing the hill and sat down and had breakfast.

It was a nice cool day after the rain and rather cloudy which made it much pleasanter for walking. We all five of us rode a good deal of the way back in the cart. The road was something terrible in places. You would not believe it possible for any cart to go along it without upsetting. Of course we were fearfully jolted, but it was quite exciting. The driver seemed rather amused at our excitement.

These bullock tracks have furrows sometimes more than a foot or two deep and huge holes and rough places...

Monday May 8th

We had decided to go for two nights to the Gokteik viaduct which is one of the wonders of Burma and the world so we had chota with porridge, tripe (ordered by the doctor for Mr L.) and eggs at 7.15 and then packed our things. We had to take bed-clothes with us and all our food as it can't be got there and the cook and the boy and Gawlah and Guy as Mrs Lister does not like leaving him, so it took a little time to get ready...

Our train went about 10 am... We descended all the time through the jungle for about 1,000 feet till we reached our destination at 12.30. We had sandwiches and papya with us which kept us going. Papya is a nice juicy fruit of the melon variety only softer.

We walked up to the Railway Rest House a little way from the station... This place is quite in the jungle, there is no village at all. On the way in the train we had wide views of hills and valleys, but they always disappoint one after Switzerland, because I feel to want snow and bigger trees and running water. The Railway Rest House is very nice. It contains several suites of rooms... bed-room with 2 beds and bathroom and sitting-room...

At 3.45 we had a cup of tea and biscuits and then set off... There is an enormous gorge, somewhere about 1,500 feet deep, practically sheer down, its sides covered with trees; and at the bottom is a lovely river rushing over rocks with maidenhair and other ferns growing on them. At one point in the gorge there has been in past ages a landslip, which makes a kind of barrier across it and in this barrier there is a vast cave and, on the top of it, the railway has made a viaduct with about 13 supports and about ¼ mile long. At the other end of the viaduct from here, the train goes through a tunnel in the rock and passes along the edge of the gorge... There is quite a good pathway winding down the side of the gorge to the bottom with wooden seats at intervals. It has recently been mended for the L. G. to go down.

We saw one or two pepul trees which are very interesting. They send up a number of shoots round the trunk of another tree and these shoots gradually join together till they form a kind of envelope round the original trunk. Up above you can see the branches of both trees and their different leaves.

At the bottom of the gorge there is a long winding wooden bridge which leads into the cave between two high pinnacles of rock at the entrance. One of the pinnacles is a stalagmite and is half covered with green creeper and half with petrified creeper which has been turned to stone by the action of water dripping from the roof. The wooden steps and pathway wind along the side of the cave past wonderful natural basins and tanks formed in the rock full of lovely clear water, right into the dark recesses at the back of the cave till a small opening, through which the river makes its way out at the back, is visible. The cave is simply wonderful. I have never seen one nearly so grand. It is an enormous height and very long and the sides are formed of rock fluted with the action of the water. It is like a vast cathedral, only the river flows through the bottom and water drips from part of the roof.

When we came out of the cave we walked... along the bank of the river and found a little white cross marking the spot where a soldier was drowned last October...

Tuesday May 9th

We had chota about 7.15, then we went out as it was a perfectly glorious morning. We walked across the viaduct along the railway lines. There is a good ledge along the sides which saves one from falling... Of course it is a terrific height to look down on the gorge (870 ft below) and the river. After we had crossed we climbed through the jungle to the top of the hill on the other side, but we could not get any view because of the trees. We found one or two pretty flowering trees. On the way back Mrs Lister and I, instead of crossing the viaduct, went along a winding path a good deal overgrown with trees to the bottom of the viaduct which stands on top of the cave. It looked an enormous height from below... to the top of the viaduct.

We had breakfast about 10.30 and then lay down till about 12.30 and again went down the gorge. It was magnificent in the sunshine... I went as far back in the cave as possible and clambered a good long way over the rocks after the path had ended, but it was impossible to reach the other entrance because the river which flows at the bottom was too wide and strong to wade across and it was not possible to find a footing along the rocks. I got very wet and dirty - there are so many basins in the rocks filled with water. Po Kah, the Listers' cook, who had come to bring over our tea-things, told me to come into a crevice to get some peculiar white porous stone. I climbed up a rock, but found myself nearly in a tank of water and when I managed to avoid that I came into a shower-bath of water pouring from above so I gave up the attempt...

...After tea we paddled and then Mrs Lister and I bathed - The water was very nice, but the current was rather strong and we had to be careful, especially as a soldier was drowned there. We wore vests and knickers as we did not bring bathing-dresses with us. I sat and read Ivanhoe afterwards (I am taking it for Literature next term)...

Wed. May 10th

J. and I went down beneath the viaduct. We wanted to find a way to the other end of the cave but could not because the jungle was so thick. So we climbed up the other side and rested at the top and came back across the viaduct. After breakfast we lay down and then went to the station for the train at 12.30... We reached Maymyo between 3.30 and 4 and took gharries home...

Saturday May 13th

...Janie caught a chill probably through staying in the baths too long, so I had to go to the Ainleys alone for tea. There were 4 Territorials there. We had a very nice tea, I expect because they are Yorkshire...

Sunday May 14th

J. was still very poorly. She seemed to have something like dysentery. Miss Cooke says there is an epidemic of it - a germ carried by flies.

Tues. May 16th

...Janie seemed no better so we sent for the doctor. Colonel Hammond was away, so Major Stewart came. He seemed to think it was dysentery and that she had better go to hospital as we could not give her proper treatment. These houses are most uncomfortable to be ill in, especially for an internal complaint like that...

Mr L. told me that the school is going to pay our passage out, so we shall not have to refund.

Wed. May 17th

...I cycled to the hospital. J. seemed much better and quite comfortable, tho' rather dull. She had 2 injections in her arm. The charge is quite moderate for the room. As her salary is 105 rupees a month she has to pay a rupee a day. They charge a rupee for every hundred up to a maximum of 6 rupees a day.

Thurs. May 18th

...Mr Lister was poorly again with a return of sprue. He has never fully recovered from the former attack. He does not diet for long enough. Mr Saxby came in for a while. He must be having a trying time. People are hinting apparently that he has received an explanation as to why his commission is cancelled and is concealing the reason...

Sunday May 21st

Church. The Bishop took the service. He has rather a nice voice... Janie re-appeared from hospital in a gharry just before breakfast. She seems fairly strong considering she has been in bed for a week.

Wed. May 24th

Finished packing... Mr Lister came with me to the station as Mrs L. was very tired. The Parr children were travelling by the same train but they went 2nd cl. and I went first. There was an American Baptist missionary in the same compartment. She has a Vernacular or Anglo-Vernacular School at Mandalay. She was very interesting to talk to. I asked her a good deal about the Buddhist religion and she seemed to know more about it than some of the other people I have asked... When we finally reached the plains after about 2½ hours there was a strong wind blowing which at times felt fairly cool, but at other times was rather like the blast of a furnace... We reached Mandalay about 2.15, half an hour late.

It was rather a business getting coolies to look after the Parrs' luggage and mine. At last I got them and luggage packed into 2 gharries and I cycled to the Parsonage to try and get the keys from the school store-room... I found Mrs Wright at school and she looked after my luggage. Mr Saxby came over and brought me iced-lemonade in a thermos which was most refreshing. We sat and talked for some time. The Bishop had written to him saying that the General has received an explanation (about the cancellation of his commission) and that he must write for it and show it to him. It is rather a mistake on the part of the Bishop, as Mr S. naturally resents interference as he is not in the least under the Bishop and was not appointed by him...

It seemed pretty hot, but the temperature on Mr S's verandah about 5 o'clock was only 101 and Mandalay has been lately about 115, but I expect I feel it worse after Maymyo. My bungalow seemed very desolate after dark. I an all alone in it and there are no purdahs (curtains), as they are all still at Maymyo in use, and so on all sides are open doorways and there is only one lamp available and the dinner was very badly cooked and I did not much want it because of the heat and my things were all packed up, so the room was more desolate than ever.

Mr Saxby came over in the middle of dinner and stayed and read me a poem he has just written which I like very much. It is the soliloquy of a mother who has sent her son to the front...

I really did feel a little nervous after he had gone, but, of course, the servants are not really very far away. However, it is rather startling to hear so many noises and to find bats running over the floor and flying about. Then it was so hot in bed that I could not get properly off to sleep till about 2 o'clock. There was a strong wind blowing which made all the doors and windows all over the house which don't fasten properly bang incessantly and I was very sticky and thirsty.

Thurs. May 25th

Ma-Mi wakened me about 7 am. I had to get up to let her in as we had locked up the house very carefully the night before. It seemed hot even at that time of the morning and I did not feel to want any chota. Of course the food here seems rather horrid after what we have been having at Maymyo.

I had to go to the Parsonage to see if I could find the school spoons, forks and knives which Mr Lister has locked up somewhere. Mrs Wright, I believe, and the children, certainly, are having to eat curry and rice and everything with their fingers. I daresay they don't mind but I don't like their doing it... I could only find 5 or 6 forks. I was very hot and tired when I got in. At home one can hardly realise what it is to be thirsty nearly all day and to have nothing that really quenches thirst. Warm water is practically useless. I am afraid we shall have to indulge in ice... I had to lie down at intervals during the afternoon, it was so horribly hot. I went down to the post about 7 pm... and when I got in there was a most wonderful tropical storm - no rain and very little thunder, but lightning all over the sky, illuminating everything most gorgeously. There was also awaiting me Mr S's thermos full of iced lemonade and you can't imagine what a treat it was to have something really cold... He came a little later to see if I was frightened of the storm.

CHAPTER VI

A SECOND WIND

"Friday. June 2nd. 1916. School re-opened. It poured during the night. The rains have certainly broken... The buses are troublesome at present. We have new drivers who don't know yet what to do and the mules are very stubborn and won't go."

On her return from Maymyo, Doris Easton was flung back into the familiar morass of problems; the squabbles; the nastiness of the cheap food; the uncertainties about the school's future for it was now deeply in debt; and, on top of all this, the rainy season which, though it tempered the heat, brought with it depression and sickness. Yet the diaries suggest a new resilience. She seems to have come to terms with her work; to be trying fresh ways of stimulating the children's interest - Girl Guides, a prefect system for instance - and to be entering more fully into such activities as were available. Among these were the Teachers' Association, newly-formed by Mr Saxby, The Temperance Society run by the Methodists, the Volunteer Hall Dances. Her natural courage and good sense, which had flagged a little during that bewildering first term, were once more firmly in control.

Apart from Mrs Wright's incompetence the worst burden was the continuing friction between Mr Lister, Mr Saxby and Bishop Fyffe. This she found hard to bear, particularly the rows between Mr Saxby and Mr Lister. She liked both men and regarded them as friends. Both were pig-headed, impetuous, and easily-wounded. Too often she was in the unenviable position of listening in confidence to the complaints of each against the other.

When his commission was cancelled, Argyll Saxby returned to the headship of the school to the joy of his pupils. Mr Lister publicly acknowledged his popularity at a parents' "At Home" held on June 1st 1916, the anniversary of the school's opening. "He mentioned how delighted the boys were to have Mr Saxby back and how one boy wanted to have the holidays cut short when he heard Mr S. was returning." This was generous of Mr Lister, for only three days earlier there had been an angry scene when he had asked Mr Saxby to be responsible for the bus-drivers and mules who were now going to live in the school because the army was no longer able to provide for them. Mr Saxby's refusal was inconsistent since "when he consented to come back, he told Mr Lister that he must have more power in his own hands and not have him interfering so much... Of course I try to show him Mr Lister's point of view... but although I think Mr S. unreasonable and a little selfish, I do know from experience that Mr. L. is extremely trying... Poor Mr Saxby - he is indeed in a horrid position. All sorts of rumours are going round about him - one circulated by Captain Monk to the effect that he is a German spy!" Here is the underlying cause of Mr Saxby's sore touchiness, his failure to get a commission. That and resentment at Mr Lister's imperious manner. In fact he was perfectly prepared to take charge of the mules and their drivers and did so with his usual efficiency.

The mystery of Argyll Saxby's commission rumbles on through the pages of the diary, causing a new rift between the Bishop and Mr Lister who sided with Mr Saxby when Bishop Fyffe demanded an explanation of its cancellation. "Mr S. has laid the explanation before (the School Governors) and they are perfectly satisfied, but he does not wish the Bishop to know, because it is a well-known fact, by all accounts, that the Bishop does not keep things to himself... Mr Lister says that he won't break Mr Saxby's confidence and that as the Bishop refused all connection with the school at the beginning, he can't claim it now." This impasse was resolved through the mediation of Mr Price, a clergyman from Meiktila, who managed to persuade Mr Saxby to send Bishop Fyffe his papers with the explanation.

And what was the explanation? The diary never fully reveals it. My mother knew but kept the secret. However it appears to have had something to do with Mr Saxby's appointment to a former post which had never been confirmed and a consequent suspicion that he had been dismissed. In the end he left the school to go to England to enlist.

The school re-opened on Friday June 2nd in pouring rain which formed huge pools in the playground and seeped into the classrooms. There were difficulties with the buses, for the new drivers did not know what to do and the mules were "very stubborn". The boarders went down with ailments, mostly minor, some serious. Edith

Bentinck was admitted to hospital with malaria where Miss Easton, visiting her, saw "the tiniest Burmese baby imaginable. It was a month old, but looked like a wizened doll." There was illness, as well among the staff: one of the masters at the boys' school died in hospital from malarial jaundice. When news came of Lord Kitchener's death, Mr Saxby requested a black band to be sewn onto his uniform which Doris managed to supply from "an old black alpaca petticoat" of her mother's which had already provided bands for the netball team. The Lieutenant Governor on a visit to Mandalay was shown round the school by Mr Lister. Doris trailed round with the Commissioner, Colonel Aplin, the Aide de Camp and his private secretary and one or two others, "It was rather a farce my being there as Mr Lister did all the talking and I did not say anything." However the Lieutenant Governor, "a fat red-faced man not unlike a book-maker," ordered a holiday for the children. The day-girls went home: the boarders had, of course, to be occupied:

"J. and I took the boarders to the top of Mandalay hill. There are about 900 steps up to the top, I think, and booths on the way up with mineral water and flowers. There are one or two enormous gilded statues of Buddha. We had a splendid view, from the top, of the plain and the mountains bounding it and the Irrawaddy and the Fort and moat. There was a strong breeze. The girls bought me a number of sticks with roses and flowers fastened to them. I suppose they were really meant for offerings to the Buddha. They also bought me some dear little baskets and tiny water-pots."

Although Janie had now taken over the responsibility from Mrs Wright, the servant drama continued. "The lugulays all came to me and said they wanted to leave. The servants are an endless worry. One of them insulted and threatened Mrs Wright, another did something or other to the paniwallah's wife, and Mr Saxby thrashed one of them. Then last night they stoned his house and another of them has been stealing Mrs Wright's chickens and so on." The grand climax came on July 6th. "I found that fine fusses had been going on. Mr Saxby's boy had informed him that Mrs Wright had been selling rice and curry to the servants (of course it must be school rice and curry) and making sweets for the children and selling them to them. (Even if she does not use school sugar, which I should imagine, she must be using school firewood and, of course, spending time which ought to be devoted to her work). Then a small Indian boy, brother to Mr Saxby's 'boy', who had come as a lugulay and was trying to do the work quite nicely, had run away because, he said, Mrs W. had beaten him, and he could not be persuaded to return.

Then the lugulay who was locked up for insulting and threatening Mrs W. was discovered to have said she hit him... Then the paniwallah had quarrelled with the other servants and Mrs W. (without permission) had said he might sleep in the other compound and so the dhobi had no buckets to fetch the water etc. We decided that Mrs W. must go. Even if she is not dishonest, she has been doing practically no work and she muddles up everything and quarrels with all the servants..." Mrs Wright was duly given notice and went on July 21st - "great relief".

The school term ground on its way. The girls' sewing was inspected and approved by Miss Laughlin, head of St. Mary's school, Rangoon and, later, the academic work by Inspector Cocks. "He thought the children very good, quite above the average." There was alarm over a pariah dog which was thought to be going mad, but escaped before it could be shot. Examination papers were set and marked: the school now qualified for a £60 p.a. government grant. The term ended at last in September. Doris had pressing invitations to visit Rangoon for the fortnight's break from Miss Laughlin and from Mrs Fyffe, but in the event could not stay with either, as the train she was travelling on was stopped by floods. She spent a few days in Maymyo instead.

The dilemma Doris found herself in of two invitations for the brief September holiday is indicative of the way her social life was widening. She appears now to have overcome her scruples about attending Eurasian functions - what did it matter what people thought of her when her own conscience approved? "There was a sort of social and dance at the Volunteer Hall to say goodbye to some sergeant who was off to Mesopotamia... It was quite pleasant. They were practically all Eurasians and our mistresses went and I was rather glad to go for that reason as I like to see how they behave. I danced every dance I was there... Eurasian dances are very proper. Your partner does not sit with you at all. Directly the dance is over he takes you back to the identical seat you came from next some lady friend and leaves you there." There was a "pleasant evening" at the parsonage. "Mr Edmunds played the piano, Mr Liddell sang and I played the violin. Mr Scot... gave some very amusing recitations. He seems to have a whole stock of them." On this occasion she met Dr Sheldon and later his wife who was also a doctor. She found, too, congenial companionship in the Mackintoshes... "Her husband and she are very fond of reading... They have been in Mandalay about two months. She was in the Jungle a long time and says she has got rather independent of other people and does not much mind the Mandalay people being unsociable. Just as she was going to drive me home, he came in. He looked a very attractive man, so pleasant and boyish. He is in the Public Works Department. This is not considered so classy as the Indian Civil Service, but I must say it is people belonging to the former who are more friendly..." Even the "aristocrats", after whose recognition she wistfully aspired while remaining fiercely disdainful of their snobbery, proved to be more approachable. She was invited to dinner by the wife of the Judicial Commissioner... "a very nice dinner with pink ice for pudding..." and even Mrs Aplin, the Commissioner's wife, expressed a desire for a call. Miss Easton, who seems to have resented what she regarded as patronising condescension, remarks acidly: "I suppose she wanted to see if we were fit for polite society. We stayed about ten minutes and she asked the usual questions as to whether we liked Mandalay and whether we went to the Club etc." However, this contrasts forcibly with her first impression of the Cuffes whom she met at the Grossetts' house the following February. Of Lady Cuffe she comments "She is such an aristocrat and not in the least a snob."

A treat which came their way rarely but was always appreciated when it came was a ride in a motor-car. "Mr Grossett wanted to take us for a motor-ride. J. and I and Mr Lister went. It was simply glorious; we went about 20 miles altogether and the country was really very pretty. The hills looked so lovely rising straight from the plain which is really quite green now with fresh paddy shoots. Of course we had to come back the same way. That is the worst of an uncivilised country. There are practically no roads, just one or two connecting the main towns which may be several hundred miles apart." Mr Grossett took them out on future occasions, always recorded with enthusiasm in spite of the uneven roads on which "we jumped up and down" and the hazards of punctures. Their pleasure in these little excursions underlines how circumscribed physically was their life in Mandalay. However Doris certainly did more travelling by car in Burma than she had done in England: perhaps more than she was to do when she returned home. She had by March 1917 become sufficiently an expert to compare the smooth action of the Overland with the rough ride in a Ford!

In the diary the companionship of Janie is so much taken for granted that it is scarcely mentioned. The pronoun "we" always includes her. Sometimes Miss Easton might be a little irked by her constant presence and be glad when her absence afforded the solitude she craved, but it is plain that in her she had a staunchly loyal friend. Janie was lively and attractive. In wartime, romances can develop very quickly and this happened in Mandalay. The first hint came on August 1st 1916. "We went to dinner with Colonel Penny... There was another lieutenant in the Punjabis there, a young man called Goldburgh or some such name. I did not much enjoy the evening... We had a little music after dinner and came away about eleven o'clock. Colonel P. and Mr Goldborough walked home with us. The latter seems rather taken with J. and asked her if he might call." Three days later there was another encounter at a meeting held in the Palace. "Someone brought us two chairs and as luck would have it put us just behind the two chairs where Mr Dunkley and Mr Goldborough were sitting... I was rather sorry as it looked as if we had gone to sit near them on purpose, especially as Mr G. later came and took a chair near J. He walked home with us. He is from St. John's Oxford and is in the Forest Department here, an I.C.S. (Indian Civil Service) man." By August 24th Lieutenant Goldberg was on his way to the Middle East and Janie was smitten by a vague malaise for which Dr Sheldon suggested a few days at the Parsonage. Janie travelled there in a gharry: Doris cycled alongside. They called on the way at the station to pick up a parcel. "When we opened it at the Parsonage it proved to be a leather blotter with silver mounts and J's initials which Mr Gordon Goldberg had sent her from Rangoon on his way to Mesopotamia. There is supposed to be an understanding between them, but whether it will come to anything I don't know."

Meanwhile far away in England another romance was developing between Mildred Easton and Theodore Wilson of Kendal, Westmorland, where Mildred was working as a matron in the Stramongate Quaker school. "The mail came, but I am always disappointed now because Mildred does not write and I can't get all the details I want about Theodore. I don't yet know what his business is, whether he is well-off, why he is exempted and whether he has a moustache and what colour his hair and eyes are and I think it will be unbearable if they have the wedding without me." Mr Wilson worked for his uncle's woollen firm, the Castle Mills, in Kendal. He was not exempted from the army: in fact quite shortly he went out to the front in France. He and Mildred were married on Nov. 8th 1916. There was, of course, no question of Doris being able to be there.

The diary records the daily, weekly, monthly round in minute, sometimes repetitive detail. The tedium of life is faithfully reproduced as well as the irritating and amusing and fascinating events which also form a part of existence. For that reason I have not told my mother's story entirely in extracts from her journals, choosing instead to intersperse passages of summary and narration which can move swiftly through her pages. But the only way to experience the full flavour of her busy Mandalay life is to let her actual words draw one into it. The next chapter is a kind of rag-bag. The reader may dip and skip at will, though to travel through it in orderly, leisured sequence is equally possible and probably more rewarding. From time to time the record glints with a liveliness and humour which confirm that Doris Sarah Easton had gained her second wind - particularly her wicked account of the Temperance Society entertainment and her full, vivid description of the visit of the Viceroy, Lord Chelmsford.

CHAPTER VII

TRIALS AND TRIUMPHS IN MANDALAY

Among the "scraps" some sombre, some cheerful, in the ragbag of the diary, for Sept. 1916 - April 1917, are four larger patches which dominate, though all belong to one month - The Temperance Entertainment; the Durbar for Lord Chelmsford, Viceroy of India; the visit to Mrs Aplin, wife of the Commissioner of Mandalay; and the summons to Rangoon to stay at Bishopscourt.

Besides these nothing but snippets. It is easy to miss the one for January 20, 1917, which records an invitation that was to change Miss Easton's life.

Sat. Sept. 16th 1916

...Spent some time altering the time-table as we have to do without a third mistress in the kindergarten - we can't afford it. I think we are in very low water financially. I never feel at all sure that this school will be a permanent thing. Government is curtailing its grants because of the war.

Monday Sept. 18th

School as usual. It was a frightfully hot day but fortunately there was a heavy thunderstorm after tea which cooled the atmosphere... I had various little presents from the children - another very nice horse, a little Shan bag, 2 huge Burmese cigars a foot or two long, 2 huge fruits as big as melons, like oranges inside etc.

Tues. Sept. 26th

...Really the animals here are incorrigible. Twice I found a huge bullock in the girls' bedroom standing between their beds, and then, at night, the frogs make such a deafening noise with their continual croaking that one can hardly hear what is said. Every night the servants have to put the hens to bed as they can't go themselves. They throw them onto the top of their houses to roost and the hens make a great commotion.

Sat. Sept. 30th

...Mr Saxby fetched me over to see the boys' school which was more flooded than the girls'. There was a deep pool in front of it and some of the boys dressed in shirts and shorts were playing football in it and falling down and swimming in between and having great fun... Worked. I could not help watching the little lizards climb over my books and gulp down all the little flies they could find. The mosquitoes and flies are very troublesome just now owing to the standing water outside. The chorus of frogs is incessant and the bull-frogs make a monotonous boom at regular intervals. I feel hungry just now - I suppose because it is suddenly cooler - and I long for a good square English meal...

Fri. Oct. 6th

...Mr Lister is having a great disturbance with the Bishop. As the Bishop has interfered so much with the school and made himself chairman of the Committee, Mr Lister says he must be responsible for getting another head-master at the boys' school when Mr Saxby goes at Christmas. Mr Lister says he wants to resign the principalship of the schools, but the Bishop says if he does go, he will not give him a Government chaplaincy. The Bishop wants him to remain principal and also to do the teaching which is madness as he would be certain to break down... Mr L. went to Meiktila on Monday to consult Mr Price, another chaplain, rather a clear-headed, sane man.

There are various breaches on the railway line owing to floods, so he had quite an interesting journey. At some places the embankment was washed away and the metals hanging over a chasm. They had to cross in a trolley and get into another train. They walked about 7 miles at one point...

I have to pay 50/- a year income-tax. It is trying.

Sunday Oct. 8th

Church. Read. Hymn Singing. Miss Pearson came to tea. Miss P. says the Lieutenant Governor does not want any lady to appear twice in the same dress during the Viceroy's visit and they are to get dresses from England, not get the dhobi to make them one. One lady finds it cheaper to go to England on a visit than to get dresses, shoes and stockings to match. He also said he considered the ladies here dressed very badly... they wear their dresses too long. It seems ridiculous to make such a fuss in war-time.

However he seems to be a good man for the position. He has a great deal of go. Apparently he goes about in disguise and finds out the corruption and bribery that goes on. Miss Pearson thinks that even the English officials are not above it. The Burmese police often seem to connive at robberies and so forth.

Oct. 27th

(The Listers) are definitely going away on Tuesday for 2 months... In about a fortnight Mr Price is coming here and he will take over the principalship of the school. The Listers don't know what will happen after Christmas.

Wed. Nov. 8th

I got two letters from Mother. It was really very nice receiving them on Mildred's wedding-day as it made me seem near to hear details about what was going to happen. After tea I worked hard as I wanted to be free after dinner to follow the wedding which would be 8.10 pm by our time. Of course it was a miserable day for me.

Fri. Nov. 17th

...After dinner unpacked my blue silk dress. I am taking out the lining and making it much shorter and I think it will look better.

Tues. Nov. 21st

The dhobi brought me a dress. He has really made me an extremely pretty one. I gave him my pink flowery dress as a pattern which I think is the best thing to do. J's does not seem very successful.

Fri. Nov. 24th

Mr Price came up to the school. He really has changed with Mr Lister though no one knows for how long. He came to talk to me about the Scripture exam and I was rather annoyed because he wants to have an oral exam throughout the school... I foresee that Mr Price is going to be more of a handful than Mr Lister. He is a very determined man, exceedingly High Church and very fond of fighting with people. He is very much liked, though, because he really is a very nice man in spite of it all.

After: Mr Saxby came to drill the girls in forming fours etc for the Viceroy's visit...

Sat. Nov. 25th

...Did my blue dress. It was rather tiresome to get the kilts right again. I had to take them off to take out the lining.

Miss Butt came to see me during the morning to bring me the dress I am to wear at this Temperance entertainment. The dress is a blue Grecian dress. I am given a typed speech to deliver. I am afraid it will be rather a poor show.

Mon. Nov. 27th

Lessons as usual. Composed a speech on Temperance for the entertainment on Friday.

...Miss Butt was having a rehearsal at the Volunteer Hall, but we had to wait ages as the volunteers had just come in from practice and were buzzing about the hall... finally we gave up the attempt to rehearse in the big hall and went upstairs where there were only a few ladies and rehearsed our speeches. It was rather embarrassing as the Bar was next door and men kept coming in and looking upon us. Of course the Wesleyans don't have anything to do with the Club so I don't suppose they minded, but I do know a good many of the Club men slightly...

Fri. Dec. 1st

Supervised Examinations etc. There are innumerable "worries" at present in connection with the Viceroy's visit and Prize Giving and exams. All the compound has to be cleared of rough shrubs. A man came to ask why ours had not been done... The Government Officials are nearly off their heads, I fancy, with anxiety about the V's visit. You see Mandalay is a seditious place. Last Christmas a conspiracy was planned which would probably have led to a rising almost as bad as the Indian Mutiny if it had not been discovered in time. It was arranged by the Punjabi troops, at a certain Mohammedan festival, to give the Territorials drugged drinks and then rise and seize the town. However, some of them quarrelled and disclosed the plot. The Punjabi troops have gone to Mesopotamia now and we have Gurkhas. There are no Burmese soldiers as Burmans do not believe in war; being Buddhists they won't take life if they can help it. I fancy now, however, some Burmans have been enrolled as sappers and miners and of course many of them are slack about keeping the Burmese customs.

After tea I dressed for the Temperance meeting and tried to make my blue Grecian dress look as respectable as possible, but it was too short, too tight, and an ugly blue...

The meeting was supposed to begin at 6pm, but I think it was considerably later as three Territorials had promised to sing and not one turned up, so Miss Butt with her usual courage went searching round the volunteer club and seized hold of one poor young territorial and told him he had got to do something.

The programme began with a piano solo... Then came our Temperance Dialogue. Miss Merrick B. A. (Principal of the Wesleyan High School) was the spirit of the Twentieth Century and was dressed as a queen. Round her sat the three doctors of Philosophy, Medicine and Political Economy... I stood up as I had to speak first and an American Baptist Mission boy stood by me holding up the Royal Temperance Legion banner... The boy gave a recitation and the curtain dropped.

The poor territorial sang, but he could not really sing at all well. Then... Miss Backhurst sang... and then we attacked the territorial again... He had no music so we had to suggest songs he could sing without the words... We finally hit on "Where my caravan has rested", but I think he la-la-ed some of it. You see we felt obliged to provide some music, as the meeting had been advertised as "The Spirit of the Twentieth Century: Entertainment and Music" and it seemed rather a fraud. Then the Rev. Bertie Adcock (Wesleyan Minister) gave a speech on Temperance from a Patriotic point of view...

There was a large audience - no Church of England clergymen or missionaries. *They* don't believe in abstinence. I can't understand the point of view of people like Miss Patch and Miss Dunkley... Miss Butt finds the drinking habits of English people out here a great stumbling block in Missionary work, especially among Mohammedans who are such strong teetotallers.

Sat. Dec. 3rd

...We had to get up at 5.30 am for the rehearsal. It was pitch dark and pouring... Then we walked to the pandals (wooden seats) erected for the eight thousand school children who will watch the procession between the South Gate and the Club... We got there about 7.30 am and marched the children to their seats which were of course soaking and waited there till about 9.30 because the Vernacular schools came late... Mr Sherman, District Superintendent of Police, galloped up once or twice and looked at us, and Mr Symms, Inspector of Vernacular schools, looked at us and that is all that happened... we did not reach home until 10 am...

Monday Dec. 4th

We had another rehearsal at the pandal from before 7.30 till 9.30. However, it did not seem as long as Saturday. It was a nice bright morning... The Burmese school-children really were a sight worth seeing - thousands of them all in bright colours and then some little Mohammedan and Parsi children and pongyis (monks) in their gorgeous orange garments.

We gave the children a holiday for the rest of the day...

Wed. Dec. 6th

Got up about 5 am. Packed off the children and mistresses at 6.30 and J. and I went to the station for the reception with Mr Saxby... There was a fine pandal erected near the platform with a shade over it made of orange and red paper in Burmese design and pillars covered with gold leaf. His Excellency, the Viceroy of India and Burma, Lady Chelmsford and their daughter arrived at 8.30 am prompt in a special train. Along the platform were arranged 4 huge white parasols, flounced, and 6 gold ones (this is the mark of royalty in Burma) and he walked between them. He was followed by 10 men in red coats with gold braid, carrying gold maces and white horsehair plumes.

The Lieutenant Governor also sat on the platform and various magistrates and officers in white with lovely red cockades in their helmets and a Burman in the old Burmese general's costume which consists of a sort of coat with capes covered with gold and other colours and a curious kind of helmet with gold flaps down the cheeks.

A speech was made to the Viceroy about the town and its needs and he made one in return and was presented with the speech in a silver casket and a silver figure. I do not know whether it was a Buddha.

The Viceroy has a nice face, he is a tall thin man. His wife is tall and thin too, but the daughter rather plump. She had on a pink straw hat with pink roses and a white dress. Of course the speeches had to be translated into Burmese. Lord and Lady Chelmsford could not help laughing at the sound of it. Burmese has such a curious intonation and occasional bellows at the end. There was one Burman of note who was so fat that he had two chairs to sit on.

We got out early and watched the people get into their carriages. Of course the bodyguard was lined up outside. The native lancers look fine in their uniform. We got a gharry again and drove back through crowds of Territorials, and Burmese children. A Burmese crowd is very attractive in the bright sunshine because of all the gay colours.

Our tickets for the Durbar had not arrived. We applied 2 or 3 weeks ago and were told we should get them if there was room... We had almost given up hope of getting them in time when they arrived at 1 o'clock... We dressed and had tea and walked with Mr Saxby to the Palace. It was a glorious afternoon, bright sunshine but cool breeze. We had to be in our seats at 3.15. We were right at the back but we could just see the throne. It is made of silver gilt and was used for King Edward and the Prince of Wales and has been sent here from Simla. The palace itself is beautiful with its gold pillars and red roofs.

As we were at the back we could see all the troops lined up outside. Then the Shan chiefs - Sawbwas - drove up one by one; some were in carriages with brilliant yellow sunshades over them and bright coloured seats for the driver. So many shots were fired from the battery as each one of importance entered the Palace. Their dresses were magnificent. Some had on these long coats with several capes on the shoulders and queer kinds of gold head-dress like a large flat plate with a cup on it and then a spike in the cup. Some of the head-dresses were all crusted with jewels and the material of their garments was wonderful. Green and gold shot cloth and all sorts of brilliant colours decorated with gold.

After the chiefs the General came in, then the Lieutenant Governor and finally, after the Royal umbrellas had lined up, the Viceroy, his wife and daughter entered. Of course guns were being fired off all the while to announce their appearance. Numerous Burmans and a few Shan chiefs and one or two Englishmen were presented to the Viceroy and decorated with gold medals, and gold chains, swords of honour, etc, for services done to the country. Then the Viceroy read a long speech about the state of the country and what had been done in it and what remained to do. He said that the communications of the country were not good, which is perfectly true. There are very few roads and railways. He also said the Burmans were very loyal and not one joined the conspiracy at Christmas. This long speech had all to be translated into Burmese which was very tedious. But it was all over at last and the Durbar ended.

The dresses of the English people were not particularly striking, though some were very pretty and dainty. I wore my new white voile with Mildred's sash and my black hat which looked very nice.

Played the piano for the children and told them about the Durbar. We went to bed early as we were very tired.

Thurs. Dec. 7th

Afternoon: It was the Garden Party at Government house. I wore my blue silk dress and new black hat. The Party began at 4 o'clock. The garden is close to the North moat and there were boat races going on during it. The crews were very picturesque. The canoes were of bright colours and there were 20 or 30 men inside them. Some of the crews were almost naked and others had on blue jackets trimmed with gold and green and gold turbans. There was one crew of women. Some of the canoes were paddled in the ordinary way but others had a hand-rail down the middle and the men caught hold of it with one hand and with the other held the top of the paddle and actually worked on it with their leg.

At one end of the garden was an industrial exhibition - examples of Burmese work in the process of making and finished articles for sale: silver things, brass, jade, amber, soap, cloths, wood-work, pottery.

There were also some of the mountain tribes standing about. It is practically impossible to describe their costumes, they were so varied. Some of them had great twisted rings nearly a foot deep round their necks. Some had bamboo twisted round their foreheads. A good many of the dresses were black with deep borders of different coloured patterns. Some of the girls had red cloaks hanging from their foreheads behind with a deep border of pale blue silk and a patch of blue silk in the middle...

Friday Dec. 8th

School. Corrected exam-papers, did reports etc. Evening. There was an entertainment at the Shan Camp, so J. and I cycled there. There were a large number of bamboo huts built around a large circular space. In the middle of the circle was a canteen with refreshments, and round this there was a wide path marked off with strings of lights shaded with red and yellow paper. In this pathway all sorts of dances were going on. It was very weird to see it all in the light of the full moon with no other light except these little red and yellow lanterns hung round everything.

The most remarkable thing was the animals, great monstrous creatures like the pictures one sees of ante-diluvian creatures. They were really made of wood covered over with thousands of shreds of coloured paper and spangles and had two or three men inside, but it was quite uncanny to see the way they twisted themselves about and rolled over on the ground and butted with their great gold horns. There were cocks and hens and tigers and leopards. All the time these numerous animals were going round in a circle, there were groups of Shans and other tribes doing strange dances. Some were dressed in pink turbans and white garments and were dancing a sort of slow Burmese dance. Others were dressed more like gipsies and were doing a sort of figure dance, the women carrying fans and the men das (short knives). There were one or two men almost quite naked, twisting themselves about and throwing weird shadows on the ground and others doing sword dances. Then there was one group of very wild people, very black skins and with a thick mop of coal-black hair, dressed in very dark clothes, black trimmed with dark blue, who went round in a circle and uttered wild shrieks at intervals. It almost made you shudder to think of meeting them on the lonely mountains. Of course all the time there were Burmese gongs and drums and cymbals being clashed.

There was one little group of 5 or 6 doing a slow figure dance who had quite a nice reed instrument to play for them, consisting of 5 or 6 pipes. It really played quite a tune and had a pleasant mellow sound. There were hundreds of English people, Eurasians, and Burmans in the crowd watching the performance. The English people looked very swell in evening dress and gorgeous evening cloaks. Of course there are a great many Maymyo people here now.

We got home about 11.30. It was a gorgeous moonlight night.

Sun. Dec. 10th

Miss Patch and Miss Dunkley came to tea as it was Janie's birthday. We had quite a pleasant tea-party. Miss Patch said she thought I was the best dressed person at the Durbar! Quite a triumph isn't it? When I only had a white voile dress dhobi-made, M's sash and the new black hat. Of course the sash and hat were very good, but you must remember people here think nothing of spending pounds and pounds on their clothes. One lady is said to have spent £100 on her clothes for the Viceroy's visit. Church.

Tues. Dec. 12th

I had a very pressing letter from Mrs Fyffe asking me to go and stay with them at Christmas as the Bishop wanted to see me particularly about the school. He offered to pay my expenses as he wanted to see me on business...

Wed. Dec. 13th

I got up for Prayers and did reports with some of the mistresses, but I felt rather ill and went back to bed. Miss Patch came up to see me in the afternoon and Miss Dunkley later. They were very kind and suggested I should go and stay with them for a few days, but of course I can't leave till Prize-giving is over.

Thurs. Dec. 14th

...Went to the other bungalow to rehearse... did reports with Miss Backhurst and then lay down again. The food question is such a difficulty here when one is ill. Nothing is appetising J. had written to Dr Sheldon, the Railway doctor, to ask if he could give me a tonic and he came up to see me about 5.30. He was very kind. He said I ought to get away at once to Maymyo or Kalaw, right away from school, but of course he knew I could not leave till term was over.

In the middle of his visit Mrs Aplin arrived. She is the wife of the Commissioner and is inclined to be snobby. She thinks herself a very great person. She said she had tried two or three times to call on us before, but had never found the house till then. She offered to drive me in her carriage to the Dispensary to fetch the medicine the doctor was prescribing. I was a little doubtful about going but thought I could manage it. However, when I went to get ready, Dr Sheldon said I was not very steady on the legs and had better sit in the garden instead. So Mrs Aplin and J. went. Mrs Aplin said she would be very pleased for me to spend a few days with them. But she is so condescending about any kindness that she does that she spoils it.

Dr Sheldon really is very cunning. He said he would wait and see me into a chair and then, directly the other two had gone, he proposed taking me for a spin in his motor with his wife.

He said Mrs Aplin would have to wait 20 mins at the dispensary for the medicine to be made up, but she could put it down to her credit.

Mrs Sheldon has just come out from England. She has a very sweet face, quiet and attractive. She is a doctor too. We had a pleasant drive and finally picked up their little son. Dr Sheldon gave him to me to nurse. He is such a perfect darling - just 3 years old and a very fine boy. He talks so prettily and nicely.

Fri. Dec. 15th

I felt rather stronger, tho' not very well... I had to be present for the Prize Distribution.

Mon. Dec. 18th

I had become so yellow that I thought I had better go and see the doctor and find out if I was getting jaundice. I went down in a gharry, but he had gone to Maymyo for the day.

Tues. Dec. 19th

Dr Sheldon came up and said I had jaundice slightly. He advised me to go to Mrs Aplin's so I went in a gharry after breakfast. The ayah took me to my room as Mrs A. was out with Mrs Owens. It was a treat to be in a nice clean room with spotless white curtains after our dirty building. My bedroom was not in the least grand, quite ordinary furniture, but it was very comfortable. I stayed in my room lying-down till tea-time at 4.30. We had a nice dainty tea in the drawing-room. The colour scheme is black and pink which is rather effective.

After tea we drove round the hill in a carriage and pair with 2 footmen standing behind us and then we went to the club and stayed there about 2 hours. I talked to various people and quite enjoyed it.

Wed: Thurs: Fri: Dec. 20-22nd

Very much the same programme each day. Chota in bed about 7 am. Remained in bedroom until 9.30. Breakfast. 10.30 - 1, knitting, reading, talking in the Drawing-room. 1 o'clock - tiffin (milk and fruit). Rest in bed-room till 4.30. Tea. Short drive. Club. 8.30 dinner.

I had a long talk with Mrs Lister on the Thursday evening... The Bishop and Mrs Lister have smoothed things over and Mr Lister is going to be chaplain for the river stations which means he will only be at Mandalay about 5 days a month. A Mr Anderson, who has left his Eurasian wife behind in India, is going to be chaplain at Mandalay and Mrs Lister and he will live at the Parsonage as independently as possible...

I was a good deal teased at the Club for my "swank" in driving about with the Commissioner and his wife in their carriage and pair.

Mrs Aplin is very nice-looking and she dresses beautifully. Colonel Aplin is a very fine-looking man and I found him very pleasant but I should imagine that he is very hard...

We had delicious food all the time and I felt very much better. The doctor told me I could tell myself what to eat and probably I should want to avoid fatty things, but I could eat and enjoy practically everything without feeling at all sick... Of course I can't have had jaundice badly because I am hardly yellow at all now...

Thurs. Dec. 28th

I finished packing... After breakfast I went down in a gharry to the Parsonage and Mr Lister came to the station with me to see me off. He had booked a seat for me beforehand. I got a return ticket for 1¼ fare as it was the Christmas holidays. I was in a first class coupe the whole way and was very comfortable indeed. Fortunately it was cool so I did not mind having the windows shut during the night. I do not like leaving them open when I am alone as thieves may climb through at wayside stations. I left Mandalay at 1.15 pm and reached Rangoon at 8.15 am on Friday morning...

...At 3 o'clock Mrs Fyffe let me have the motor-car and go out to see Miss Henderson... principal of the Normal school... really under Miss Laughlin who lives at the big S.P.G. school in Rangoon itself. I had tea with Miss Henderson and she poured out all her troubles to me. Miss Laughlin apparently makes life very hard for her and she has been very unhappy... It seems to me that one of the greatest problems of missionary life is that missionaries can't get on with one another. I suppose it is really due to the bad effect that the climate and strain have on the nerves...

Sat. Dec. 30th

Mr Fyffe had to take the Bishop to the hospital to have an abscess on his face operated on...

Miss Cook came to tea at 3.30. She has come down from Maymyo for her holidays.

We took a gharry and went to the Jubilee Hall to a Red Cross Fete which was on the whole exceedingly dull... We saw some Indian dancing which was most boring. A girl came on and droned out a song with about 6 notes in it and beat time to it with her foot and kept putting her handkerchief to her nose, first with one hand, then with the other. We thought she must have a cold in the head, but when, after 15 minutes of this, she finally departed, another girl came on and did exactly the same sort of thing, so we came out...

Monday Jan. 1st 1917

Miss Cook and Miss Summers came... and we went in the Phaeton to the Lakes... it was just glorious on the Lakes. There was a lovely pink sunset. We came in when it was dark and sat on the balcony in the moonlight and drank ginger-beer and ate potato chips and nuts...

Tuesday Jan. 2nd

...Mr Hardcastle, the Bishop's financier, a clergyman, has returned from Moulmein. After tea Mrs Fyffe asked him to take us to the Shwe Dagon, an enormous pagoda all covered with gold at the top of a hill... There are numbers of steps leading up to it with stalls on both sides and an enormous platform round the base of the pagoda itself with hundreds of shrines and images of Buddha. Some of the shrines are ancient and some modern. Many of the latter are hideous because they are trying to ape our style of architecture. Some of them are just square rooms with 30 or 40 different sized images of Buddha inside. There was one rather curious construction, a huge pole with a kind of rest house at the top, and, at the bottom, figures of two men assisting a third to climb up the pole. I don't know whether it symbolised the soul's mounting up to Nirvana, the goal of the Buddhist religion.

After we left the Pagoda we walked across the golf-links to the Gymkhana, Lower Burma club, where Mr Hardcastle talked to a lady about tennis and drank some kind of "liqueur". I think he is rather a "nut"...

Thurs. Jan. 4th

...There is a lovely tennis court at Bishop's Court. We played till about six o'clock and then Miss Henderson took me down in her rickety phaeton to the hospital as the Bishop wanted to see me. Miss Henderson and Miss Clarke have been on a jungle tour for a few days with Mr Purser and Mr Caldecott. They say it was most inspiring, just like the Acts of the Apostles. Mr Purser apparently is very fluent in Burmese and he sits down and the people throng round him and follow him and those who are Christians bring up fresh enquirers and people wanting to be baptised. At one village they slept in a Burmese house. They were given an absolutely empty room with just mats on the floor. They had meals under the house with cows etc looking on. Miss Clark told me that the work is simply waiting to be developed and an enormous amount could be done if there were more workers. It is very refreshing to hear of life somewhere, because in Mandalay missionary work seems so dead.

I found the Bishop in his pyjamas and dressing-gown, but of course that is nothing here...

Mon. Jan. 8th

...We caught a train at 7.50 to Thazi where we had to change... We travelled in a most luxurious first class carriage to Mandalay which we reached at 1.20. At the station there were the cook who had come to see to our luggage, a mother who wanted to ask me if her daughter might sleep at school and Mr Anderson, the new chaplain, rather agitated about the school and wanting to come up and see me that same afternoon.

I had a fairly long talk with Mr Ince (the Eurasian master at the boys' school). He seems rather down. He will be in charge at the boys' school till a master can be found and he does not like it... It looks as if the beginning of this term would be as great a muddle as ever.

Fri. Jan. 12th

We re-opened school, but a great many of the children were not back...

Sat. Jan. 20th

...J. and I had a letter from a Mrs Lee at Taung-gyi asking if we would spend the hot weather with her. Mr Potter, the middle-aged inspector of schools whom we met at Meiktila, had told her about us. I think he was rather taken with J. The Lees have a school for sons of Shan chiefs...

Tuesday Feb. 6th

...J. and I cycled to the Club. It was rather interesting as there were a good many people there. Also Lady Cuffe who has come down from Maymyo. She is such an aristocrat and not in the least a snob...

Tues. Feb. 13th

...Just after I had gone over to the other bungalow to take Prayers there was a frightful dust storm. The windows and doors banged and the hurricane was terrific and everything got covered in dust and we ate dust in our soup and drank it in our water. At last the rain came in torrents which was a great relief...

Sat. Feb. 24th

Mr Grossett and J. came up in the motor to know if I would go to Amarapura with them. I thought it was an opportunity not to be lost, so I went and it was a glorious ride. Amarapura was the old Burmese Capital till 1865 when it was moved to Mandalay. Of course there are no English houses there or only one or two as the English did not take Upper Burma till 1885, so it is quite a purely Burmese place and people looked at us with interest. Probably some of them have hardly ever seen a white woman before.

After we got out of Mandalay the road was very uneven and we jumped up and down. Mr G. had to leave us in Amarapura and cycle out into the jungle to see some work. We went to a huge white Pagoda and climbed the steps up to it and then went down to the side of the water, an overflow from the Irrawaddy, and tried to get into some tiny Burmese boats. We took off our shoes and stockings but could not manage it. Then we went into a Burmese house and watched a girl weaving silk, with a hand loom.

When Mr Grossett came back he took us to the weaving school and the superintendent explained it all to us. The Government pays R15 a month for these 60 or so Burmese girls to come and learn silk-weaving properly and they have to buy their own looms and carry on the trade at home. Just when we got back to Mandalay, the motor punctured and we had to take gharries...

Tues. Feb. 27th

...A number of our children have baby squirrels now. They feed them with milk from a bottle with a piece of rag stuffed through the cork. It is rather pretty to see them feeding. They hold the cork in their hands...

Wed. Feb. 28th

...Mr Anderson is very happy because one of the teaching brothers from Moulmein Church School is coming to be our headmaster next term.

Thurs. March 1st

...These baby squirrels of the girls are rather a nuisance. One of them woke up between 9.30 and 10 and began crying because it was hungry and I had to let the girl call up a servant to see if any milk could be found at the other house...

Fri. March 2nd

...I went to Club and met J. We did not stay long as we were going to the Bioscope after dinner with Miss Dunkley to see the Battle of the Somme pictures. I did not really want to go, but felt I ought to see them. I was so frightfully sleepy that I could not really take them in...

Sun. March 4th

...In church I suddenly saw Mabel Parr make a dive at the seat behind her and I thought she was going to stop a small child speaking and then to my horror I saw her pick up her baby squirrel which she had taken with her to church and which must suddenly have jumped from her shoulder on to the seat behind. I was so afraid that it might begin crying because these baby squirrels can make a great deal of noise when they are hungry.

I was invited to Dr Sheldon's to dinner on Saturday to take my violin, but received a note on Saturday morning saying that Mrs Sheldon had to take her little son (who is only 3) to the Pasteur Institute at Rangoon, so I suppose he must have been bitten by a mad dog.

Thurs. March 15th

...After dinner played the violin. I take off my dress and sit in my camisole. It is much the coolest method.

Sat. March 17th

...I cycled to Miss Butt's to have breakfast with her. The wind has begun now which goes on blowing on and off till the rains begin in June, so the clouds of dust are flying on the roads and get into one's eyes, nose and teeth, and of course it will go on getting hotter and hotter and dustier and dustier. It feels pretty hot now although it is only just over 90 degrees in the shade.

I had a very pleasant time with Miss Butt. I think she is a wonderful woman and a true missionary and she does missionary work as one imagines it to be at home - I mean preaching in villages and selling Gospels on the railway stations and taking Scripture lessons in the village schools and visiting the Leper asylum, and she is so extraordinarily humble with it all... I came away about 1 o'clock and went to the Court House to pay our income-tax. It is a nuisance having to pay income tax every month. I have to pay 4/2 each month...

Sat. March 24th

Two of the boarders were thought to have chicken pox so Mrs Wakely took them to the hospital... They had to turn out some children suffering from measles and they only have room for one other if we get any more cases...

Sun. March 25th

Another girl started with spots, so after church I told Mr Anderson that I thought we had better write to the parents and ask them to fetch the boarders home at once...

Mon. March 26th

Mr Anderson and Mr Ince came in to see me before school and we decided that we had better close school and postpone the exams till the beginning of next term and send the boarders home as soon as possible...

Thurs. March 29th

...After tea Mr Watson (who has a match factory near the shore, we have met him once or twice at public functions) came and fetched us in his motor. He took us right away out of the town to the canal and we went for miles along the bank of the canal on what in England would be called a towing-path, but these canals are only for irrigation, not for transport, so there are no barges. It was very pretty and we saw some lovely birds - glorious blue king-fishers and snipe and a heron and a crow-partridge. Then we went right along the Maymyo Rd for about 20 miles. The first 16 were on the plain, but the last 4 miles we ascended 1,000 ft. It was a little alarming as the road winds backwards and forwards along the face of the mountains and we had to make numerous hair pin turns. When we got up about 1,000 ft we turned and had iced ginger-beer and ginger-bread. There was rather a thick heat haze or else we should have had a glorious view of the mountain ranges and the valley of the Irrawaddy. We came back at a good rate. It was rather tiring as Mr Watson's car is a Ford and does not go as smoothly as Mr Grossett's which is an Overland. Also there were such numbers of bullock-carts and the road is very narrow and winding and sometimes precipitous at the sides. It is marvellous the way bullock carts squeeze themselves half down a ditch to let a motor pass. We saw a field all on fire. We got back about 7.35.

Sat. March 31st

...We get our vegetables from the prison now and in the term every morning a very swell warden in a butcher-blue uniform and staff conducts a convict in chains with a basket of vegetables to the school, but this morning I saw the warder coming alone with the green stuff under his arm...

Sun. April 1st

...We went to the Novitiation of a Burmese boy. It corresponds a little to our Christening. Each Burmese boy must undergo it. The priests shave his head and put on him the orange robes of a priest and then he has to go 7 hours or 7 days or 7 weeks or 7 months etc to a monastery.

Unfortunately we did not see the actual ceremony, but were there only for the social part. There was an image of Buddha of white alabaster. (By the way Buddhists are not really idol-worshippers. They have an image much as I suppose Roman Catholics have images, just to assist them in their prayers).

There were about 12 iron bedsteads with mosquito nets, mattresses and pillows and a priest's robe in each that the family were offering to the monastery. There were crowds of Burmans in the outer room sitting round little tables and on carpets on the floor with all sorts of dainty Burmese food and fruits in pretty little bowls in front of them. Of course there was also a Burmese band.

In the inside room were the Eurasians and English people. The little boy himself, a child of 8 or 9, was dressed in beautiful Burmese silk and had numbers of lovely jewels in his dress. There was a huge christening cake and other delicious little cakes and sweets and ices. We each had a pretty silk scarf given to us and the gentlemen had silk handkerchiefs. We also (had) a Burmese cheroot and cigar given to us...

After dinner I shortened some knickers, as it makes them much cooler to have no elastic at the knees but wide open...

Wed. April 4th

Went to town to do some shopping. I went to see a Miss Scott, a teacher from the A.B.M. (American Baptist Mission) school... Mr Anderson has arranged for Mabel and Freddie Parr and George Kerr to lodge with her as they are wards of the school... Poor Mabel feels it very hard not being allowed to go home to her father whom she adores. He has a Burmese wife who is a very bad woman and may not have anything to do with the children, but he does not live with her but with another Burmese woman...

I called at the hospital before I came back. After breakfast Mabel and J. helped me sort and dust the library books and put them in my big box. The ants have eaten two or three. It is almost impossible to preserve them in a cupboard like ours made of cheap wood and the cockroaches, too, make a horrid mess of them. I found a little scorpion which we killed.

Easter Sunday April 8th

Service at 7.30 am. The church looked very pretty. After Church I went to hospital. I saw Colonel Penny, the civil surgeon, and had a little chat with him. He said he had a motor at Kalaw and would like to take me in it up to Taung-gyi but did not know whether he would be able to. We have to go by motor or bullock cart the last 40 miles as there is no railway...

Read. We have had a dog at school for some weeks with a broken leg and have been asking Mr Anderson to get him killed, but he has not done so. Of course, the Burmans, being Buddhists who believe that souls of people may go into animals, don't like killing them. These pariah dogs who hang about the kitchen are a great nuisance. I am always afraid of their going mad and biting the children and this particular dog with the broken leg must have suffered terribly as the bone is growing out. Fortunately, however, Janie thought of asking Captain Hele (who is in command of some of the territorials and has been attending to her teeth as he is a dentist from Carlisle by profession) and he sent round three soldiers and one of them shot the dog...

CHAPTER VIII

A DELIGHTFUL TIME IN BURMA

> "April 25th. 1917. We felt very sad at leaving the lake-bungalow. We had so enjoyed the time there - I never thought I could have such a delightful time in Burma."

The quotation from the diary is geographically inaccurate. The hot-weather holidays of 1916 and 1917 were spent not in Burma but in the Shan states, at hill-stations popular with the British and amply provided with fine colonial buildings. Taunggyi, which Janie and Doris were able to visit through the services of the "stout and middle-aged" Mr Potter, H.M.I., had been founded by Sir James Scott, writer of "The Burman: his life and his notions", still a classic work on Burmese culture. The town stands some 4,000 feet above the central plain and takes its name (taung: mountain, gyi: big) from the craggy tree-covered cliff which rises another thousand feet or so above it.

When the British annexed Burma, while exercising an overall control, they allowed the chieftains of the hill-tribes to rule their own territories. This contrasted sharply with their treatment of the Burmans of the plains. There all higher administrative posts were held by foreigners. It was a policy which, by encouraging divisions already in existence, made unlikely a concerted attempt to drive out the invader, but it was a policy which, after independence, was to put obstacles in the way of achieving a unified country. However that lay in a future totally hidden from Doris Easton.

The visit began with all the bustle and confusion inevitably attendant on journeys at that time and place.

Monday April 9th

Finished packing and locking up, etc. We sent our luggage down to the station in a bullock cart. Mr Ince's boy whom we are having as our own servant went with it. J. went down in a gharry as her bicycle was punctured, and also the beds which Mrs Lee had asked us to bring were left behind by the bullock carts. Mabel Parr came up to school to see me, so I wheeled my bicycle and walked down with her nearly all the way. It is nearly 2 miles and it was about 12 o'clock so we had all the mid-day glare.

We went in the same compartment as Miss Dunkley who was going to Rangoon. It was 2nd class but very comfortable. Mrs Grossett sent down to the station some jam puffs and curry puffs for us, also apples and oranges. Mr Anderson also came and saw us off as he had to get the school keys and at the last minute Colonel Penny came up and asked me to take a parcel to Mr Price who has had a bad nervous breakdown and is at Taung-gyi. He also wanted us to deliver a message at the Hospital at Thazi about a motor which he has there. He has 4 motors altogether.

We left at 1.15 and reached Thazi about 5 o'clock. Miss Dunkley provided us tea, bread, butter and cake and mango-fool on the way so we had plenty to eat.

We had to get out at Thazi and spend the night there. Fortunately some of our children live at Thazi and they generally come to the station and meet the trains. Of course there are only 2 or 3 a day. The children were very useful in helping with our luggage...

Each Government Department generally has a bungalow at stations where government officials can stay if there is a room. We went to the Public Works Department one.

It was quite empty. Of course there was a caretaker who provided us with water and lamps. We got some dinner - ham and eggs and iced ginger-beer at the station.

We were both feeling rather tired and done up, so went to bed very early. The boy slept in the passage outside our room. It was a dirty gloomy sort of bungalow and of course very hot in bed. I was wakened 3 times by a mosquito inside my net, biting me all over. Fortunately I had left the lantern burning so I managed to catch each of the three, but it was very irritating.

Tues. April 10th

We did without chota and packed up our things and then the carter of one of our school-boys brought up some men to carry them to the station. We went down about 9 am and had some breakfast. It was a 5 course meal and very nicely served... Miss Sumner and Miss Hearn and a Eurasian girl arrived about 9.30 from Rangoon... We left Thazi about 10.40. The second class carriage was very uncomfortable and there were 5 of us and all this luggage, so I did not enjoy the journey at all, and of course it was very hot. I believe the scenery was very fine part of the way... but we were too tired to look at it much.

We arrived at Kalaw, a favourite hill-station, about 4.15. It is about 4,500 feet high and pretty country with hills and fir trees. We got out there and had tea. Miss Butt and Mrs Vickery were on the station. Miss Butt is staying with Mrs Vickery who is a Wesleyan living at Kalaw. She said she would like to ask us for the night on the way back. Kalaw seemed beautifully fresh and clear. Then we went on in the train to Aungban which is the terminus of the railway.

There were two mail motor-cars there to carry letter bags to Taung-gyi, so we packed as much of our small luggage in them as possible and had to leave the rest at the station to come on the next day, then we climbed in with the luggage ourselves and started off for the 40 mile motor-ride.

We left Aungban at about 5.45 and reached Taung-gyi about 8.30. I felt a little nervous with a native driver as the road was very winding and rather narrow and of course there were numbers of bullock carts, however the man seemed pretty careful. The country was glorious - great rolling peaks in the distance. It is such a treat after seeing nothing but plains and huge mountains covered with trees from top to toe to see bare hills like moors.

The sun was setting as we went along and the light was very pretty. The country is very English... only on a much larger scale... You can go miles and miles without seeing a human being or a house anywhere around you. We only passed two or three villages the whole way. Taung-gyi is in the Southern Shan states, so the people are Shans not Burmans...

We stopped at one or two Shan villages to get petrol, and people crowded round the car. It was weird. I suppose travelling by stage-coach was like it, but I should think it would not be quite as easy to

FROM THE EASTON FAMILY ALBUM

The Reverend Edward William Easton and his wife Sarah
with Gertrude and Mildred in 1886.
(page 7)

Gertrude Easton (aged 7)
and Mildred Easton (aged 6)
in 1891.

Doris Easton

Mandalay Hill
(page 57)

Burmese boats on a festive occasion.
(page 104)

Pagoda with guarding chinthe.
(page 138)

Jungle pagoda and derelict zayats.
(page 159)

ARTHUR PERCY MORRIS

'A Mr Morris has arrived... He seems quite jolly'

April 11th 1917

Principal of Insein Technical Institute 1912 - 1924.

(page 131)

Village Craftsmen. A.P.M. was the Provincial Art Officer responsible foe encouraging local crafts 1914 - 1924.

(page 145)

WEDDING IN MANDALAY
Dec 20th 1917.

Doris Sarah Easton
1917

Arthur Percy Morris
1917

Doris Sarah Morris in her wedding dress.
(page 157)

Po Khin, servant to A.P.M.
from 1905 - 1924 and his wife, Ma Gyi.
(page 162)

Tea with Sir Otway and Lady Cuffe.
(page 141)

Mong Kung, May 2nd 1920.
Shan village: ladies at the well.
A water-colour painting by D.S. Morris when on tour.
(page 207)

En-route for Nawngleng. Po Min makes cakes of unleavened bread for breakfast while the oxen and travellers rest.
A water-colour made by D.S. Morris. May 5th 1920.
(page 213)

On tour. A boat trip.

Homeward Bound. Passport photograph
of the Morris family. March 1924.

plunder a motor-car. The solitude and vastness of the country was wonderful. Occasionally we passed little groups of mat houses with several bonfires lighted beside them, I suppose to keep away wild animals.

At last we began to climb again and we went up and up and up more than 1,000 ft till at last we reached Taung-gyi which is higher than Kalaw. The views must have been magnificent but there was no moon and we could not see much. Occasionally there was a flash of lightning and there were a few fires scattered here and there over the landscape.

We stopped in the motor agent's house in Taung-gyi and left Miss Wall, the Eurasian girl... and then they drove off the motor with the letter bags and came back to take us to the Lees. J. and I are sleeping in a room which is really the children's day nursery... Miss Hearn and Miss Sumner have another room. Mr and Mrs Lee are sleeping in a mat hut in the garden. Some people called Broadbent who are on a cycling tour are living in tents for a few days in the garden and Miss Napier is living in the school building.

The Lees keep a school for the sons and relations of Shan chiefs. They have about 85 of them. They are on holiday now, they have 10 weeks holiday once a year and that is all. You see it takes some of them about a month to get home. Some of them go on elephants and some on ponies and some in bullock-carts. Just lately many of them have bought motor cars, but Mrs Lee say they often break down as they get wild Burmans to drive them...

Wed. April 11th

...J. and I went to take the parcel to the Prices. Agnes, the youngest daughter, came with us. She is 7, the next one, Nellie, is 10 and the eldest, Mary, is 11. They are such bright attractive children. They all wear their hair in one plait and have a sailor suit and shoes without stockings... The Prices were out, so we left the parcel and Agnes went home and we went for a walk. Taung-gyi is so pretty. There is a great craggy mountain in front of the Lees all covered with trees... and then the air is so fresh and cool.

We had breakfast about 10.30 and then walked around the garden with Mrs Lee. They have 13 rabbits whose eyes are not yet open and

3 cats and a dog. Mr Lee is a very quiet man and is busy now correcting examination papers. I think he is something of a scholar. Mrs Lee is very nice and kind. She is not a society type of lady. After breakfast wrote and lay down. We had tea in the garden - a nice homely kind of meal...

A Mr Morris arrived, he is head of an engineering school near Rangoon. He seems quite jolly. After dinner we sat in the dining-room and talked.

It is so nice to be cold at night and have 2 or 3 blankets. I heard the cuckoo several times during the day.

The Lees grow their own coffee in their garden.

Thurs. April 12th

Our big boxes, bicycles and beds have not come yet. They are coming by bullock cart which takes 2 or 3 days. I do hope they will arrive safely. Boxes are often robbed on this lonely road. It is an expensive journey here. We each had to pay Rs 5 for our seat in the motor and then they charged Rs 10 for bringing all our small boxes and I suppose the bullock-cart will cost Rs 6 or Rs 8.

We had tea in the garden and then Mrs Lee and the three children and we four went a very pretty walk along the side of a hill through a wood.

We played with the children at skipping in the garden when we came back and then I stayed in our bedroom and ran a tuck in a skirt. It is so nice being free like this. We can do just what we like.

Mr Potter came after dinner and we played animal snap and ordinary snap and we were very lively. Mr Morris and Mr Potter are both very jolly.

Fri. April 13th

Sat out of doors and studied Burmese. After breakfast did some sewing. It poured with rain, but it had cleared about 2 o'clock and we all went about 600 or 700 ft down the hill to a cave. The servants came to carry the tea-basket. We had lovely views on the way down. We could see a big lake in the distance. In the cave there are two big images of Buddha, one white and one black and candles burning in front of them. There were some pilgrims in the cave who were going to stop there for the night. After tea some of us went exploring to the back of the cave which was a good long way. The servants carried lanterns and we had to pass through low passages. Three times we had to crawl on all fours. There was one hole where we had to lie down flat and wriggle through. There were stalagmites which sounded hollow like a drum if you tapped them. On the way back from the cave we met the three ponies, so J. and I and Mary rode them. I had never ridden a pony before, but I enjoyed it very much. The man led it a good part of the time. The ground was fearfully rough and uneven, but of course these mountain ponies are used to it.

The Shan women dress quite differently from the Burmese, and they have such lovely brown complexions. They look as if they were in evening dress because they wear such low necks.

Sat. April 14th

We started out for a walk about 8 o'clock, but met the bullock carts with our luggage, so turned back to see to it. It was on 3 carts. We had to pay Rs 6 which was not out of the way for 4 of us.

Unpacked and read. We meant to play tennis but it poured with rain. It had cleared about 5 o'clock and Mr Morris took J. and me for a ride in his motor-car, as he wanted to test the strength of the engines. We went about 20 miles. Mr Morris is, I should think, between 30 and 40; he is very merry and interesting to talk to as he is keen on his work and being an engineer knows a good deal about the country. The worst of him is that he has such a squeaky voice.

We saw a man riding a buffalo. I believe it is rather difficult, as they twist round their heads and scratch you with their long horns, so you have to sit quite close to their tails to be out of reach.

Sunday April 15th

After dinner Mr Potter came in and I played the violin. Mr Morris accompanied me, but he could not read difficult pieces well so I had to limit myself to easy ones.

Monday April 16th

Mr Price wanted to go to Kalaw to see Dr Sheldon who is there for a holiday so Mr Morris offered to motor him there. He said he could take two more so Mrs Price asked if I would like to go to make up the quartet. We started about 8am... Mr and Mrs Price sat behind together, Mr Morris and I in front... It was a glorious morning and the air was delicious. We descended about 1,600 ft to the valley. The road was very winding but Mr Morris is very careful. Then we had to cross the valley which is about ten miles wide and then begin ascending again. The soil near Thamakan is a lovely red like Devonshire soil and there are rolling downs. We stopped at the P.W.D. bungalow to tell a Mrs Ashton who was stopping there that we wanted tea at 3 o'clock... Then we went to Aungban... and to Kalaw through roads shaded with fir trees a little like Bournemouth. We went to Kalaw station where a good many English people were gathered. They generally go to meet the trains... One girl, whom Mrs Price introduced me to, was living with her mother and little daughter and nurse in a railway carriage on the platform, there being no houses available. Her husband is in the railway...

The Refreshment room had not much food, so we telephoned to Miss Owen at the Hotel. She is sister of Major Owen who came out on the Ava and runs the Hotel. She said she had no food to give us, but she could provide porridge, eggs and bacon, sausages, curry and rice and, as we considered that plenty of food for us, we went up to the Hotel when we could succeed in dragging Mr Price and Mr Morris from the people on the platform...

We had an excellent breakfast in a very nice room and then Mrs Price and I sat in the drawing-room while Mr Price went to see Dr Sheldon and Mr Morris went to do business... We were all to meet at the station at 1.15 but Mr Price was very late...

At last Mr Price came and we... motored to Loian and stopped at a bungalow there to pass the time of day with Mr and Mrs Ross...

We blew the motor horn to wake them up which was rather unfortunate as we also woke the baby who had had a bad night with teeth. There are 9 adults and 9 children attached to the house, either in the building itself or in annexes in the garden. It is so difficult to get rooms in the Hills in the hot weather.

Then we motored on to Thamakan where the Prices have a house... It is absolutely lonely - just two or three Shan huts and one or two English houses. We went to the P.W.D. (Public Works Department)... Mrs Ashton and Miss Farrington who were staying at the P.W.D. bungalow gave us tea...

After tea we again started on and continued, but we stopped at the P.W.D. bungalow at Sinhe to greet Mr. Stirling, the resident of Taung-gyi. (I suppose the resident means the head of the station). He was not there, however, though his elephant was eating grass outside. But we saw a Mr Brown who used to be in Government Service but is now adviser to one of the Shan Sawbwas (chiefs). This country is divided up into a number of different states and each chief has a certain amount of power, though of course he is under the British Government and has to pay about 25% of his revenue to the Empire.

We got in about 6 o'clock. They made me play my violin after dinner, but I was very sleepy and did not want to.

Wed. April 18th

...We had some very nice tennis after tea. Mr Potter only played one set, but Mr Morris stayed on some time... It was a very cold night. I had to play the violin after dinner...

Fri. April 20th

We went for a motor picnic starting about 7.45... It was a glorious drive, about 26 miles long. We left our own food and wraps at the P.W.D. bungalow at Thamakan and then went on to the caves. About 40 excited Shan men, women and children came with us and carried great torches made of stacks of sticks tied together. We went into 3 caves. I think the first was the most wonderful. The stalactites and stalagmites were marvellous. It was like a great cathedral with numbers of columns and the torches gave such a weird light to it all.

The second cave had a very sloping roof and we had to stoop very low to get through it. The river flowed through it and Mr Morris and Major Owen waded through, carrying the children on their back as they wanted to get to the other side. Some of us climbed out of the third cave by a kind of chimney and climbed down the rocks which was rather exciting. Then we went back to the bungalow with a crowd of Shans following us. They were very interested in the car...

After we had fed and packed up, Major Owen's party went home and we walked 2 or 3 miles along the road which led to a magnificent gorge. Miss Sumner made a painting of a bend in the road with a grey crag skirting it. Mr Morris got one or two very pretty orchids - he knows a good deal about the flowers here... Motored home, arriving about 4.15.

Sat. April 21st

...It was Agnes' 8th birthday and at her request we had a book tea. I think Agnes had a thoroughly nice birthday party. Mr Price is very good for entering into games and of course Mr Morris is very lively. Mr Potter would not run about as he is middle-aged and stout, but he is quite good fun.

Sunday April 22nd

Service at 8 am... After tea I played hymns while the others sang, then we went to service at 5.30 and when it was over motored to Sinhe which took about half an hour and put up at the bungalow. There were 3 bedrooms at the bungalow so that was all right. Mr Morris took a cook and 2 boys and we took one boy so the servants got dinner in really nice style and then we went to bed. These bungalows always have crockery but of course one has to take one's own food...

Monday April 23rd

We had chota about 6 am so that our bedding could be packed up and sent off our bullock carts at once as they travelled so slowly. Then we all went for a walk along the embankment of the canal leading to a lake. It was very pretty country and a glorious morning. We walked about 4 or 5 miles and got back about 9 am and set off in the motor to Yaungwhe, the capital of one of the Shan states. It only took about half an hour to reach it.

We stopped on the way to look at a pongyi-kyaung (priests' school) where there was an interesting pagoda. The walls of the passages were decorated with different patterns in coloured glass and figures of coloured glass. There were hundred of niches in the walls, with a tiny image of Buddha in each.

At Yaungwhe we went first to Mr Browne's house. He and, I think, one other Englishman are the only white people who live in the town, but the houses are quite nice and comfortable-looking. We left the motor at Mr Browne's and then went to the Sawbwa's Guest house, a very nice bungalow, very well kept with a number of novels to peruse. We had breakfast there and then sat and rested till the bullock carts were re-packed about 12 o'clock and then we walked down behind them to the river-side where two dug-outs were waiting for us. Dug-outs are long boats on a level with the water, with a bamboo shelter in the centre to protect you from the sun. The servants went with the luggage in one boat and we went in the other. There were about 6 rowers in each, Inthas, which means "sons of the lake". The lake is called the Inle lake and is about ten miles long and five wide with mountains on both sides.

For some time we were going down a narrow river and we saw some buffaloes bathing, but then we got into the open lake itself and it was lovely. We did not sit under the shelter of the boat, but in front, and we had a nice cool breeze although the sun was hot. There were hundreds of floating islands in the lake. Of course they are really only masses of grass and weeds, but the people arrange them in straight rows and pin them down with long bamboo poles, so that they can put fishing nets between them.

It took us about 1½ hours to reach our destination. The rowers stood all the time to paddle with one foot and one hand, balancing with the other foot and leaving the other hand free. I suppose in fishing they use their disengaged hand to spear the fish with their long tridents.

There were two bungalows in the middle of the lake where the water was not very deep, only about 8 ft. They were made of bamboo and built upon long sticks driven into the bottom of the lake. There were 2 bedrooms with dressing-rooms in each bungalow, so Mr Morris decided to let us have one bungalow and to take the other himself. There were several yards of water between, so he had to come backwards and forwards in a boat. Ours had a huge verandah like the deck of a ship where we had our meals. Each bungalow had a little gallery at one end with a kitchen, shed for the servants and a lavatory.

We sat on the verandah and talked till tea was ready and after tea Mr Morris went over to his room in the boat and I had a bathe. The others could not come in because they could not swim. I had to swim the whole time, of course, as there was no shallow water and no resting-place. The only way to rest was to hang on to one of the sticks on which the house was built. I did enjoy myself immensely. The water was so clear and warm and of a dark green colour and a space round the bungalow was enclosed with a green floating hedge, so it was like swimming in a garden. I could not get back into the house because the platform was so high above the water, so I had to shout to the durwan (caretaker) to bring a boat and I managed to scramble into it and climb onto the steps.

After I had dressed and tidied up, I sat on the verandah and read for some time and then Mr Morris came over and we all read Browning and then he gave us a Burmese lesson. I don't know whether he is a very fluent Burmese scholar, but he was able to tell me a great many things I wanted to know about the language. It is a great pity that there are not more government officials like him. He is so nice with the Burmans and has great faith in their possibilities and believes that there is a great future before the Burmese craftsman instead of thinking him quite useless as so many people do. He himself took an engineering degree in London university and is now head of a Government Engineering school in Rangoon. But he has also been created a sort of Superintendent of all the industries of Burma and he has to encourage Burmese industries and see what the people are capable of and so on. He seems interested in Art of all kinds and gets up Art exhibitions in Rangoon. He believes unlike many, or most I might say, Government people that we can't possibly raise the country to our moral standard without Christianity and he considers that Government ought to provide Christian teaching in Government schools.

The cook gave us an excellent dinner. Of course all our food was brought with us. The only trouble was that numbers and numbers of little insects swarmed around the lanterns and candles and got into our food. After dinner we sat and talked for some time and were very merry and then Mr Morris went off to bed... and we brought our beds out onto the verandah, as the bedrooms were stuffy and had no windows, and rigged up mosquito nets.

I can't describe how glorious it was to be right in the middle of miles and miles of water and to see the mountains in the distance behind and before with scattered jungle fires on their sides, while on the lake itself there were a few bright lights from fishing boats...

Tues. April 24th

It was glorious waking up about 5 am to see an orange glow in the sky behind the mountains and to feel a splendid breeze blowing all round over the water and making the mosquito nets flap like sails. One feels so fresh after sleeping out like that.

When we had dressed, Mr Morris came over for chota about 6 am and then we started off in one boat to go right to the very end of the lake to a place called Nampam. It was lovely on the water at that early hour, the mountains were all grey and misty and threw a lovely pale grey reflection onto the water. It took us about two hours to get to the end. We had all 12 rowers in one boat, as they were anxious to come to Nampam bazaar and of course, we did not need the two boats...

We got out by a pongyi-kyaung and looked round and Miss Sumner made a little sketch of a group of pagodas with a "flame of the forest" tree nearby. (They have bright scarlet flowers). The monks did not much like our sitting on the steps of the monastery as of course they have no dealings with women, however they gave way in the end and were quite hospitable and took Mr Morris in to give them medical advice on a pongyi who was ill. Miss Sumner happened to have two aspirins, so he gave them to the man and told them to keep him on milk, though as he apparently had asthma it is doubtful whether they would do him much good.

When Miss Sumner had finished her sketch, we got into the boat again and were rowed down a creek to Nampam bazaar. We passed numbers and numbers of houses built on sticks in the water close to the shore. There were some built on the land too, but I suppose during the rainy season they would be surrounded by water.

The bazaar presented a very interesting scene. There were numbers of straw-thatched shelters under which the people were selling their wares. Others merely sat outside under large reddish umbrellas. We strolled round and Mr Morris talked to the people about their goods and asked where they came from and so on. Besides vegetables and food stuffs there were Shan bags and silks and cotton materials and lacquer work, and iron work and numerous odds and ends. We excited great interest and quite a crowd pressed round us at one stall when Mr Morris was talking to a seller. When we grew tired, we went to the zayat (resting place which consists of a roof on pillars with a wooden floor) near the water where the servants prepared breakfast. We squatted on the floor like orientals and ate our food while a number of Shans sat near and watched us. We felt that we were not giving a very good illustration of European table manners as we had to balance our plates on our laps and manage as best we could.

When we had seen all we wanted to at the bazaar, we went back to our boat. While we were waiting for the servants, I got into one of the native canoes and paddled it about standing up at the end like the natives. I did not try to work it with my foot, though, as it is so difficult to balance on one leg and the water was full of weeds just there and not at all easy to manipulate. Then we went to see a man across the water who was a silver-smith. It was like Venice as we had to paddle about between the houses till we found the right one. We went upstairs into his room and sat on mats on the floor. The staircase and floor was made of bamboo poles tied together, so it was rather slippery to walk on. All our crew and a number of villagers came too into the room and our host provided us with fans and cheroots (which we did not smoke) and showed us various articles in silver that he had made. Mr Morris bought a very nice tobacco-case made of silver inlaid with darker material for one of his masters who was leaving the school. He was also thinking of buying a necklace with a fringe of very delicate gold tracery for his sister whom he is very fond of, but I don't know whether he decided to get it or not.

Next we went in our own boat to another house to buy some live ducks as Mrs Lee had asked us to bring some back. Beef is the only meat procurable at Taung-gyi. The ducks were swimming about and had to be caught which involved an exciting chase. The fifth one gave great trouble, but a small boy swam about the water and chased it and by going underneath the water he managed to catch it unawares by the leg and drag it to the boat.

We at last got away about 2 o'clock - it took us over 2 hours to get back and we were rather sleepy and glad when the voyage was over. After tea I had another glorious bathe and dived once or twice from the platform. When I was dressed Mr Morris came over again and we read Browning and talked about it and then Mr Morris read aloud to us a book called "The Tall Ship" by Bartimaeus - stories about the navy which were very interesting - while I mended stockings and the others knitted till dinner-time.

After dinner Mr Morris told us old legends about Burma while we all sat on the floor at the top of the steps leading down to the water.

Wed. April 25th

We had chota about 6 am and packed up our things for the homeward journey. We felt very sad at leaving the lake-bungalow. We had so enjoyed the time there. I never thought I could have such a delightful time in Burma.

Thursday April 26th

We had chota about 6 am and packed up. Miss Sumner and I tackled Mr Morris about paying our expenses, but we could not persuade him to let us pay more for the use of the bungalow. He paid the whole of the cost of 2 bullock carts and 2 boats and all the food except what Mrs Lee gave him to bring, so I should think he must have spent 50 or 60 rupees, probably more, as he would have to tip innumerable boatmen and bullock cart drivers etc etc.

We left in the motor about 7 o'clock and reached Taung-gyi between 7.30 and 8. We stopped at the club to read the news and then went on to the house. Read. Wrote till breakfast time.

Sat. April 28th

Mr Morris motored J. to Kalaw as he was going to fetch Mr and Mrs Ross and their little girl up to Taung-gyi for two nights. He really asked me to go with him, but I felt that, as I had gone to Kalaw the last time, it was not my turn, so finally he asked J. instead...

Sun. April 29th

Mr and Mrs Lee were going to the wedding of a Sawbwa's son on May 3rd. It had been arranged that Mr Morris and we four were to stay at home to look after the children. However Mrs Lee asked me if I would like to go with them, so I accepted at once, as I believe it is a very interesting spectacle...

Thursday May 3rd

A party of us started off about 8 o'clock to see the Sawbwa's wedding. The Sawbwa sent one motor and a driver so Mr and Mrs Lee and Mr Potter went in that, I went in Mr Morris's car with his Burmese servant and a good deal of baggage, and Dr and Mrs Taylor who are staying in Loian came in their own motor with servants and baggage. We could not very well take any more passengers because of all the food, water and bedding we had to pack in, also the road was so bad after we got to Sinhe that it would not have been safe to be heavily loaded.

For 4 or 5 miles the road which was just a cart track was really very bad, chiefly because it belongs to the Yaunghwe Sawbwa and he won't mend it because he does not want trade into the Yatsauk Sawbwa's territory to be made too easy. There were great ruts in the roads and ups and downs and it needed careful driving. However we got on quite all right and it was not at all unpleasant. We all stopped about 10.30 beside a stream and had breakfast - sausage pasty, hard-boiled eggs, bread and butter, pate de foie gras, short-bread and coffee from a thermos.

I enjoyed the ride very much in spite of the roughness of the track. The country is lovely - undulating and wooded but very vast and practically uninhabited. Mr Morris is very interesting to talk to. He has a sister out here who has just been married and he seems to think the world of her. He is very anxious that she should learn Burmese, as he thinks English married women out here can do so much to help the people, more really than the Government officials themselves if they will learn the language...

We arrived at Yatsauk about 12.45 and went first to the Sawbwa's palace which is an old wooden building with turrets and pergolas. There was a ring of chairs round a carpet in the middle of the room, so we sat down with the Sawbwa who was dressed in a pink turban, white cotton jacket and full bright blue satin pantaloons and he talked a little in Burmese. We were offered golden bowls of water to drink, but we only sipped a little as it is dangerous.

Then we went away from the town in our motor to the camp which had been built for us. There were a number of huts made of bamboo and thatch. There were three big ones with 2 rooms in each for sleeping rooms and a central room, connected by covered ways with 2 of the huts, for a dining room. Then there were other buildings for kitchens and servants. Mr and Mrs Lee and Mrs Taylor and I shared one hut. Mrs Taylor and I had a room between us. The floor was raised above the ground and built of bamboo sticks covered with bamboo matting, so it felt rather wobbly. The whole camp was under the shade of some fine mango trees and there were a number of bamboos round us. Bamboos grow 20 feet or more high, but their growth is like ferns, as they bend gracefully at the top... Mr and Mrs Gordon were already there... Mr G. is in government service and often camps here.

About 2 o'clock Mr Morris motored me out about 3 miles to see a camphor plantation, where Mr Wickham lives, the only white man I suppose for 40 or 50 miles. It is lovely rolling country with glorious red soil, but it must be fearfully lonely. He is a very tiny man, very jolly and cheerful. His camphor has only just begun to yield, after years of work.

Friday May 4th

It was still pouring with rain about 5 am, but cleared up later on... Dressed for the wedding. I wore my blue silk as Mrs Lee thought they would like bright colours. Mr Morris took us in his motor to the town, which is perched on a hill, and we went into the inner room of the palace and were provided with golden bowls of water, oranges, biscuits, cigarettes. The Sawbwa shook hands with us all, also his wife, and his daughter, the bride, and the bridegroom who is the son of one of the chiefs of the Northern Shan States, and various royal ladies. The bridegroom had a very nice face. He wore a pale blue satin turban, a long white satin coat and full, pale blue satin trousers. The bride had a pale flowered mauve ingyi (blouse, shirt) and pink flowered lungyi (skirt) and yellow scarf and blue flowers in her hair. She looked very dainty and pretty as the colours were delicate.

Then they went outside, and, accompanied by men carrying the gold umbrellas which are the mark of royalty, they went on to a bamboo building where a Burmese band was playing amid a crowd of people. They went up some stairs and through two lines of astrologers all dressed in white, who held silver bowls in their hands full of sacred leaves, into an inmost room and sat down on each side of a sort of raised seat. Then the astrologers in turn came and read out a report in Burmese on the propitious moment. The chief astrologer was very gorgeous. He had on a mauve turban with gold spots and a deep blue-purple robe with gold embroidery and full black satin trousers.

After the reading some of those present tried to feed the bride and bridegroom with curry and rice, but they would not touch it. At last they were made to sit on the raised seats facing one another and Mr Lee and Mr Gordon were called up. Mr Lee had to tie a white silk scarf round their hands to join them together, then two of the astrologers read marriage hymns which they had composed. Then the scarf was untied and they were again fed with curry and rice from the same bowl and this time they did partake of it.

After this a man rose and read out a list of the presents and the value in money (a very embarrassing custom I think. However they did not price the presents given by the Lees and the gentlemen). I believe they had 6,000 rupees worth. Some messengers from neighbouring states came up while we were there and presented the Sawbwa with piles of rupees. We came away about 11 o'clock and they held golden umbrellas over us while we walked to the car...

When we got back Mr Morris asked me if I would go for a walk with him to explore the country. We went for some distance among the hills. On the way back we were caught in a heavy storm and drenched to the skin. After tea it cleared up and the others went out for a walk, but I stayed in and read. After dinner we had a pwe (festival) outside our hut. About 50 girls came and danced Burmese dances for us. A number of villagers came too to watch. I was very tired and not in a mood for it. Burmese dancing is very monotonous.

Saturday May 5th

We packed up and left about 7.30... There were four motors going back as Mr Browne and Mr Wickham joined in to our cavalcade. Mr Morris was very nervous about the road. I don't think he had had much sleep during the night, however we got on all right. The first few miles were pretty bad as there was deep red mud and the car zigzagged from side to side and once we stuck so I had to get out... We reached Taung-gyi at about 12.30. Lay down. After tea did writing...

Monday May 6th

Wrote letters. After breakfast Mr Morris and I had a long violin practice. Lay down and read. After tea we meant to play tennis, but rather suddenly I felt very giddy and dizzy and my head got rather bad, so I lay down for some time and had my head bathed. When I was rather better Mr Morris took me out in the motor with the children for half an hour. It was a lovely evening. We had dinner at 7 o'clock and all of us including the children went for a moonlight walk. I was anxious to go as the moon was glorious and I thought it would do me good... Mr Morris helped me all the time and I really felt better as my head grew easier. He has been so kind and natural, not at all as a rejected lover might be expected to behave.

Wed. May 9th

Mr Morris motored the four of us to Yaunghwe. We went to Mr Browne's house and took him out for a little ride to see the estate of a Rangoon gentleman... We came away directly after tea and reached Taung-gyi about 4.30. After we had dressed and changed we played some tennis and then Percy and I went for a walk.

I explained to him the evening before that I was not trying to avoid him any longer, as I wanted to get to know him better and see if I cared for him or not. Of course I said that, if he thought it would make it harder for him in the end, I would not do it. He said he would take the risk... He teases me a good deal, because I told him that I did not think I was suited to be the wife of a government official and he says he can't see why a poor government official should not have a good wife as much as anyone else. Of course he is very anxious that good women should be in the Government service as he thinks they might help the country so much... He would like to do his 8 years longer out here to earn his Government pension, but after that he says he would go wherever I wanted, although I believe he would much rather go on working for Burma as he is so fond of the country and people... He had a brother killed at Gallipoli who seems to have been rather brilliant. He was in the diplomatic service... Their father was in China in the tea-trade, but at present the father and mother live at Herne Bay in Kent. The father wanted to send his sons to the university, but lost a great deal of money through the failure of some shares, so Percy began working about 17 with engineering firms and worked up for his London B.Sc. degree in his spare time. Of course he had to work most frightfully hard. He is very fond of his mother and father and younger sister who is out here, but he does not know his other brother and sister very well as they have been abroad so much. He wants me to let him tell his mother all about it, and I said he could, but I do not wish him to talk to people here. I am afraid they all know his feelings towards me, but they don't know whether I return his affections or not. He is wonderfully kind and considerate, just the sort of man to spoil a girl because he is so unselfish and clever with his fingers that of course he is always ready to do the odd jobs that generally fall upon the woman.

Thurs. May 10th

J. had a letter saying that her brother in France was dangerously ill, so we went to the Post Office to send off a cable, asking them to cable back how he was...

After tea we played tennis and then Percy and I went for a walk. After dinner we had music.

Friday May 11th

...About 4 o'clock two elephants came to take us for a picnic. Mr Lee had borrowed them from Mr Gordon as we said we should like to ride one. They had a sort of mattress on their backs fastened with ropes and the driver sat on their necks with his feet on their ears. The elephants knelt down and we climbed up by means of a little foot ladder. Mr Blythe (visiting clergyman) and I and Mary and Nellie (Lee) sat on one and Miss Hearn, Janie and Percy and Agnes on the other. I was a little afraid the motion might make me seasick, but it did not at all. It really was most comfortable and one had such a lovely view as we were so high up.

Mrs Lee, Mr Potter and Miss Sumner walked as they did not like to ride. We went along the side of the hills for 2 or 3 miles and had tea among some trees beside a stream. Then we mounted our elephants again and went on to a little village among a grove of bamboo trees on the red hills. This red soil is really lovely. We got back about 7 o'clock and P. & I went for a walk till dinner-time.

Sat. May 12th

Went to the Club, as J. had heard from Miss Dunkley that her brother in Mesopotamia was wounded and she wanted to see if it was in the paper. She had not seen it before, but found his name in the Gazette a few days back. It is very dreadful for her to hear of a second brother so soon after the other one...

After tea Miss Hearn and I played tennis, the final of the tournament. I won the first set 6-4 and the second 6-1. Percy umpired for us and I expect his presence encouraged me, because I played much better than I usually do.

Mon. May 14th

We had to pack up as the bullock carts were going to start off with our luggage. After breakfast Percy and I played for a time and then we all went up to the Prices... There was... a Captain Nairn there. He and his wife and two little children are on their way to Keintung 300 miles away on the border of China where he is to do police duty. He was taken prisoner by the Germans in Africa and released on parole, but the authorities say he can do police duty. They will travel by bullock cart, or mules and elephants and will have to carry all their money with them - paper money is no use out there. I suppose the journey will take over 3 weeks. Bullock carts only do about 12 miles a day...

After tea Percy and I started off for a walk at once as all our tennis things were packed. We went along through the woods and climbed to the top of a very high hill. The more we are together, the more we find in common. He is very interested in education. He thinks it is partly hereditary. Many of his ancestors were clergymen and probably had teaching to do and his grandfather kept a school. His father's ancestors were vicars of Padbury. In politics he is rather like Dad - not entirely on either side, though he feels very strongly about certain points such as the Disestablishment of the Church. He is very much against it.

Besides being principal of the Government Engineering College & Art Officer for Burma, he is secretary to an Industrial Commission which is considering the advancement of the industries of Burma and, when the war is over, he will probably receive the post of Director of Industries for Burma. It is strange to think of him holding all these posts as he looks such a boy and has the charm and brightness of a boy of 25 or 24. He seems to be able to make friends with people of all ranks... He must have something in him to retain his simplicity and sweetness after 11 years of this country... Percy has been feeling lonely for years and praying that he might find someone he could love... He told me that when he used to dream of his ideal woman, he felt that the first thing was that she should be very good and next he would like someone with brains.

We had breakfast at 10.30 and then we five had to say goodbye to Taung-gyi and set off in the motor. P. had undertaken to motor us all as far as Thazi instead of our going in the mail motor-car...

It was rather a hot drive but very pleasant. We reached Loian which is two miles from Kalaw about 2.15 and dropped Miss Hearn and Miss Sumner at Mrs Browne's estate... Then we motored on to Kalaw to the Vickerys' house which is a very pleasant place on the top of a hill. She had asked us there to spend the night with her... P. & I went for a walk among the pine trees.

Thurs. May 17th

About 7.30 P. took me out in the motor, so that we could have a little time together. I think he was feeling down. He said he was very very anxious about the next two months as he felt I should probably come to a decision by then... He is nearly 37 and this is the first time he has been really in love. He said he had not given me presents as he did not want me to think he thought it would make any difference...

We got back to Loian at 10.30. The Vickerys have Family Prayers (the only house I have been to in Burma where they have them) and then we motored to Loian to fetch Miss Hearn and Miss Sumner... Then we began our journey. It is about 60 miles from Kalaw to Thazi and the road winds along the side of magnificent gorges hemmed in with towering tree-covered mountains. We left Kalaw about 12.45 and stopped at Nanpandet about 2.45 for tea. We got crockery from the P.W.D. bungalow and made a fire beside a lovely river flowing through the forest. Then we all paddled - the water was delicious - and started off again about 4 o'clock.

The heat grew more and more fierce the nearer we got to the plains. There was a strong breeze, but it was a burning one. We reached Thazi which is on the plains about 6.20 and went to the Irrigation bungalow. The atmosphere was stifling and the water in the filter was warm so we could not drink it. We had to go down to the station and get a drink there. Then P. and I went out for a little alone till dinner time... The heat was terrific. It was horrid to wake up at 5 in the morning all soaked with perspiration...

Friday May 18th

We had breakfast at the bungalow at 8 am and then went to the station. P. was coming to Mandalay with us as he had to go to Maymyo to see the financial Commissioner... Of course we had a very hot journey and reached Mandalay at the worst time of day about 2 o'clock. I suppose the temperature would be about 110°... Mr Anderson met us and told us there was no matron at the school. (Miss Brennan had left to get married). He had secured one but she had collapsed in two days and gone away... P. and we two went in a gharry. He came up to school with us and then went on to the Club where he is staying the night. Our house was locked up and very dismal. We felt stifled... Percy came about 4.30 pm and had tea with us and then left as Mr Anderson was coming to see me. Mr Anderson came about 5.15 and said Mr Grossett had a scheme for turning the Parsonage into the Girls' school and building on to it. I had hoped that Mr A. would have arranged to amalgamate the girls' school with the American Baptist Mission and I was rather disappointed to hear him talk of building...

Percy came back at 6.30 and we went for a stroll along the Fort walls. I told him I did not see how I could possibly leave the school unless Mr Anderson joined it to the A.B.M. as they would never get another head-mistress. I think we both felt rather down, but he is wonderfully sweet when I am depressed. He is so understanding about the difficulty I should feel leaving my work. But he is rather upset at my being here and says it is "a rotten place" and "they don't deserve to have me".

Sun. May 20th

We had to go to Church in a gharry as our bicycles were still at the shop. We called for them on the way back. The man said there were 20 punctures in mine due to the little thorns which strew the ground at this time of year...

Percy came at 4.30 to take me out. He is rather in doubt as to where his duty lies and wants my help. Mr Thomson, the financial Commissioner, is anxious that he should devote himself to the work of this industrial commission and become Director of Industries as soon as the post is created which would put in his hands the organisation of all technical and industrial education, but it would mean his giving up his engineering school and personal contact with the students and he did not know which he ought to do. I suppose the Directorship is a bigger post and would give him wider scope, as he would have to organise schools all over the Province. I should imagine the Directorship would be rather an important post, but Percy is very humble and makes very little of himself, so I don't know exactly how important a person he is. He is rather attracted by the Directorship because of the scope it would give him, but he is very anxious to find out what is right for him to do, so I hope the way will be made clear. He need not decide just yet.

When we got back, he motored J. and me to Church. There was a terrific storm, first dust, then thunder, lightning and rain. I am glad the rain has come, but I was disappointed it happened in church as I wanted Percy to hear Mr Anderson at his best. The storm was still raging when service was over. We waited for some time and then P. took us home. The lightning was magnificent.

Percy came after tea and took me out in the motor... He is returning to Rangoon tomorrow. I believe he is a very sincere Christian. I told him that if we were married, I should want us to be able to go to Holy Communion together and, of course, he has not been confirmed in the Church of England as he belongs to the Congregationalists. He said he was thinking of joining the Church, but he should have to think it out for himself and see whether he really believed the articles of the church. He could not just join because he wanted me to marry him and, of course, I respect him all the more for that...

Wed. May 23rd

Wrote out a time-table for the new matron. She seems to have some go in her, but is rather untidy looking... Miss Dunkley came to see us. She has been doing evangelistic tours in the jungle and enjoyed it immensely. Many of the women had not seen a white woman before and they brought their sick to her to be doctored and implored her to come back again. She is feeling very sore at having to come back to her school work which she dislikes very much.

Friday. May 25th

We re-opened school and when we had settled down had lessons as usual...

Sun. May 27th

...Miss Dunkley came for tea and we told her about our visit to Taung-gyi. Percy's letter arrived while she was here, so I could not read it properly. We write to one another every day. It is wonderful how much there is to say. He says that God who gives the love will give the solution of our difficulties.

CHAPTER IX

JOURNEY'S END...

Epilogue to alphabet written by Miss Sumner and Miss Hearn in Taung-gyi:

"And now we must to work again
In Rangoon, Mandalay, Insein.
Perhaps you think the story's done,
For two 'tis surely just begun,
The links they forged this holiday
Shall bind them closer through life's way.
To the two the three give greeting -
May journeys end in lovers' meeting."

Mr Morris was right: the difficulties which stood in the way of the marriage were resolved one after one.

Though the diary was intended to replace a weekly letter to the family, it is supplemented from time to time by private letters which give a clearer impression of my mother's feelings and scruples. On May 5th, 1917, the day after the Shan wedding, she wrote:

"Mother darling, Mr Morris asked me to marry him yesterday. He said he had been waiting for me so long and praying about it and he knew at once that I was what he wanted. Of course I have known him hardly a month, but I suppose he pressed things because after we leave here it will be practically impossible for us to see one another unless we are engaged as he lives at Insein near Rangoon, 300 miles from Mandalay. I told him that I did not think I could marry because you wanted me at home and because I came out here as a missionary and did not like to give up my work, also that I did not care enough for him to marry him..."

Of the three reasons given for refusing Mr Morris, the last was the least serious and she knew it. She had sufficient insight into her own nature to recognise that she was less likely to "fall in love" than to grow, quietly, steadily, into a deepened affection for the man she already admired and trusted. All she needed was time.

More serious to her was the separation her marriage in Burma would involve from her family and especially from her mother. Both her parents were elderly. Mrs Easton was now over seventy and not particularly well. Her life had been a constant struggle to make ends meet. Though her situation financially had been eased a little by taking paying guests and by making a home for her not very considerate sisters, the demands upon her time and energy were beginning to tell. Her daughter feared that if she married Mr Morris and stayed in Burma for the eight years he still had to work to gain his government pension, she might not see her parents again.

The most serious difficulty, and the one which Mr Morris was bound to respect, was her belief that she had a vocation to missionary work, a call she would be unable to obey if she married a government servant. My parents were deeply religious people: there was no question of committing themselves to a relationship if this meant setting aside a commitment to God. There were principles they could not give up even for each other. Yet Mr Morris believed that his wife would be engaged in work as important as that of a missionary; and Miss Easton could see, only too clearly in view of the number of mission schools in Mandalay, that St. Mary's would not be greatly missed. Nevertheless she had a warm sense of loyalty to her school and could not leave it without being certain that her children were provided for.

Before the Taunggyi holiday was over, it was fairly clear to Miss Easton that she did "care enough" for Mr Morris to marry him. With characteristic good sense, she had made opportunities to be alone with him: their evening stroll together became an almost necessary ritual. It is noticeable how quickly in the diaries he becomes "Percy", a name "which I don't much like", she tells her mother, and goes on to give a candid but not unsympathetic description of his physical features. "He is nothing special to look at. He is only about two inches taller than I am and very thin, but I think his face grows very attractive the more you look at it. He has a very nice nose and mouth, but his hair is rather thin. You see this country does pull one down..." The "squeaky voice" which once irritated her is now less obtrusive. "His voice sounds a little croaky sometimes, though, as a matter of fact, I very seldom notice it now." On May 13th, less than two weeks after she had rejected him, she writes in a second letter to her mother, "I feel I do love and care for him very much." However she adds that she thinks it too soon to make a definite decision. She wanted to test her feelings in the humdrum of work, away from the heady enchantments of the Shan hills. Meanwhile she would not permit an engagement - officially that is; in fact all the European society of Mandalay was buzzing with it - until her parents gave their consent.

Slowly, almost imperceptibly, her doubts melted away. On July 1st, since letters were impossibly slow, she allowed Percy to send a cable to her parents asking them to sanction the engagement. The reply arrived on July 7th 1917. "The cable from home came about 2 pm. I had been hoping and praying it would come as I did not want to keep Percy waiting any longer. I had made up my mind about it and felt that we ought to be engaged. He came up about 4.30 and I showed him the cable in my little office, and he put on my ring. He chose it himself and brought it up hoping we should become engaged. It is five lovely diamonds set onto a gold ring with little platinum clasps. He wanted to have all diamonds and no coloured stones. Then we went and sat on Mandalay hill..." Mandalay hill had been their special place ever since the return from Taunggyi. Time and again the diary records their visits in search of quiet and privacy, on the surprisingly numerous occasions that Mr Morris found his business brought him to Mandalay. They had passed together between the huge white chinthes, the mythical lions which guard pagoda entrances, walked the coolly-shaded covered stair-ways with their bright intriguing stalls and, once, at least, they had climbed the 1729 steps to the very top with its breathtaking view of the plain and the Irrawaddy and the hills beyond. It was natural they should seek the hill again as betrothed lovers.

If Doris was still a little troubled about her vocation, she must have been reassured by a drive with Lady Cuffe who, after telling her that Percy was "one of the nicest and best men she knew and she did not think there was another man in Burma she was so fond of", went on to say "I should be doing as much real missionary work as his wife through the force of example and the influence of a good home as I could by actual teaching." She was encouraged too by the pleasure all her friends took in her engagement - Miss Patch who had been so pleased and excited when Doris returned from Taunggyi (for "everyone knew... that Percy was in love with me, long before he proposed to me, almost before I knew it myself"), Mrs Grossett, the

Price's. On the Sunday the diary records, "Of course people saw my ring in church and the mistresses stopped... to congratulate me afterwards... Lady Cuffe asked if she might kiss me and Percy said they all called her 'mother in the East', so she said she hoped she was going to have another adopted daughter... Before church Mr Anderson came out and said to me, 'May I congratulate you at last'".

The practical problems regarding the school were solved - not easily nor without setbacks, but solved they were. Mr Anderson who had taken Mr Lister's place as vicar of St. Mary's was more of a realist than his predecessor. He saw clearly that there was only doubtfully room for the school in Mandalay, though as a new head to replace Mr Saxby had been appointed, the boys' section of the school was likely to continue at least for a time. He had come round to Miss Easton's view that the American Baptists should eventually take over the girls, particularly as Mr Baldwin, head of the A.B.M. school, was willing to allow Church of England children to have church teaching. "I told Mr Anderson that I did feel strongly that we ought to cooperate as our numbers had been steadily decreasing since this time last year. I also discovered from him what I rather suspected he thought, namely that a small school like this, so crippled for funds, ought not to be paying for anyone with my qualifications. He said it was a big salary (it is not really, it is very small considering I am headmistress and have to save up all the time for passage and furlough) and the work is very elementary. Of course the work is exceedingly elementary and there is not the least need to have any one with a degree and I believe he thinks that even if the school continues they ought to get someone without a degree and pay her less." It was perhaps not very pleasant to Miss Easton to discover that she was regarded as an expensive luxury, but it must have done something to lessen her sense of guilt. Meanwhile Miss Cooke, who taught in the S.P.G. girls' school in Maymyo, was eager to take her place, for in her present post she was not allowed much scope and felt that, at 40, it was time she had more responsible work. Unfortunately she could not be released until December. Doris first thought this would mean postponing the marriage until February or March as she would not be able, while teaching, to complete her preparations. As it was she was finding it difficult to concentrate on her work. However at some point she must have persuaded herself that, with a little extra leave, she could be ready for a December wedding.

The familiar grind of school continued with its familiar problems and irritations: the constant punctures in bicycle tyres: the heat which made the children languid and enterprise a near impossibility: troubles with servants and matron: children's illnesses ranging from chicken-pox to plague from which one of the day-girls, a friend of Mabel Parr's, died: the creatures - scorpions, white-ants destroying books, bats. "The bats are very troublesome now. They flop about my study and worry me when I am working. I captured one and kept it under my waste-paper basket until I was ready to get into bed, it was such a nuisance." She soon found that her engagement to A. P., as he was known to his friends, was a source of gossip and excitement all over Mandalay from Club to Mission Compound. Everyone she met seemed to think she was exceedingly lucky to have won the affection of such a good man. She suspected, too, that they considered she was marrying above her station, since Percy was an important Government Official with a yearly salary of £800, and she was only a mission teacher. It was a relief to discover that a real aristocrat like Lady Cuffe approved of her. "She said she would be only too glad to do anything she could to help me and she felt she was going to be very fond of me too. She implied that there were not many people whom she would think good enough for Percy, but she was very happy over our engagement."

Doris was happy too but distinctly nervous about meeting Percy's friends and a little anxious about her clothes when they were invited out to dine. Naturally she wanted to make a good impression. "It is very awkward not having a nice evening dress. The one the dhobi made is not at all satisfactory and Mildred's black one is so long and big." This black dress, however, won Percy's approval: he liked it best of her dresses "which shows his good taste, because although it is old-fashioned it is much the best-made I have." In August they were both invited to spend a week-end with the Cuffes in Maymyo. This was something of an ordeal for Doris, but the chatter of Lady Cuffe's sister, Mrs Watson, helped to dissipate her shyness, while the simple if elegant style of their living took the edge off her awe for these Anglo-Irish aristocrats. My mother was no snob, but all her life she retained a deep admiration for good breeding. "The Cuffes have a pretty drawing-room, full of Lady Cuffe's water-colour paintings and lovely Burmese curios. Sir Otway is such a nice kindly gentleman, so friendly and easy to get on with... I think the Cuffes live very simply. We had a very plain dinner and no cake for afternoon tea. Lady Cuffe is devoted to her garden and spends a great deal of time on it... I heard Sir Otway reading the Bible aloud to Lady Cuffe after we had retired to our rooms." Later she met Percy's sister, Dorothy Chapman, and Dorothy's brother and sister-in-law, Alice and Harold Clayton. Alice was Arthur Chapman's sister and so could be regarded as related through Dorothy to the Morris family.

Now that they were officially engaged, it was easier for them to be seen together in public. When Percy was able to be in Mandalay, Doris snatched what time she could from her work and they went out in the motor-car, sometimes accompanied by Janie or school-children. One Saturday they crossed the Irrawaddy in a Burmese country-boat and saw King Bodawpaya's pagoda which he left unfinished when he died in 1813. "We went up to the top of a huge pagoda which one of the kings began building. He only got as far as the base, but had it been finished it would have been something like the pyramids for size." When they were alone they spent time in the happy pursuit of finding out more about each other. Doris read "Sylvie and Bruno", one of Percy's favourite books.

She found that his family, like hers, always had Family Prayers. She was pleased that he had decided that he could join the Anglican Church and was hoping that, if they could go to England soon, Mr Easton would prepare him for confirmation. Meanwhile they went to church together and both took communion "for it was an order of the bishops of India that clergy were to administer to communicants of all denominations." In politics, like Doris's father, Percy was not wholly in favour of either the Liberals or Conservative party, though he inclined to the latter. They did not always agree. Doris supported the suffragettes, Mr Morris was opposed to votes for women: he felt it would be a mistake for them to cheapen themselves by becoming involved in politics. It was an instance of a kind of Victorian idealism which had already alarmed and touched her. "P. and I went again to Mandalay hill. Sometimes I feel almost afraid because he has such a high ideal for me. He said he wanted me to be a light to a great many people as he was sure it would be a help to them to know me as "a mother in the east" (like Lady Cuffe) to the young men who come out here and are faced with such great temptations."

Work and courtship run side by side in the diaries, not always smoothly but with a growing conviction of the rightness of the engagement. To Janie Openshaw fate proved less friendly. Her affair with Gordon Goldberg was causing anxiety to her friends, and the contrast between the happiness of Percy and Doris and the uncertainty of her own relationship was telling on her health. Poor Janie, so loyal, so attractively young and lively! Doris's marriage meant for her the loss of a companion and must have made her the more eager to become engaged herself. The diary records on Saturday June 9th: "She has been having a worrying time with anxiety about her two brothers (both fighting: both reported in hospital) and her love affair with Mr Goldberg[2] and I am afraid there is trouble in store for her. He wants to get leave in India and meet her there and she has asked if she may get a substitute and go, but people think it very inadvisable." A few days later, however, a telegram came telling Janie that Gordon was unable to get leave, so "the Indian affair is at an end." A relief to her friends who were aware that there had been other "affairs" in which Lieutenant Goldberg had been involved, but to Janie it must have felt like the blocking up of an escape-route. A few months later she did leave the school and went out to India to marry Gordon, but once more his leave - he was serving in Mesopotamia - was cancelled and Janie was left stranded in a strange country without friends. The marriage finally took place but meanwhile she had to endure a restless, anxious period of waiting. My mother maintained her relationship with Janie long after they had both returned to England. The two were very different in personality and interests; probably in other circumstances they would not have become friends; but those troubled months in Mandalay had forged an enduring link between them. In the diary Janie emerges as a distinct character, even though she is swallowed up in the "we" which always includes her until the arrival of Percy gives it a different significance. She is prepared to argue with Mr

---

2 The exact form of Gordon's name remains uncertain throughout the diaries. Later, presumably to remove the German - Jewish association, he changed his surname to Golding.

Lister on Doris's behalf; she is fun-loving, entertaining company, and she complained when Miss Cooke took over the school
that "they never have any fun as we used to"; she is certainly spirited it must have taken courage to defy her friends and cross to India to marry Gordon - perhaps a little headstrong and impulsive: after all in 1918 she was still under 25. Apart from a half-hearted criticism of her romps with the "masses" on board ship and a hint that she is too "young in mind" to be a support, the diary conveys scarcely a breath of censure. I believe she gave more support than Doris altogether recognised in her unconscious acceptance of a friendship which was superseded only by the more satisfying relationship with A. P. Morris.

The end of the June to August term came at last. For the two weeks' holiday at the beginning of September, Mr Morris planned to take Doris and his sister Dorothy on tour along the Irrawaddy, combining business with pleasure. Unfortunately Dorothy, in the early stages of pregnancy and missing acutely her husband who had been called to India for military training, was advised by her doctor against accompanying them which left them without a chaperone. In the end Mrs Price, wife of that clergyman who had counselled Mr Lister and Mr Saxby in their quarrels with the Bishop, agreed to go, but meanwhile Doris had accepted an invitation to stay with the Claytons in Maymyo where Dorothy was living. This visit was shortened to a week-end which passed very satisfactorily in consulting the two ladies about her trousseau. Alice offered to make "six pairs of drawers" if provided with the stuff. "She has a very nice pattern she showed me... I showed my clothes to Alice as I wanted her advice... They gave me addresses of places in India where I can get hand-embroidered undergarments and hand-made lace. It is very strong and stands the dhobi very well."

Miss Easton was determined to be impressed by Dorothy: a sister dear to Percy must be worthy of respect. The diary notes her good taste in dress... "a pretty white coat frock and a very becoming hat." Later the same day, after a rather engaging entry ("Percy and I went out in the motor and I tried my hand at steering. When I can do that properly I am going to learn to control the engine and brakes"), she records, "Dorothy looked very pretty and dainty. She wore a white chiffon and net dress and a pearl pendant that Arthur gave her." Doris discovered that her sister-in-law had been brought up in France which perhaps supplied the reason for her "chic" appearance, and that all the Morris family worshipped their mother "because she is such a saint and so charming".

"...Dorothy is distinctly attractive. She does not look more than 20, though she is really nearly 32. She is not exactly pretty - she has rather a long nose which spoils her, but she has an exceedingly neat pretty figure and dainty hands and feet and she dresses very daintily and prettily and speaks rather prettily. She had very fair hair and very blue eyes... I should think she has a good deal of character and independence. She only came out to be married last November. She was doing V.A.D. work in England and very much wishes she were back there, now that he husband has gone to India and will probably be sent to Mesopotamia. It is very hard for her being out here in Burma, because a married woman here can't keep her own house if her husband is away and Dorothy does not like Club life. During the few months she has been married she had been touring nearly all the time with Arthur, her husband, in the jungle..."

On September 4th 1917, Percy, Doris and Mrs Price set off by steamer from Mandalay down the Irrawaddy to visit Nyaungu and Pagan, where they stayed at one of the bungalows provided for officials of the Public Works Department. Doris found them much less comfortable than the boat. "The subdivisional officer, a Burman, met us with a green cart drawn by bullocks which took us up a steep road to the district bungalow... The bungalow was very dark and dreary. It was raining outside and we only had 2 or 3 candles to light us. It makes one realise how lonely it must be for unmarried men, who have to spend nearly all their days touring, spending their nights at these dirty rat-infested bungalows out in the jungle" She had her first experience of sharing in Percy's work when she walked with him, his clerk and some other Burmans to some pottery villages. "The ground was thick with mud and very slippery and it was not at all easy walking... We looked at sites for a tile factory as the government is going to build one here. We came back in a boat. It was just a rough Burmese one and we had to sit on the bottom as there are no seats except for the paddlers." Next day they saw the potters working. "It was very interesting to watch men moulding huge pots like those in Ali Baba and the Forty Thieves..." Their inspection of crafts included a visit to a weaving-school and to the thugyi's (headman's) compound to see the lacquer workers as "Percy had to find out all about them. They gave us chairs to sit on and a crowd of them sat on mats on the ground and explained how they made their bowls and boxes... We went to the house of one of the best workers and saw the whole process. The article is first woven of bamboo or horse-hair. Then it is covered with layers of thitsi (wood oil). Sometimes they put on about 26 layers and each takes 4 days to dry. Then they scratch the designs on it with a pointed instrument. It is marvellous the way they draw with such accuracy and precision with only a few rough measurements and the designs are often intricate. After the design is scratched it is coated with a red colour and allowed to dry and when that is dry, it is washed off, but red, of course, is left in the scratches. Then another design is engraved and filled in with green and so on with the colours required."

Business was combined with sight-seeing. Pagan is an ancient and beautiful place with its thousands of pagodas, ruined but lovely, its grey-trunked palm trees and distant views of the silver Irrawaddy and the mountains beyond. It became the seat of the first dynasty of Burmese kings in 1057 when Anawrahta conquered the Mons capital of Thaton. For nearly two hundred years it was a great Buddhist centre until a foolish ruler defied Kublai Khan and killed his ambassadors. It is a strangely numinous place - like Delphi or Iona. When Doris visited it, she felt this atmosphere of holiness. She writes of the Ananda pagoda, called after the favourite disciple of the Buddha; "It is more like a cathedral because there are long corridors inside running round the central square block. On each side of the square is a shrine with a gigantic standing figure of the Buddha in gilt. Windows let in to the upper storeys of the building throw light on his face... There is more of an atmosphere of quiet sanctity about the building than in most pagodas.

"On the four sides there are huge gates of black and red finely carved..."

They visited other pagodas, "differently constructed from the usual type as they have corridors and terraces outside so that it is possible to walk round inside the building and mount by flights of steps from terrace to terrace outside right up to the door at the top. With most pagodas it is not possible to go inside except just to the recesses at the sides where the image is placed." The Thatbyinnu was one they climbed, and the Nanpaya where Manuha, the Talaing king, was imprisoned by King Anawrahta and forced to become a monk.

They also visited, travelling in a bullock cart, the Petleik pagoda and saw the terra-cotta tiles "carved with illustrations of stories of the life of the Buddha in his previous existences. Really they are a number of old folk stories from Northern India which people connected with Buddha after his life. The collection of stories is called the Jatakas. Buddhism came to Burma partly from the north and partly from the south via Ceylon. The southern form is the purer but all Buddhism is mixed to a certain extent with animism and nat worship and so, in some pagodas, you see figures of nats at the entrances. Sometimes the idea is that the nat was converted to Buddhism, but I think some of the people worship nats still." ("Nats" are nature spirits appealed to and placated by the Burmese.)

Not only were the pagodas themselves interesting: the views from the top rewarded the effort required by the climb, particularly in evening light. "We went for a walk and then climbed to the top of a pagoda and watched the sunset. It was simply magnificent. We had such an extensive view and the colours were wonderful, impossible to describe - sky and water and land all took on the most glorious tints. We stayed up there till it was nearly dark as Percy had his electric torch to guide us down." On another occasion, she records an evening walk when they sat on a headland "while Percy read aloud to us some of the travels of Marco Polo. There was a glorious sunset, a great wall of leaden blue cloud and nearly all the colours of the rainbow in the sky and water." Reading - and often reading aloud - was to be a common feature of the Morris's life on tour. On this occasion they had, as well as Marco Polo, a book on Buddhism which Percy read to the ladies while they sewed or knitted.

The holiday came to an end in mid-September. There was still time enough, though not ample time, to get ready for the wedding: or so Miss Easton thought when she was once more engulfed in the business of school.

CHAPTER X

SCHOOL WEDDING IN MANDALAY (DEC. 20TH 1917)

"It is rather disappointing about the measles... We have had to arrange for the reception to be held at the Volunteer Hall. I daresay some people won't like any children to come to the reception for fear of infection, but I am not going to keep them away." (Entry for Dec. 16th 1917).

Mon. Sept. 17th

Re-opened school. Lessons as usual...

Sat. Sept. 22nd

Miss Butcher (teacher), J. and I walked down to bazaar. I wanted to get some embroidery to put on my old petticoats which are quite plain...

After tea I saw the dhobi and gave him enough work to keep him busy for a week... I cut out pictures from pattern books to give him. He seemed rather pleased because I gave him a pair of pyjamas to make. Several ladies here wear them on tour as they say they are much better. Also on voyages.

Mon. Oct. 1st

...After tea I set the children to wash the motor as it was thick with mud. It was a hard job but they worked well...

...The children asked if they might go into the town and see the lights as it was the light-feast. So Janie and I walked down with them. The streets were gorgeous with lanterns and animals and flowers of coloured paper all lit up with candles. It was a lovely moonlight-night too, but we were very tired by the time we returned. Worked.

Sat. Oct. 6th

After breakfast gave out pocket money etc... Percy arrived from Monywa, so after tea we took five of the children who helped to wash the motor, out in the car. I think they enjoyed it very much...

Wed. Oct. 10th

Lessons. It was a terribly hot day. J. and I did not feel at all well. I think we both had fever - our legs ached so and our heads were hot.

Thurs. Oct. 11th

I still felt very hot and poorly and my limbs ached a good deal. However I gradually recovered during the afternoon...

Fri. Oct. 12th

I was surprised to find the children remembered it was my birthday. I had to kiss the dormitory all round when I went to inspect it in the morning...

Percy arrived from Maymyo about 5.45... He was having a card case made for me for a birthday present, but it was not yet ready. He gave me some lovely hand-woven white silk... The mistresses (gave) me a lovely tea set of Japanese china for my birthday... I really did not expect anything at all as they will I suppose give me a wedding-present. Some of the children gave me a purse and a tray for the tea-service. Janie gave me a sideboard cloth.

Sat. Oct. 13th

...Percy came about 4.30 pm and we took Janie and the two Parr girls for a long motor-ride. We went nearly 30 miles. Mabel had never been before. They appreciated the scenery very much. These children don't see much outside Mandalay...

Wed. Oct. 24th

Lessons. After tea sat in the garden and pinned some tucks in petticoats which were too long...

Sat. Oct. 27th

...Percy arrived from Pakokku about tea-time. After tea we took Janie and 2 or 3 of the children for a motor ride. Percy came to dinner at school.

Sun. Oct. 28th

Church... Janie and I had breakfast at the Club with Mr Price and Percy. Read and lay down. Wrote letters.

(At this point there is a break in the diaries - one of the very few, which is explained in a series of letters to Mrs Easton. The first written on Sunday, November 11th was headed General Hospital, Mandalay)

My very darling Mother,

I have had a very bad time but I am thankful to say I am much better now and I hope to be let out of hospital in a few days and go to Maymyo to stay with the Claytons. I have got Malaria fever and they say I must have got it from mosquito bites during my September holiday as it is a nasty kind of Malaria which one does not really get in Mandalay. I started being ill a fortnight ago tomorrow and I was at school till the Sunday. I ought to have gone to Rangoon that week to see about my dress, but I fell ill two or three days before we meant to start. Percy came to Mandalay to fetch me and had to stop and help nurse me instead. I don't know what I should have done without him when Janie was in school. One day I kept feeling faint and it was a great comfort to have him. My temperature was 103 and 104 on and off and it does make one feel bad.

Dr Sheldon was very good about coming, but he thought I had dengue (a kind of influenza) and did not detect the malaria. On the Sunday Percy had to go on to Rangoon and the doctor thought I was better as my temperature was normal when he came in the morning, but it went up again and all that day I lay in bed feeling stifled with a temperature of 104; in the evening it got to 105 I think. So Janie sent for Miss Patch and she said we had better have Dr Sheldon again. When he came he said I had better go to the hospital, so he carried me down to his motor and he and Miss Patch took me there.

Colonel Penny who is in charge of the hospital was away and there was no spare room, so I had to sleep in a sort of passage. Dr Sheldon still attended me as the Colonel was away. When he discovered from examining my blood all the malaria germs, he ordered them to give me injections of quinine and since then I have improved steadily...

Mr Price had been most kind too always coming in. He has taken prayers with me once or twice. He has found someone to do my work at school and has engaged her till the end of the term, so that is a relief.

The £40 from Uncle Harold arrived safely. It is good of him to give so much and it is an enormous relief to have it to spend. The prices of things out here are perfectly appalling. You must not think, Mother darling, of paying for the cake. It would distress me very much. I can't get it under £7 and if I want ornaments on it, it would cost £2 more. Of course I shall do without ornaments...

c/o Mrs Clayton, Maymyo, Sunday Nov. 18th

My own darling Mother,

I came up here on Thursday morning, but the journey and change of air upset me rather and I have not been quite as well. I am in bed, that makes nearly three weeks now and it is very hard to be patient when I want so much to be up seeing to my clothes. I really don't know what is to happen about my wedding-dress and other best dresses. You see I meant to go to Rangoon a fortnight ago and I am afraid it will be at least another fortnight before I am fit and that will be only 3 weeks before the wedding...

Nov. 25th c/o Mrs Clayton, Maymyo.

My darling Mother...

I am much better now. Percy came up last Tuesday and it has made a great difference. He could not stand the strain and anxiety of waiting for news and not having good reports any longer. He was getting really run down himself so he wired on last Monday he was coming the next day. It has been a great help to me, because he has been able to take me out for little walks according to my strength and now I am able to walk by myself and go quite a fairly long distance...

The doctor said last Monday when he came that he thought I should be fit to have a school wedding in Mandalay, so we are going on with preparations, at least Percy is. He is doing it all, sending out invitations, ordering the food and the cake etc etc. Just providing light refreshments for the children and the guests will come together with the cake between £30 and £40; things are a terrible price here. I expect I shall have to pay Percy back out of the £50 I have in the War Loan. It is rather unfair to him that he should have all this arranging to do and he has a terrible press of work with the Industrial Commissioners coming over from India in January and his Art Exhibition also coming off then. Of course our honeymoon is one of his government tours.

You see Government Officials don't have any holidays, except they can apply for a few days off in the year which is called Casual Leave, because at the end of every 4 years they are supposed to be able to have one year's leave on half pay. Percy is due 3 years furlough as he has been out 12 years without any, but of course when the war is over and he does get leave he would not be able to take more than 6 months or so because of the money loss.

I wish he could have a proper holiday... He is rather down just now about the Engineering School, because he had worked up the tone and discipline so much and now since they have put a Eurasian headmaster in and given him so much touring to do... the discipline has gone back and the boys have got slack...

Percy hopes to be able to take me down to Rangoon on Thursday to do my shopping. I think I shall be equal to it if I do not rush about too much and of course we shall have the motor car to go from shop to shop. That is exactly 3 weeks before the wedding. I do hope they will be able to get my wedding dress and other dresses made in time, it is leaving it all very late...

Percy had managed to get a house in Insein (pronounced by most people Enseen, tho' I believe the correct form is Insane) quite close to the school. It seems to be a fairly nice house, 3 rooms and a verandah upstairs and 3 rooms downstairs, but houses are fearfully expensive. He has to pay about £80 a year for it, although Insein is quite a small place.

I don't think it is any use my telling you the names of places we shall visit during the honeymoon. It is in the neighbourhood of Taung-gyi where we stayed in April with the Lees and we shall probably go there for a night or two. We are also going for two or three nights to the bungalow in the middle of the Inle lake where we went before in April. The tour will last just a fortnight so we expect to reach Insein on Jan. 3rd.

Dec. 2nd. (Letter to Mrs Easton written c/o Mrs Taylor, Insein)

Percy brought me down from Maymyo to Mandalay on Wednesday and I spent the night at school and then we left for Rangoon on Thursday, arriving Friday morning. We had a very comfortable journey and I stood it quite well... I am still not certain of how much I can do without making my head ache. Also I have not quite got rid of a cold I caught at Maymyo... I am staying with Mrs Taylor, the doctor's wife at Insein... Mrs Taylor is trying to fatten me up by giving me a lot of milk. They keep their own cow and so I get really nice milk. The Taylors are very kind. They have two darling little girls, Vivian aged 5 and Peggy 3...

Insein is very pretty. It is quite a small place and very quiet. There is glorious country just outside and it is a lovely motor ride from Insein into Rangoon. It is 13 or 14 miles by the nicest road but only 9 by the other.

Percy motored us into Rangoon yesterday and Mrs Taylor took me to a dress-maker, whom she finds very good, to make arrangements about a wedding dress... I am going to give Percy gold cuff-links and gold studs for a wedding present. He is coming with me tomorrow and we are going to do one or two things together and to have breakfast with the Listers who are now stationed at a church in Rangoon. They did not want to go there at all as they liked Shwebo very much. The Bishop came back a month or two ago and he is making these changes...

I have received the £3 and the £32. Thank you very much indeed, darling Mother and Daddy, but it is too much for you to give. Of course I am very, very glad of the money, there is so much to pay for and now I have the hospital bill in addition, also the salary of my substitute, Miss Hosy, which will be between £10 and £15, I am not sure which, and possibly doctors' bills. I do hope Dr Sheldon won't charge me anything. He came twice a day sometimes and once I think he came three times. He did not charge me last year, but of course he may think that as I am marrying Percy he can charge me this year... I tell you this, darling to show how much I appreciate your present, not because I am really worried... But I don't like to think of your denying yourselves, darling, to give me all that because in war time it must be so hard to spare it.

The Bishop is holding a Confirmation this afternoon and Percy is going to be confirmed so I hope to go to it with him...

Dec. 9th. (Letter to Mrs Easton from St. Mary's School)

I have arrived back at school again at last yesterday afternoon and I am thankful to feel nearly myself once more. I have so much to tell you and I don't know how to find time to tell it. My things seem rather a muddle and there is so much to be done and now some of the boarders and a number of the day scholars have started with measles and we don't know where to have the wedding-reception as people will probably be frightened to come here. Do you know that we have had to send out between 150 and 200 invitations? That is exclusive of all children... You see Percy has so many friends all over the country and he has to send a certain number of courtesy invitations to particular government officials.

I think I got on quite nicely with my shopping in Rangoon but the prices are appalling, I don't think they can be as bad in England. I will quote some to show you what it is like out here - over £5 for 3 single blankets for myself when touring - 3/- for a pair of quite poor white cotton stockings, 3/4 for an absolutely plain ordinary nailbrush, 15/6 for a wedding veil (plain medium size) 7/- for wreath of orange blossom.

I don't know what the price of small huckaback towels is at home, but I gave 13/- for half a dozen.

My wedding dress which is very simple, made of georgette and taffeta silk, is going to cost about 8 guineas and a pale blue silk ninon evening dress is to cost about the same. I think they will be very pretty...

I bought at a native shop an evening coat of Chinese embroidered silk a sort of peacock blue embroidered with various pale colours £2/6/4 and, which was perhaps rather extravagant, a lovely white Chinese silk dressing-gown embroidered with large pale pink flowers and a peacock on the back. I have bought no new hats except a straw-covered topee to go away in. (The straw-covered ones are much more becoming than the canvas ones). That is about all I bought in Rangoon.

From a Mission in India I got a few lovely hand-embroidered undergarments. For the rest I am making out with old ones and dhobi-made ones. I got 5 white lawn blouses from India beautifully embroidered and I have got the dhobi to make a few print every day dresses and white skirts.

Percy has some very nice drawing-room furniture and a piano and some most beautiful Burmese curios - ivory boxes exquisitely carved, bronze statuettes and two silver bowls engraved by one of the best silversmiths in Burma and numerous other delightful little pieces of work. He has a set of Burmese bandsmen playing their instruments done in silver, which he puts round his table centre when he gives dinner parties. I say we must bring them home to show Dad the queer instruments the Burmans play. Of course he collects these things not only because he is fond of art, but to encourage the workmen and also to show other people what the Burmans can do, so that they will give orders for work.

Insein is a very pretty place and the country round glorious. It gives the effect of moors because it is so wide and open and one feels rather high up.

Janie is going to be bridesmaid and Mr Boedikker, the man with whom Percy has been sharing a house in Insein since he gave up his own, best man. The Bishop has promised to marry us. Sir Otway will give me away...

Dec. 16th. (St. Mary's School, Mandalay).

...It is rather disappointing about the measles. I do not suppose there will be more than a dozen children at the wedding now, as we have sent all the boarders home... Then it has been a worry, too, because some of the English people are nervous and we have had to arrange for the reception to be at the Volunteer Hall. I daresay some people won't like any children to come to the reception for fear of infection, but I am not going to keep them away.

Of course in a way the measles may possibly be a blessing in disguise because it obliged us to put off both the prize-giving and an entertainment in aid of "Our Day" which we were giving at the Volunteer Hall and I don't think Janie at any rate could have stood the strain, as, of course, she has had a hard time all these six weeks while I have been away and it would have meant extra work for me too... Of course, I have not got my clothes as ready as I should have liked. There are numerous odd jobs such as running tucks which have had to be left undone and not a single thing is marked, but, of course, I can't help it.

...Percy is coming to Mandalay today, I think, as he has some work to do here and he wants to help me with my packing. He will be able to do all my books at any rate. Of course he is doing things for me that my family would naturally do, but one can't think a great deal of conventional practices in a country like this. I suppose it was improper his looking after me when I was ill here, but I don't know what I should have done when Janie was in school all day. In fact Dr Sheldon, Mr Price and Percy all had to help act nurse in some degree. Dr Sheldon told me afterwards he was rather amused one night when he was trying to give me some water out of a feeding-cup without spilling it over me and found afterwards that I had not got any because he was not holding it properly.

I have been to dinner twice with Arthur and Dorothy this week. He is posted in Mandalay for two months training as Lieutenant in the Sappers and Miners and then expects to go to the front.

Of course Percy is much more original and less conventional than Arthur or Dorothy. For instance they are both very fastidious about their clothes and appearance and Percy is so devoted to his work and so interested in everything round him that he does not pay much attention to his appearance and he does not like spending money on his own clothes. I know I shall have to look after him in that respect. He looks very nice in his evening suit, but he won't wear it more often than he can help, though as a matter of fact both Alice and I think he looks nicest of all in his everyday costume which consists of shirt, coat and shorts...

(From Dec. 20th, my mother took up her regular diary again).

Thurs. Dec. 20th

Wedding Day. I did not feel at all well. Miss Sumner and Miss Hearn who were staying at school for the wedding helped arrange the presents at the Volunteer Hall and also helped me dress. Mrs Grossett, Mrs Anderson and our mistresses decorated the Church and Lady Cuffe and Mrs Watson, her sister, saw to the arranging of the Volunteer Hall and the reception...

My dress was made of georgette and taffeta. It had broad bands of taffeta round the skirt and was trimmed with silver lace and orange blossom. I had a wreath of orange blossom round my head and my veil thrown back over it. Janie had a white georgette dress trimmed with blue and gold embroidery and a blue velvet sash and velvet ribbons on her hat and a gold rose. Stella (Lister) and I got her materials in Rangoon and the dhurzi (tailor) made the dress.

My dress was made by Madame Adele of Rangoon. For a going away dress I wore a coat frock made of thick white silk hand-woven which Percy gave me on my birthday. I had a topee covered with white straw and lined with blue straw and a very pretty blue veil of silk ninon - not over my face, topee-veils hang down behind. Madame Adele made up the silk for me, also some of the white material that I had brought out from home. She also made me an evening dress of very pale blue brocaded silk and ninon, trimmed with rose-bud trimming.

The ceremony was to begin at 11 o'clock. Lady Cuffe, Mrs Watson and Sir Otway came round with two motors between 10.30 and 11 and brought our bouquets. Lady C. said I looked very sweet. Janie went with Lady C. and Mr W. in one motor and I went with Sir Otway who was going to give me away in the other. Sir Otway was so nice and kind and chatted so pleasantly that it made me feel less nervous. They were singing "Thine for ever" when we went up the Church, and Percy was singing too, so it reassured me. We got through the service very well, and I quite enjoyed it. People said afterwards how nice it was that we both sang and that I spoke up so clearly.

The Bishop gave us a very nice little exhortation and then we sang "O Perfect Love". After the service Percy and I motored round by the Chapmans before we went to the Volunteer Hall to see Dorothy who was not well enough to go to church. When we reached the Hall some of Sir Otway's Burman friends held gold umbrellas (which by the way is a sign of royalty in Burma) over me while I walked from the motor to the building. The room upstairs where we had the reception looked very nice. The presents had been very nicely arranged and the bridescake was very pretty and everything went off without a hitch. We had to keep well up to time as we were going to catch a train at 1.15.

We had got the Vienna Cafe to provide iced coffee and cakes and sandwiches besides the wedding-cake. I would not have champagne (as is, of course, the custom out here) so, when Sir Otway proposed our health, people ate it in wedding-cake instead of drinking it. Percy made a very amusing little speech in reply to the toast, thanking those who had helped in the event eg the Bishop and Mr Lister. He roused much laughter by saying that he hoped all the Bishop's undertakings of the same nature would have a similar result at which, of course, the Bishop pretended to be very indignant.

Brides and bridegrooms out here generally seem to stick absolutely still in a corner by themselves at their reception, but I was determined not to as I think it is so silly, so Percy and I walked about the room and talked to people. I don't know how many were there, about 60 or 70 I should think. There were only about half a dozen children. Of course the staff were all there and some of the parents and a fairly large number of the English people. Janie told me that everyone said what an exceedingly pretty wedding it was and how happy everyone seemed and her dress was much admired.

I changed my dress in the Sergeant's room at the Volunteer Hall and left Miss Sumner to look after my things. Percy and I motored to the station where one of the Railway Officials had lent us his inspection carriage with bathroom and kitchen attached. We left Mandalay about 1.15 and reached Thazi between 5 and 6. Our carriage was disconnected there so that we could spend the night in it.

Fri. Dec. 21st

We went on by train about 10.30 to Kalaw which we reached about 4.30. We stayed the night with the Vickerys...

Sat. Dec. 22nd

It was so cold that I could hardly dress, but of course one enjoys it and there is brilliant sunshine all day which makes the air warm and pleasant. After breakfast we set off in two motors with our servants and luggage for Yaunghwe... and then went on by boat to the Lake bungalow in the middle of the Inle lake. Of course we had to take our Cook and food etc with us.

We stayed four nights there. Each day we rowed to land and had a walk or sat and sketched and after tea I bathed and we had reading. I got the dhurzi (tailor) to make me a very pretty bathing costume, a bright blue poplin trimmed with black. Some of the evenings and nights were very cold, but we managed to keep fairly warm.

Percy gave me a Christmas stocking on Christmas day to amuse me. He had filled it with a very great variety of things - onions, potatoes, sweets, eau-de-cologne, hair-lotion etc etc and one or two lovely things - a gold filigree necklet (Burmese work) and a beautiful card case made of silver and a carved ivory vase. It was great fun opening all the packets.

Wed. Dec. 26th

We went on by boat to a place called Taungdo. There was no bungalow so we had to stay in a zayat. A zayat is a roof supported by pillars with a floor a foot or two above the ground, but with no walls. Sometimes they are made of bamboo matting, sometimes of wood. Of course when an English officer is touring he generally sends notice of his coming, and the headman of the village gets the villagers to hang carpets and mats round the sides of the zayat, so as to afford some privacy. Taungdo is not on the lake but on a river which drains from the south end of the lake. Our zayat was right in the middle of the bazaar in rather a public place and I did not much like it. However we were really quite comfortable although it was bitterly cold. Of course we had carried our own camp beds with us and two chairs and a little table.

Thurs. Dec. 27th

We went on by boat to Leme which took us about 3 hours. The river is very beautiful and Leme itself is a charming little place on the river. We had a nice little zayat to stay in close to the water. There was a monastery quite near but no other houses so we were nice and private.

Of course the little yellow-robed boys who were learning to become priests took a good deal of interest in us, but we did not mind them. The mountains come fairly close to the river at Leme and it is altogether very pretty. Each evening we had a big wood fire outside our zayat and sat near it in the moonlight and read. We stayed two nights there. Percy wanted to see the potters at a village near by and collect some pottery for his exhibition.

We also went by boat to a place called Saga, about 3 hours down the river and paid a visit on the Sawbwa. He was a shy-looking youth who lived in a sort of English house. His room was a strange mixture - the walls had framed English advertisements for pictures and there was a gramophone and a mirror covered with a lace curtain. Percy talked to him in Burmese for some time - (most Shans speak a certain amount of Burmese) - and then we paid a visit to the village school where a few funny little Shan children were sitting at long tables.

The custom in the schools is to make all the different classes repeat the lesson aloud at the same time while the schoolmaster (of course there is only one) sits down with his book and seems to pay no attention.

The Shan states are not in Burma and are not really governed by the English, though the English see that the Sawbwa keeps his state in order.

Sat. Dec. 29th

We went by boat from Leme to the lake bungalow. It took us about 10 hours and was rather tiring. Of course we were only in a dug-out with a shelter in the middle, paddled by leg-rowers. The cook, who was in another boat, got us some breakfast and tea. It was very wet, misty and rather cold. Percy did a little shooting on the way and got two teal.

Percy is a very good snipe-shot, but we did not see many snipe, and the wild duck were too wily to let our boat come close to them. We spent Saturday and Sunday nights at the lake bungalow.

Mon. Dec. 31st

We set off about 8.30 in our boats but there was a thick mist and after about ¾ hr. we found ourselves back at the bungalow - the boatmen had made a circle. However we got on all right the next attempt and reached Yaunghwe about 11 o'clock... then set off in a motor for Taung-gyi. The mist had cleared and the sun was shining so the ride was glorious. We reached Taung-gyi about 1.30 and put up at the Circuit House (a public bungalow where Government officials of a certain standing can stay). We had tea and dinner with the Lees. Between tea and dinner we climbed the Crag, as we wanted to re-visit our old haunts.

Wed. Jan. 2nd

We left Taung-gyi with our servants and kit in two motors about 7.45 and drove to Loian near Kalaw. It was bitterly cold at the start and the wind felt quite icy. At Loian Mrs Browne has a boarding-house. She is sister to the Yaunghwe Mr Browne... We had breakfast with her and then caught the 11.30 train at Kalaw. We had a compartment to ourselves all the way.

Thurs. Jan. 3rd

Reached Rangoon 8.15 am after quite a comfortable night... When we reached our house we found a welcome party there... and had breakfast with the party which had collected - namely the Listers, Mr Sherratt, Miss Sumner, Miss Hearn and Miss Slocumbe (another teacher at the Diocesan school) and a Captain who was staying with the Listers. They left soon after breakfast and we began putting the house in order...

Fri. Jan. 4th

I spent a good deal of time getting the house cleaned... The wife of Percy's boy fortunately knows English and is useful in many ways. Her name is Ma Gyi. She is quite a character and I daresay will be somewhat of a trial. Her husband, Po Khin, has been with Percy all the twelve years he has been here and Percy thinks a great deal of him. I think he has been a very faithful servant, but I don't suppose I shall find it easy to order him about. Of course with a bachelor he could do as he liked and had a fairly easy time. I don't think he liked my coming at first. Percy said he thought he was a little jealous...

Sat. Jan. 5th

I had another very busy day. I went through Percy's store of tinned foods. Of course they have to keep a certain amount for touring, but I was much amused at the quantity and variety of his things, tinned meats, tinned fruits, tinned jams, tinned cheeses, tinned soups and queer things that neither of us knew what they were. I think he needs someone to look after him. I think Po Khin had been fairly careless...

Sun. Jan. 6th

We motored into Rangoon for Holy Communion... On the way back one tyre punctured and Percy had a very bad time over it, as someone had stolen his repairing things and he had to stuff the outer tube with hay and grass instead of putting in the inner tube...

CHAPTER XI

THE GOVERNMENT OFFICIAL'S WIFE

> "He teases me a good deal, because I told him that I did not think I was suited to be the wife of a government official and he says he can't see why a government official should not have a good wife as much as any one else."
>
> May 9th 1917.

Mr Morris's bachelor days with the faithful Po Khin to look after him were at an end. So was his wife's career. Many years later she commented to me that marriage was harder on a woman than on a man, because, being expected to devote herself entirely to a new role, she had to sacrifice so much more. Doris did not, it is true, give up all her educational work. She took English classes in the Engineering school and introduced these Burmese and Indian boys to a simplified version of "Tom Brown's School Days" which she thought they would enjoy. She was asked by the Diocesan Board of Education to set and correct Scripture papers for the Bishop's Prize. When a university for Burma was under discussion, Mr Potter H.M.I., sought her advice. "In connection with the new University he has been put on a training course. I do think it is stupid the way they have omitted to put any women on these University committees. There are numerous women in the country with both degrees and training diplomas while I don't suppose there is a single man here with the latter and most of the men in the educational service have been out here years and cannot be very up to date in their ideas. Besides the University will affect women as much as men and the question of halls of residence is most important for women."

These educational commitments did not come her way until the autumn of 1918. Meanwhile much of her time in Insein was taken up with running a home for her husband. Po Khin, who had worked for Mr Morris since he first came to Burma in 1905, was inclined to be a little jealous of the new bride. His wife, Ma Gyi, had been doubtful whether a mere school-teacher was socially acceptable as a wife for her master, but she had been re-assured when she learned that Miss Easton was the daughter of a Church of England clergyman. Yet, though Ma Gyi was a strong character, stronger than her husband, perhaps almost as stubborn as my mother, and there were occasional clashes, she soon became devoted to her new mistress: and where his wife led, Po Khin followed. Other servants drift in and out of the pages of the diary, these two are constant; the last glimpse shows them weeping on the wharf as the boat carried my parents and their child back to England never to return.

Now that she had time to supervise them the servants did not present Mrs Morris with the kind of problem she had faced in Mandalay. She asserted her authority by getting rid of the cook: he was spending too much on his "bazaar" without the result justifying the expenditure. She experimented in the kitchen herself under Ma Gyi's disapproving eye - not very successfully. The guava jelly proved obstinate about setting: when she tried her hand at butter the milk turned out to be too poor: it was difficult to make the light-weight sponges and scones of home in a wood-stove. One feels the servants must have sighed with relief when their "thakinna" turned her attention to making curtains and doing a little gardening.

Now that she had more time, Doris set herself very earnestly to learning Burmese. The diary records an almost daily study of the language even on tour. Her first teacher was Percy's clerk, San Lun, who frequently accompanied them on their travels. Later Mrs Luce, the Burmese wife of Professor Luce of Rangoon College, gave her lessons. She also talked with Ma Gyi and began to acquire a little confidence and fluency. It was not, however, until December 1921 that she passed the government examination in Burmese written and oral "for which I get RS 200. Ma Gyi was very pleased when I told her and said there was no one like her thakinna, that Lady Cuffe knew a lot of Burmese, but did not speak as correctly as I did."

Then, of course, there was all the business of entertaining, the leaving of cards, the calls, thc attending and giving of dinners. The couple gave their first formal dinner on May 30th 1918. It went off very well though unfortunately it was a night for "creeping things innumerable". "Of course people in England would think it absolutely unbearable to have beetles etc crawling up your garments and down your back and swarming on the floor." The guests on this occasion were Miss Hearn and Miss Sumner, Mr Boedikker (Percy's "best man") and Dr Taylor. The whole affair is reported in affectionate detail in the diary:

"Percy took in Miss Sumner; Mr Boedikker, Miss Hearn; and Dr Taylor, me. The table looked very nice. We have a hanging lamp of beaten copper, hand made, and we put a petrol lantern inside. On the table itself we had a branch candlestick with pink shades. We had the silver Burmese Band figures ranged round the table centre as a decoration. We had quite a simple dinner - soup - fish - duck and tinned green peas (we get a duck here for two shillings) tinned pears and a white mould (made of gelatine and whites of eggs) and custard, cheese and biscuits and a little dessert (just coconut sweets that the cook makes and monkey nuts roasted. That is the usual sort of dessert here. One does not eat proper fruit in the evening as a rule. It is not supposed to be good). Of course one does not eat tinned things very often as they are rather a luxury, but tinned peas, and tinned cheese and tinned fruits are very nice.

We had two plain silver vases on the table with pink flowers. We used our fish knives and forks for the first time... Their blades are silver and their handles carved ivory. Of course they are all hand-made. They cost £10 - a Mr Phillips here gave them to us. We had the pudding in an entree dish and the fruit from a glass dish and a silver stand (the glass dish takes out and you can put in a bread-board instead. It is rather a nice thing). We have some very pretty little dessert knives and forks. We had them brought with the finger bowls though we did not really need them. We have 2 or 3 sets of finger-bowls, but we used some Indian brass ones that Percy's sister in India sent us... We have some pretty dessert plates made of delicate grey Japanese china... We had coffee brought round during dessert in little Japanese coffee-cups. We have some little coffee spoons made of Burmese silver with little Burmese figures on the top which makes them rather like Apostle spoons. Janie had them made for us. We had ice brought round in a little silver bucket with silver tongs to put it in the glasses.

Of course all these things are wedding presents...

After dinner we sat in the drawing-room and talked. The conversation did not drag at all, but Percy and I gave them a little music... I wore my pale blue evening dress. It is very pretty, much prettier I think than my wedding dress. It is made of a most delicate pale shell-blue brocade silk with a very pale blue ninon tunic over it and has some very pretty lace on the bodice and a very narrow trimming round the tunic of pale blue, heliotrope and pink rosebuds (very small and pale of course)."

On another occasion, soon after their return from their honeymoon, when they had dined with the Listers, she had worn her wedding-dress. "Of course, I being a bride, had to break up the party. It is rather a nuisance, as one does not quite know when to get up..." Food like clothes always interested my mother: she lists the fare of "a very long dinner" which Mr Phillips gave at the Rangoon Refreshment room, before they went to watch an amateur performance of a play in aid of St. Dunstan's home for blinded soldiers, "anchovy olives, soup, prawn cutlets, mutton cutlets, chicken pasties, roast goose, iced asparagus, lemon pudding, vanilla ices, dessert." When she dined at Government House in January 1918, wearing her wedding dress and the evening coat she bought as part of her trousseau, she writes:

"There were about 30 people to dinner, but it was quite a nice sensible dinner, only 5 courses. The present L. G. seems a very different type of man from the last. Sir Harcourt Butler was very fast and very extravagant and though he was a very able man, a genius I suppose, he lowered the tone of society here. But Sir Reginald (Craddock) is introducing a good many changes and cutting down the expenses at Government House and so on.

There were not nearly as many ladies there as men and of course it was not very interesting. After dinner we sat in the drawing-room and talked. When the men re-appeared, the Aide-de-Camp piloted the ladies to various parts of the drawing-room and brought men to talk to them so that the ladies should not be clustered together in groups... At 10.45 the A.D.C. went up to the leading Lady, Lady Frances Stewart, and gave her the hint that it was time to go and we all followed..."

All this elegance was in sharp contrast to the Mandalay life of their first two years in Burma and no doubt she enjoyed it, just as she enjoyed the pleasant domesticity of the Insein home, walks with her husband and the two dogs, Inky and Paddy; tennis; golf; going out in the motor (which she never learned to drive); indulging in music and reading in the after-dinner quiet. Such peace was frequently interrupted by the tours which her husband's post demanded and on which for the next four years she almost always accompanied him. They were involved in one which lasted eleven weeks only a month after they returned to Insein from their honeymoon. A lull followed, largely because Percy was waiting to hear whether he could be released from his post to join the army, an earlier application having been turned down on the grounds that he was needed in Burma. But now, since the British army was desperately short of men, it seemed, to his wife's inward dismay, that he might be allowed to enlist. In fact the war ended before his papers came through.

In January 1918 they were plunged immediately into the business occasioned by the Arts and Crafts Exhibition and the visit of the new Lieutenant and the various members of the Industrial Commission. After the dinner party at Government House on Jan. 22nd, the diary records...

"We had to meet the Government House party at the wharf at 7.30 am to go with them by steam launch to the yards of the Bombay Burma timber firm to see an elephant display... Chairs had been arranged for us and we sat and watched three or four elephants at work. It is a beautiful sight. They roll huge logs along with their trunks and pick them up between their tusks and trunks and place them on a log pile. They even walked over the top of a huge pile carrying a log in their mouths and at the top one of them waited while some of the party took his photograph. He looked just as if he were posing. They use their weight in an extraordinarily skilful way to move the logs and to balance them. When a log is very, very long, two elephants carry it between them..."

On Thursday, January 25th, they went with some of the commission to see a rice mill... "The white rice is polished with sheep-skin after all the husks are removed. They use nothing but the husks for fuel in their enormous furnaces - no coal or wood and even then they can't burn it all. When we had seen everything we went back to the Jubilee Hall where Percy was giving a lecture on pottery..." When the exhibition was over and the clearing completed, the young couple set off for Mandalay to meet the Commissioners there and escort them back to Rangoon.

Mandalay gave Doris an opportunity to see Janie and to renew other acquaintances. The school, under Miss Cook, had moved into the buildings of the American Baptist Mission. She was welcomed there by the children and by Janie who was not very happy. "She finds Miss Cook trying and says that they never have any fun over anything as we used to." She dined with Mrs Grossett wearing "a dress Madame Adele made me of white sparkly material which I brought out with me and a little sort of black velvet bodice embroidered in white." She and Percy lodged on a ship which the Irrawaddy Flotilla Co. had put at the disposal of the Commissioners as this meant they got their meals free. These meals were inconveniently substantial, however. "I do dislike meals on board, because one has a 4 or 5 course breakfast at 9.30 and then another 4 or 5 course meal at 2 which is quite unnecessary and then tea at 4 and a very long dinner at 7.30."

On Saturday Feb. 2nd they set off by boat with the Commissioners so that Mr Morris could show them some of the local industries. They visited Nyaungu to watch lacquer-workers, the oil-fields at Yenang Yaung, the cotton-mills at Allanmyo, the silk-weaving at Prome. There was much of interest, but the company was "not a very lively one. It consists of Sir Rajendra Mukagee (Indian) Sir Dorabji Lata (Indian and millionaire) Sir Francis Stewart, Mr Chatterton, Mr Lowe, Mr Davis, Mr Masumbra (private secretary to Sir Dorabji) Lady Stewart and Mrs Davis. Percy and I would like to have some music but we do not know whether the others would care for it." At the oil-field apart from the modern derrick which she describes carefully - it looks like "the scaffolding for mending tram lines only it is much higher" - they saw "a primitive Burmese well, that they were digging by hand. A man dressed in a diving costume with an air tube attached to his mouth went down and dug out the mud. They drew him up with a rope for us to see. He was in a horribly oily condition. In the British Companies the men used to drill the wells are largely Americans and in times past were rather a rough lot. I believe they have quietened down a good deal now." At Allanmyo they visited the Cotton Ginning mill. "We saw numbers of Burmese women sitting among cotton seeds sorting it (when it had been combed off the seeds) and it was just like a snow scene. The same mill had machines for grinding the monkey nuts and cotton seeds into oil - salad oil. After the oil is pressed out of the nuts in huge presses, the rest of the nut remains in a cake which is used for cattle fodder." They reached Rangoon by train from Prome on Feb. 7th, but their stay in their Insein home was brief. On Feb. 16th they set out on the eleven-week tour already mentioned which took them to the Kyawkse district where Mr Morris had been irrigation engineer when he first arrived in Burma, then north of Mandalay to Shwebo and as far as Mogok with its famous ruby mines.

It is, perhaps, the tours which make the most interesting part of the diaries from 1919 onwards. In that year Doris and Percy managed at last to secure berths on a steamer - difficult because demobilisation was still incomplete - and spend an overdue furlough in England. On her return Doris dropped her practice of the diary-letter. As a result the record becomes less explanatory and communicative, a brief, at times monotonous account of the ordinary. Yet for her the ordinary was seldom dull, and even the repetitive chronicle of Insein day to day life is enlivened by intriguing glimpses. There is the affair of the palm fibre hats, for example. "A Burman near Sagaing has made some hats... Percy wanted to see if people would buy them so he ordered two dozen," the idea being that, suitably decorated by his wife, they would go on sale at the Y.W.C.A. Christmas sale. The economics of the hats pinpoints a fundamental difficulty in turning such enterprises into commercial propositions. "The man gets 1/4 each for the hats, but we can't sell them for less than 2/8 because they have come from such an out of the way place, first by bullock cart, then by boat, then by cart again and then 300 miles by train." The hats did sell very satisfactorily: the Lieutenant Governor's wife was among the purchasers. "Lady Craddock bought a hat which Percy had varnished scarlet. She said she though it was rather smart, but she made him assure her that it would not run in the rain; as she said it would be so dreadful if it did and stained her daughter's dress."

The record is enlivened, too, by short but telling portraits of colourful personalities - Mrs Bigwithers of Yamethin with her pet panthers, Mr Curly and his outsized moustache, the H.M.I. who looks as if he wore corsets "but he is not offensive." The Harveys amused and faintly irritated her with their "artistic pose". "They have orange draperies in the flat and the baby has a black toy cat with an orange bow." Justice compels her to add "however I believe that was a present." Mr Harvey was a very clever young man with a wide knowledge of Burmese history who tried unsuccessfully to conceal his interest beneath a languid manner. "Mr Harvey poses as having no enthusiasm and envying Percy his... Before we left a lady who plays Mrs H's accompaniments came in, so she condescended to play a violin piece. She won't play as a rule unless she has her special accompanist. She certainly does play very well." She mentions visiting the Kemendine school for the blind where she saw Father Jackson. Blind himself, he dressed like his Burmese boys, went barefoot and sat on the floor to eat with them. Doris was not altogether sure that it was wise for a European to behave like this. "I suppose he is very wonderful," she comments dubiously. "It may appeal to some Burmans, but probably other would despise an Englishman who followed the Burmese customs." Later when Father Jackson came to a meal in their house she was impressed by the neatness with which he ate.

Her everyday life was not essentially different from that of any middle-class lady of the period in England, though grander than she was accustomed to. The people she visited socially were almost all Europeans: only rarely are meals with well-to-do Indians or Burmese mentioned, the second infrequent enough for her to be anxious when one such occasion occurred "as to whether we and particularly Percy would be able to manage the food; however it was all right as we had very nice prawn curry and then various other dishes brought along to mix with it - fish and vegetables served in different ways." Between the natives of the country and their foreign rulers stretched an invisible barrier over which they eyed each other and perhaps made friendly conversation. Those who did cross the barrier, usually by marriage, risked raised eyebrows for themselves and some disadvantage for their children. It is a sad fact that my mother always seems to find it necessary to remark when someone with a European name is "Eurasian". For all their idealism and their criticism of the British Government in dealing with Burmese matters, my parents shared the basic assumption of the imperialist - that the natives were in our debt for the gifts we brought of a superior civilisation and technology. At times in the diary I am startled by attitudes which now seem unacceptable in two people whom I love and respect - only to remember that we too are prisoners of our period as they of theirs.

Towards their own servants, the Burmese they knew best, the Morrises showed a kindly paternalism. Po Min consulted Doris about his marriage plans. "Po Min told me the other day he was thinking of getting married and asked if I wished him to do so. Today he brought the girl to see me. I am not altogether satisfied. She is only 15 and is very poor and Po Min has been spending his money buying her a gorgeous green silk longyi and flowered muslin angyi and fancy underclothes. He has bought himself 2 silk longyis within the last two months and he must be in debt." Her fears were justified. Only a month later the diary records. "Po Min has been having trouble with his wife. When she found Po Min could not afford to give her jewels etc she went to her mother and said she would not live with him. However I believe they are reconciled now." The marriage of another employee was on a better financial footing. "Po Huaing had gone to Kalaw. He is going to marry the Loilem clerk's adopted daughter. She has R 8,000 in diamonds, R 5,000 in cash. I hope she is nice as Po Huaing is very nice."

The two servants they knew best were, of course, Po Khin and Ma Gyi. Strictly speaking Ma Gyi was not employed by them, though I suppose they must have paid her something when, later, she acted as ayah for their first child. However, to begin with it was Po Khin who was my father's boy and she, as his wife, enjoyed an independence which suited her nature well. She came as did her husband from Kyawkse in Upper Burma: some of her relatives had been employed at the Burmese Court, one of her uncles having been a masseur for King Theebaw. Ma Gyi prided herself on her knowledge of courtly language and the intricacies of Burmese dance. She was certainly the power behind the throne where Po Khin was concerned. When his mother and sister died and the family house was empty, she left Insein with her two children to take charge, making a living, like many Burmese women, by selling in the bazaar. As a result there was a sad falling off in Po Khin's standards. "We had a blow up with Po Khin. He is really getting too slack. He never bothers to put on an angyi when I call him and looks dirty and untidy and spends most of his time mooning. So Percy spoke to him. He said he would go at the end of the month. Of course we don't want him to, but we left it at that. The trouble is that he needs Ma Gyi to look after him and she won't come." Po Khin did leave. Even the warning that he would lose a promised pension if he went had no effect. He said goodbye to his mistress but left his master, after 15 years, without a word, hurting him deeply. However, the rift did not last long. Three months later in October 1921 when Percy and Doris were again on tour, Po Khin was at Kyawkse station to meet them. Next day "after breakfast I went round and had a long talk with Po Khin and Ma Gyi. They have a nice little house and keep it clean. I asked Ma Gyi if she wished to come back to us or stay there: she said she wanted to come back, but the house was the difficulty as they could not let or sell it. I said if she honestly wanted to come back Percy would try to do something. She must be having a hard time. She goes round to the bazaars in the district selling, while Po Khin stays at home and looks after the children." By the end of November these difficulties had been overcome.

"Sun. Nov. 28th

...When we got back from church we found Ma Gyi squatting outside and Po Khin followed in a few minutes with the luggage. We were very glad to see them..."

Only once after this did Ma Gyi desert the Insein household for any appreciable length of time. That was in October 1923 when her son, Aung Houet, was to go through the head-shaving ceremony in Mandalay and become a monk. "He is 7 years old - the earliest age at which it can be done. He will only stay 7 days in the monastery. The affair is going to cost 700 or 800 rupees. Ma Gyi is borrowing 200 Rs from us, but I don't suppose we shall ever get it back. They call 10 priests and give each priest yellow robes (silk) which cost about R50 a set... Then Aung Houet has to have yellow robes and a beautiful longyi also. Ma Gyi has bought one of lilac satin which cost R 40. Then there has to be a kind of stage and free food for all the guests and a beautiful silk scarf to put on the image of Buddha. I think Ngwe Saing (the daughter) will have the ear-boring ceremony done at the same time, but that is not nearly as expensive. They have to have a band of musicians for each of the children and so on. Ma Gyi hopes, of course, that her relations in Mandalay will contribute a good deal." While she was away Ma Gyi became so dangerously ill that Po Khin was summoned to his wife. She could not enjoy the festivities and, when Aung Houet had exchanged his princely robes for those of a monk to represent the Buddha's renunciation, they were unable to process round the town in an ornamental car. However "there was one good thing about her illness in that, as her friends thought that she could not get better, they all contributed more generously than they would otherwise have done." It was from Ma Gyi that my mother received her one - and only? - Burmese kiss. When, pregnant for the first time, she was setting out for England without her husband, "Ma Gyi seized my hand as the gharry went off and sniffed violently."

Mr Morris's clerks as well as the house servants (not Po Khin if they were going by boat as he suffered from sea-sickness) often accompanied them on his business tours. Among these clerks, Maung San Lun, who helped Doris with her Burmese, figures frequently. He made himself useful in other unofficial ways; lecturing the servants for his employer when they became slack; taking photographs; on one occasion, when they were in Moulmein, acting as their guide to local places of interest. "San Lun and some of his numerous cousins who live in Moulmein took us in the river steamer to Kadot, a Burmese town some distance up one of the tributaries of the Salween... They took us to see some fine tazaings (pavilions) with very beautiful glass mosaic pillars... We saw another wooden house where they had a waterborne sanitary system... We had tea at the house of San Lun's aunt. She is apparently a rich widow and has a very fine house." Later he took them to some caves, borrowing his aunt's private gharry to drive to a river-ferry. "The caves were very fine. We wriggled a long way on our tummies trying to get through narrow tunnels. Once I felt nearly suffocated and quite frightened."

San Lun had one child. In recording the tour of the Shan States in 1920, Doris remarks, a little caustically, that he brought with him his wife and child "because the child cried." In February 1921 this child became seriously ill. The Morrises went to the house, meaning to call, "but we saw brilliant lights and people in the house and then we saw a kind of bier covered with coloured paper, so we knew the child was dead." Next day Doris went with Ma Gyi to see the bereaved parents. "The room was full of relations. The child was lying there. The mother kept imploring him to speak to me and give salaams - it was rather terrible. She and San Lun were both crying. The child had a bad cold which apparently turned into bronchitis and I think it was left too late. He is their only child and they are overwhelmed with grief and there seems no comfort in their religion. Ma Gyi tells me that if the parents have been good there is a chance that the child will be born again to them, in which case he appears in a dream to them and tells them so." Next day they followed the cortege to the Burmese cemetery. "There is no enclosure and I never knew it was a graveyard. The boys (presumably from the engineering school) had made a kind of bicycle carriage for the coffin and made a canopy of coloured paper. San Lun and his wife first made offerings to the hpongyis in the zayat; then the prayers were said and all the people received presents, after which the pongyis and many of the people went away. "We did not stay to see the coffin put into the ground."

Monks' funerals in Burma were, by contrast, colourful and exciting festivities. The diaries describe two beside the one recorded in Mandalay, and note that children stayed off school to attend these occasions.

"The body of a hpongyi is going to be burnt and they are having a most gorgeous ceremony. The constructions they make are most wonderful - all made of coloured paper and bamboo. A wall was made round a large area and numerous booths and shelters and then a colossal elephant, a colossal chinthe (mythical lion) and a human figure were erected inside the enclosure some distance apart. These figures must be 40 to 50 feet high, possibly more, and their size is proportionate. They are made entirely of paper and bamboo but are very effective. Over a long low booth the figure of a gigantic snake was placed. At the actual ceremony the coffin of the pongyi (which by the way has been kept about 4 years since his death) will be raised onto each of these constructions in turn (to signify I suppose his ascent to Nirvana) and will finally be burnt on the highest.

The cremation of a hpongyi is a time of great rejoicing and numerous entertainments and fireworks. We saw one booth that amused us much. It was decorated entirely with numbers and numbers of white enamel plates (I suppose they were offerings to the priests) which really looked very effective placed on a background of green paper. Then another booth was decorated with hundreds of grey tin mugs on a background of pink."

A few days later they went to the site at night when the elephants and chinthes had electric lights in their eyes and mouths. They saw the coffin covered with gold work but empty, as the body itself has to rest on different biers in turn; and the brightly-coloured pandals where people sat and ate, watched entertainments or even slept.

"In one place they had what they called a Christmas tree, though one would hardly recognise it, loaded with things to give as presents to the pongyis. The actual burning will not take place till Sunday when the body will be put in the golden coffin and placed in an iron cradle and that will be slung by ropes from one construction to another, till finally it reaches the elephant's back and there it will be burnt. They say that the heat is not great enough to melt the gold work and the manager said he was thinking of selling it afterwards and building a free Buddhist anglo-vernacular school...

All these gorgeous celebrations take place on what has been a vast rubbish heap for the district. They have tried to tidy it up a little, but it is very smelly."

Apart from such ceremonies, Rangoon life was a fairly monotonous round of house-work, church meetings and other good works, and entertaining, for Doris; and for Percy, the wearing business of running the engineering school with insufficient staff. The nearest he got to real holidays were the tours which his work as Provincial Art Officer necessitated. These, however, as recorded in the diary, have an air of freedom and adventure about them and certainly of greater leisure than it was possible to enjoy in Insein. They were not, of course, particularly comfortable: the trains and boats were often hot and slow; travel by motor was hazardous on earth-roads which the sudden rains turned into red-mud; and even on the better roads there were hair-pin bends, precipitous edges and bullock-carts. These last were extraordinarily adept at squeezing themselves out of the way, though on one occasion "the oxen shied and went over the khud. The man jumped out but it was horrid to see them go over. Miraculously although they went down an almost sheer descent of sixty feet or so they did not lose their feet and were unhurt. The cart did not even overturn." Such carts could go where cars could not. The Morrises nearly always used them for their kit and often, padded with straw against the jolting, for themselves, though it was usually quicker to walk - Percy's frequent choice. He thought little of leaving very early for a jungle village ten miles or so away, finding out about the crafts practised there and returning in time for "breakfast" at 1 or 2 pm.

They stayed in bungalows erected by the Public Works Department or by Buddhists seeking to acquire merit by helping travellers. It was not usually possible to book a place beforehand, so accommodation might be cramped or have to be sought in village houses. The bungalows were sparsely furnished if at all: they had to carry beds, bedding, mosquito nets, cutlery and so on. Food could not always be obtained locally: an emergency supply in tins was necessary though Percy had his gun and sometimes brought back snipe or duck for the pot. Often the weather or the need to wait for some other travellers kept them in one spot for several days, so they had to be able to entertain themselves. They both enjoyed sketching and music. Doris took her fiddle and worked at her Burmese. Above all they had books which they read aloud to each other in the light of candle or oil lamp. There is something faintly absurd yet touching in the picture. While their servants relaxed and smoked and chattered and slept, jungle sounds drifted through the bamboo-matting walls, lizards ran up and down catching insects and moths and beetles swarmed round the lights, my parents got out their books. Their reading included history, psychology, Buddhism, Evelyn Underhill's "Mysticism", the book of Job in Burmese. For Sunday, since they could not go to church, they had devotional books and, if they could avoid it, they did not travel. Of all the places they visited, it was the Shan States, where they had first met, that they loved best, thought their Burmese companions sometimes found the people distressingly primitive. "Po Huaing complains that they all bathe naked, men, women, and children, and laugh at him for wearing shorts. A crowd of women and children came down to the camp and were immensely pleased because they could see themselves reflected in the glass screen of the motor car. Apparently they had never seen themselves before and they went into shrieks of laughter."

What had happened to Doris Easton's missionary aspirations? As the wife of a government official, she was not allowed to engage directly in evangelisation. She saw the wisdom of this. "One would not wish the Burmans to become Christians under government pressure or because they thought it would please government officials if they did so and bring them promotion." She did, however, involve herself in a great deal of educational and church work, led Bible study groups, was on the Y.W.C.A. committee and the committee of the Christian Literature Society. At one of the meetings of this last there was a debate about re-printing a tract written by Dr Judson (the great American Baptist missionary) which was said to be of rather an "aggressive type" and unfair to Buddhism, hence exciting antagonism even among Christian Burmans. It was decided not to reprint it.

"Personally I think the society ought to devote more attention to getting more good pure stories in Burmese. After all the British and Foreign Bible Society is circulating the Bible and I don't see what need there is of so many tracts."

Occasionally she undertook pastoral visits at the Bishop's request and once she, informally, inspected a little S.P.G. school, held in that area beneath a Burmese house which acts as a kind of utility room, workshop and store. "A great many of the children were away as there is a pongyi-pyan going on (pongyi-pyan really means the flying of the priest and refers to the fact that he is flying to heaven or in other words is dead). I stayed there nearly an hour, I think, listening while the children read and said Geography and Scripture. They learn everything off by heart. They read a paragraph of their reading books and then try to repeat it from memory. In Scripture the teacher says, "Give me the five features of sin", for instance, or "the seven points relating to Salvation" and so on and the children repeat a long answer by heart. Of course it is the method by which they learn their Buddhist Scripture and so familiar to them, but one wonders how much they understand. They were having lessons underneath the building (a mat building on sticks) and the head woman-teacher who I think is wife of the head-master was swinging her baby in a cloth slung to the floor of the room above. Such surroundings seem rather incongruous with the brand new wall-maps from which the children were learning their Geography. The maps were merely hung up on one of the wooden supports of the house."

All in all, it was a busy life, not without its satisfactions and pleasures as well as frustrations, which Mr and Mrs Morris lived in Insein, diversified by their frequent travels in Burma and the Shan hills.

CHAPTER XII

TOURING WITH A PROVINCIAL ART OFFICER

The three tours which are presented here in extracts from the diaries are representative of others. On the map they look fairly unimpressive: the distances covered are not great: the travellers did not venture very far from centres of civilisation or from the railway or river. But the difficulties of the journey, once boat or train were left behind, were considerable. To read Mrs Morris's account gives a truer picture of the hazards than to measure distances covered.

It is not always easy to identify the places she visited. Her spelling of place-names often differs from that on the available maps, transliteration from Burmese into English being a chancy enterprise any way. And many of the smaller villages are not recorded in anything to which I have access. They may well no longer exist, the jungle having re-claimed its own.

Tour in Central Burma and northward to Mogok Feb. 16th to May 4th 1918

Sat. Feb. 16th

We were going off by the evening train, so I had a very busy day getting everything ready and packing up. We went to Rangoon by the 4.17 train. The 6 o'clock up country train was very full, so much to our disappointment we could not get a compartment to ourselves; I had to go into a ladies' compartment with three other ladies and Percy had to go in with some men.

Sun. Feb. 17th

The other ladies did not mind Percy coming into our compartment, so he sat with me most of the time and we had breakfast together. We reached Mandalay about 2.15 and went round to school to let Janie know that we had come... and then we went to the Dak bungalow (a rest house belonging to the mail service)...

Mon. Feb. 18th

Percy had to go to Maymyo for the day on business... After tea I went down to the school and saw... Janie.

Tues. Feb. 19th

We left Mandalay by a train at 7.33... We had to cross the river in a steam ferry at Sagaing and catch a train there about 10.30. It was a hot journey and I slept a good part of the time. We reached Shwebo about 2 o'clock and drove up to the Price's house... After tea we went to the Club. Mrs Price drove me in her trap and Percy and Mr P. went down in a gharry. We had two sets of tennis and looked at the newspapers. Of course I was introduced to various people. Percy always finds old friends at these stations...

Fri. Feb. 22nd

...We caught a train at 2.20 to Kinu, two or three stations away and arrived there about 3.10. We had some distance to walk to the bungalow and when we got there we found a Mr and Mrs Mangell and child staying there with all their servants. It was only a small bungalow - 2 bed-rooms and 1 sitting-room made of bamboo so of course one could hear everything that went on. Also another man had come by the train to stay there. We thought we should have to manage somehow, but to my relief our clerk found that there was another place where we could stay - namely the upper storey of the Court-house... The rooms were fairly decent and anyhow it is much nicer to be by ourselves...

Sat. Feb. 23rd

Percy went out to see the collectors of soap-sand. I did Burmese. After breakfast did some writing and lay down. After tea we went for a walk to the soap-sand area. It is very interesting. There are numbers of places where water oozes out from the earth bringing with it the soap in solution. When it comes to the surface, the water evaporates and the soap lies white on the soil. Where the water oozes there is always a hillock of mud, sometimes 3 ft high and 5 or 6 ft across, and if you touch it with your foot the ground shakes. The people do not know how deep down the mud goes, but of course it is dangerous to walk across these mounds. They are like quicksands. Cattle sometimes get in, and I suppose people too, and sink deeper and deeper and the vultures collect round them trying to hasten on their death.

The people come and collect the white soap and the sandy soil which contains a good deal of it all round these mud volcanoes. The dhobis use it for washing clothes and at present an Indian gentleman is asking to have the right to be the sole collector of it, so that he can use it for making paper. That is why Percy has to examine all the soap-beds and get information from the people, so that Government may decide whether to grant this monopoly to Mr Jamal...

Mon. Feb. 25th

We had breakfast at 9 o'clock and walked to the station to catch a train at 10.25 as we were going to a station nearer Shwebo called Myingatha. We arrived there about 11.20 and walked out about 1¼ miles to a bungalow near the canal as it was a nicer one than that in the village... It was really a very nice bungalow and moderately clean, such a treat after the last which was extremely dirty.

Tues. Feb. 26th

We caught a train about 11.20 and went on to Moksogyon, a station past Shwebo... From Moksogyon we had to go 4 or 5 miles in a bullock cart to a place called Halin. It took us nearly 2 hours as bullocks go very slowly. Of course there is a great deal of jolting in a bullock cart and it goes over pieces of road that look impossible for roughness. It is marvellous that these carts do not continually tumble over into the ditch.

The bungalow was locked up and the durwan (caretaker) was nowhere to be seen, so we had to wait some time till he could be found... It was quite a nice little bungalow, though only made of matting and wooden beams.

After tea we went for a walk through the village. It is quite a big place and must once have been important. There are great bare areas of ground where they collect salt. Apparently they take the water from the salt springs, and pour it over the ground (which they have raked) to evaporate and then they take the salty earth and put it into earthen basins and pour water onto it. The water dissolves the salt and pours out of the basins through a pipe and is collected in jars. Then I suppose it is boiled for the water to evaporate once more. I suppose they perform this double process in order to get a larger proportion of salt in the water.

The thugyi (village chief) told Percy that people had collected salt here for 3,000 years and that they sometimes found old coins in the ground.

Wed. Feb. 27th

Mended stockings. Did Burmese. Read etc. The thugyi had told Percy that there was good duck shooting and that he would have a boat ready for him on some lake where he could get them, so after tea we went off in a bullock cart a very long way over an extremely rough track and after an hour or so arrived near some water, but there was no boat and no cover, so it was quite impossible for Percy to get near enough to the duck to shoot them, so we had to come home having had our trouble and a most uncomfortable ride all in vain.

Halin is rather a pretty place with plenty of pali trees and other vegetation and a great many pagodas. Pagodas, of course, like country churches are often picturesque.

Percy read aloud to me some Psychology and some of Kipling's "From Sea to Sea." After the tiring cart ride I was too sleepy to do mending.

Feb. 28th

Did mending. Studied Burmese. Wrote letters. Percy went out at 2 o'clock shooting. The thugyi of a village near the lake had promised to get him a boat. He did not come back until 7.30. It was quite dark by then and I was getting frightened. The servants were frightened too. The Clerk, Ba Gyaw, came to know if he should go out and search. But I told him to wait a little longer and then the bullock cart arrived. He had shot 9 duck, but he gave 2 to the thugyi who went with him on the lake.

Fri. March 1st

...After tea Percy and I went off in a bullock-cart to a village 3 or 4 miles away where they collect soap-sand. Part of the way it was most fearfully rough riding. One is jolted up and down and against the sides of the cart and against one another. When we came to a stream, one of the bullocks would not drink, so the driver took water into his own mouth and then spat it into the bullock's mouth.

Sun. March 3rd

We read aloud "The Jesus of History" and having finished it started a book on "Evolution and the Need for Atonement" that Mr Price lent us...

Mon. March 4th

Percy went out about 6.30 am as he had to walk nearly 20 miles to see a village. He got back soon after 12 o'clock... After tea he had to go another 7 or 8 miles to see some other place...

Tues. March 5th

We had to catch a train at 7.30 am for Sagaing. We got there about 9.15 and took a gharry to the bungalow. Sagaing is a fairly large place near the river. The bungalow was clean and tidy but very hot... After tea... went to the Club and had tennis. There were some people called Carrapiett and De Cretoche there, partly Eurasian I should think, but in small stations Eurasians are accepted at the Club...

Thurs. March 7th

Percy got up about 5.30 am as he was going to walk 20 or 25 miles. I had breakfast about 8.30 and then walked about a mile to the ferry steamer as I was going to Mandalay to shop... I walked into the town to do some shopping... then I went up to the school and had some tiffin with them... Janie has told the Bishop that she means to leave at the end of the term. She expects to go to India the beginning of April and be married as soon as Gordon gets leave. What she will do when he goes back to Mesopotamia I don't know. I suppose he will arrange for her to stay in India with friends. She is quite convinced she will be happy with him although they only saw one another for ten days...

Sat. March 9th

We left Sagaing by a train at 11.30. Went to Mimau, arriving there about 2 o'clock. Then went by bullock-cart to the town itself which is on the river about 1½ miles from the station... We left just before 4 o'clock and crossed the river in a boat with the servants and luggage. The crossing took about 1½ hours. Then we had bullock carts to take us to Ngazun a place about 7 miles away. I walked 3 or 4 miles and rode in the cart the rest of the way. Percy walked all the time. We arrived at the bungalow about 7.20 and had nothing to do but sit down in the dark and wait for the servants who were slower as their carts were more heavily laden.

The time of arriving at bungalows is not very comfortable as one is hot and tired and, of course, one can't have a "wash and brush up" so to speak as there is no water. The servants are very good and quick in making the place habitable, but they could not get us a meal ready till about 9.15 pm, so we were about twelve hours between one meal and the next...

Tues. March 12th

Mended stockings. I got Maung San Lun, the clerk, to give me a Burmese lesson... After tea we went for a walk by the river. We saw the village girls going down to the water to bathe and wash their clothes and carrying back water-pots on their heads.

Wed. March 13th

We got up about 6 am and when all was packed set off for Myotha, a village about 16 miles away. I walked about 6 miles and then rode for about 3 in one of the bullock carts till we reached Gyo about 10.40. My head had begun to ache about breakfast time and it grew worse as the afternoon went on. I suppose I had got a touch of the sun, for when I rode in the cart after we started out I felt very bad and got very sick and of course the jolting of the cart made the sickness worse. When we came to a zayat (a sort of platform a foot or so above the ground with a roof over it, built for the sake of travellers) Percy laid me down flat and fanned me and kept me there half an hour or so till the sun had gone further down, then we started again... We got to Myotha somewhere about 7.30 pm. There was a little mat bungalow with two bedrooms side by side and a little verandah. There was another Englishman staying there, but he was fortunately moving on the next day. He had come to see about the capture of a robber.

Thurs. March 14th

My head was better, but I think I had fever still, so I stayed in bed...

Sat. March 16th

Percy went off about 5.30 as he was going to walk to a village some miles away. He did not get back till about 2.30. I did Burmese and made Mg San Lun give me a Burmese lesson. Then practised my violin...

After we had been in bed a little while, we were roused by a sort of roar and shoutings. I thought at first it was a storm of rain coming, but we soon discovered that it was a fire and gongs were beating, cattle lowing, dogs barking and people shouting. There was an enormous blaze filling the sky about 150 yds away. It looked as if half the village were on fire. I thought possibly our house might catch as fires here spread so rapidly among mat houses, so I dressed fully. Percy put on boots and went off in his night suit to see what could be done. Of course there is not often any loss of life, as it is easy enough to get out of little one-storeyed huts. About 5 or 6 houses were burnt and stacks of paddy husks etc and the village fence caught. The glare in the sky was wonderful, but it had practically died down in about half an hour, so we went back to bed.

Sun. March 17th

We read aloud to one another, and had a little music - violin and singing, then wrote letters.

Sunday Night. March 17th

We partially undressed before dinner and put on dressing gowns and then about 9 pm we got on to bullock carts to travel by night to the next place. Our mattresses and bed clothes were laid out in the bottom of the cart. We had a cart each to give us more room so that we might sleep, but as a matter of fact I slept very little. I slept once for some time and when I woke up I thought the cart-man must be walking as I could not see him. Then I touched something that looked like a piece of cloth beside me and found that he was lying fast asleep and the bullocks were going by themselves.

I did not enjoy the night. The roads were very bad in some places and we had precipitous bits to go down. The cart-men lost their way entirely and took us over rough open country and I could not imagine when we should reach our destination. I was too far away to talk to Percy and it was altogether very weird and uncanny and I did not like being so close to a dirty little Burman. We went by night to avoid the heat of the sun. The distance was really only 16 miles, but we took 10 hours.

We reached Chaung-gwa, our destination, about 7 am. The bungalow was already occupied by Mr Carrapiett, however he was going off the same day. It was a horrid dirty little shed, the worst we had stayed at. I felt very exhausted all day and spent a good part of the time in bed. Travelling by bullock cart is peculiarly tiring.

Tues. March 19th

...We set off about 5 pm to go on to another village, walking part of the time and riding part. It was beautiful moonlight before we arrived at 7.30 at Dwehla. There was a fairly good bungalow there...

Wed. March 20th

We set off about 6.45 am to go to Kyawkse 9 miles away. I walked 5 miles and rode the other four... We reached Kyawkse about 10 o'clock and it was a treat to get into a well-built house with a good deal of furniture and actually curtains...

Kyawkse is very pretty, there are rivers and canals and a hill quite close which affords a relief to the flatness of the plains. Percy is very fond of it, because it was the district he came to first and was in charge of the irrigation and had to look after the rivers which are very troublesome, being flooded at certain times of year and nearly dry at others. He had of course to regulate the canals and distribution of water and punish people who stole water out of their turn.

After tea we climbed Kyawkse Hill which is about 800 or 700 feet high. We had a beautiful view from the pagoda at the top. There was rather an old looking image of a nat (nature spirit) in a shrine at the top with 2 candles burning in front of it. Of course there were plenty of images of Buddha too, but the Burmans although they are Buddhists go in for animism and nat worship also. They are not really supposed to worship the Buddha or pray to him, though I think in reality they do.

Thurs. March 21st

...Percy had to go to Rangoon for a couple of days... I decided to go to Mandalay. I caught a train at 12.37 and reached Mandalay at 2.05. I went in a gharry with my luggage to the school as Janie said I could share her room. After tea, she and I started to walk to the Club. A most fearful dust-storm came on. I have never seen anything like it. The sky was dark all over with dust, like a fog, and great clouds of dust were whirled along...

Mon. March 25th

...Did some shopping and packed. Caught the 1.15 train from Mandalay. It was very hot travelling. I had a compartment to myself. Reached Thazi about 5.20. I expected to have to look after my own luggage but Percy was there to meet me; also Po Khin. Percy had reached Meiktila in the morning. We caught a train about 5.30 and reached Meiktila between 6.30 and 7 pm and went in a gharry to the Circuit House which was a nice roomy building...

Wed. March 27th

...Mr Page, the deputy Commissioner, took us out in his motor as Percy wanted to see some soapsand in a village about 10 miles away. The road was very bad and finally we had to leave the motor and walk two miles. We found some fairly rich soapsand. It was lying very white on the ground. When we got back to the car there was a crowd of 20 or 30 persons round it and they gave us some water from the inside of coconuts to drink...

Fri. March 29th

...After tea we called on some Americans called Ludington - Seventh Day Adventists (which is quite a strong little body out here strangely enough) who keep an Industrial School. Percy is interested in the school and has been to see it before.

Mon. April 1st

We left Meiktila by train about 11.30 and reached Yamethin about 2 o'clock. The Lieutenant Governor was going to visit Yamethin and the Bigwithers (Major B. is deputy Commissioner of Yamethin) wanted Percy to help him with an industrial commission in his honour. However a day or two before, he had sent a telegram to say he could not come which was very annoying for the Bigwithers as they had made elaborate preparations... Mrs B. keeps panthers as pets and she sometimes keeps them till they are full grown. She once had two tigers, but sent them when they were big to Rangoon Zoo... She has three panthers now... She takes them on tour with her, so the villagers have to build them cages at every bungalow where they stop... Some of the servants take the panthers out every evening on chains.

After tea... we went down to the station to see Janie and Miss Dunkley who were passing through on their way to India. They got out to have their dinner, so we sat with them in the refreshment room and talked...

Tues. April 2nd

Percy was going off by train for the day to see a paper factory. After breakfast I talked to Mrs Bigwithers for some time... After tea she and I went for a walk. We walked a little way with the panthers and then went on by ourselves. I think Mrs B. was glad to have me to stay there as there is no other English lady in Yamethin. She showed me all her dresses. She keeps her own dhurzi and he sews beautifully. He makes a great many of Major Bigwithers' clothes besides all hers.

Wed. April 3rd

...In the evening Po Sein, the great Burmese dancer, was holding a pwe. They had asked him to come for the L. G. really. We went down about 10 pm to the huge tent which will hold thousands of people. I should think there were 2 or 3 thousand there, possibly more. The performance was a kind of Burmese play. Po Sein was one of the actors, but he performed several dances during the course of the performance and gave one or two recruiting speeches. He is very graceful and rather attractive. He had most magnificent diamond rings and ear-rings, which glittered brilliantly as he danced about.

The first play was over about 1.30 am. There was going to be another, but we did not wait for that.

Thurs. April 4th

We had to catch a train at 8.05... We reached Thedaw about 11.30 am...

Fri. April 5th

...After tea we went in a pony cart to a place about 4 miles off where there was a Buddhist monastery. The monasteries generally have school-boys attached who are taught by the priest, but this one had 200 or so girl students which is very unusual. It had extensive grounds and funny little buildings and sheds scattered about where the novices lived and pagodas and priests' quarters etc. There was one big hall where all the girls had their lessons and when we arrived they were all gabbling their lessons out loud - quite different lessons of course as they were all ages and sizes. They had their hair cropped quite close as nuns always do and wore the yellowy pink nuns' robes.

The chief priest was a jolly round-faced man who seemed rather proud of his school. The clerk took a photograph of the girls and nuns and one of the priests and boys but there were less then 20 boys...

Sat. April 6th

We left Thedaw about 11.20 and reached Hanza about 12 o'clock... After tea went for a walk. We could not do much reading as we had only candles and there was a strong wind blowing.

Monday April 8th

Did Burmese. We caught a train about 1.30 and went on to Mahlaing arriving there about 4.30... We went on in the train to Yesin as the bungalow was nearer there than Mahlaing.

Tuesday April 9th

Did Burmese. After tea we went for a walk. We found a little lonely graveyard where some Irish soldiers were buried who died during the occupation of Burma in 1886.

Mahlaing is a fairly large Burmese place, though of course no English people live there...

Wed. April 10th

Did Burmese. P. & I began reading the Book of Job in Burmese as we have got copies from the British and Foreign Bible Society.

After tea we went for a walk to a little lake about 2 miles away. This high rolling country is rather like English moorland and is rather attractive...

Thurs. April 11th

Did Burmese. We left Mahlaing by a train about 4.10 and reached Myingyan about 6.30. I mended one of P's stockings in the train. I find it is quite easy to do.

Myingyan is a large town and has a very comfortable circuit house...

Fri. April 12th

...About 6.30(pm) we started off in a bullock tonga to go down to the steamer. The river is very low and the bullocks had to draw us over a mile or two of soft sand. We got to one boat which we were told was the boat and found that our luggage and servants had not arrived. Percy went off to look for them and I waited... Percy came back after a while to say that they were on the mail steamer, so we set out for it. It was rather a nasty walk in the dark along the soft sand to the other boat...

Sat. April 13th

We had a little music, violin and singing as there was a piano on board... We reached Mandalay about 2 pm and went into the town to do some shopping. We had tea at the Club and walked round to the Chapmans but Arthur and Dorothy were both in Maymyo. Then we walked back to the town and took a train to the steamer. The one going to Thabeitkyin was not nearly so nice as the one we had come by from Myingyan. The cabins were small and we had no electric fans. We were again the only passengers.

Monday April 15th

The steamer reached Thabeitkyin about 8 am. There was a motor lorry waiting for us, but it took about an hour to get our luggage weighed and loaded. There were two other passengers and our three servants. It is 60 miles from Mogok to Thabeitkyin and the road ascends between 3,000 and 4,000 feet. The views are most magnificent, more magnificent I think than on the way to Taunggyi range after range of enormous mountains and deep gorges and valleys. The road twists with hairpin curves up one range and then down into the valley and up another. We saw a whole number of monkeys running about on the road at one place.

We got out at a bungalow half-way which we reached about 11.45 and the durwan gave us our breakfast. We set off again about 12.30 and came upon the mail motor-car which had broken down as the axle had broken and the wheel came off. These motors are ramshackle old things and are sometimes tied together with bits of string. It is wonderful that they do not break down more often. The drivers seem to have no nerves and go whizzing round sharp corners. We picked up two passengers although we were already rather heavily loaded. We reached Mogok between 3 and 3.30 and went to the P.W.D. bungalow, a funny little building with fire places in the rooms. The other two passengers took possession of the other half of the house. After tea we went to the club and talked to a lady there and then went for a walk.

Mogok is a mining village among the mountain tops. It is most wonderful country round, though Mogok itself is not specially pretty. In a few minutes' walk we came to a glorious view but a thunderstorm came on and we had to come back. It poured and poured with rain during the night and was in consequence quite cold.

Tues. April 16th

...After tea we went out again and wandered over the hills and gathered yellow raspberries. There are quantities here. It was dull but fine. It seems very cold after the plains and I have got a nasty cold.

It is the Burmese New Year and to shower blessings upon people they pour water over them. The children have great sport out of this custom. When we were getting off the steamer a whole crowd of youngsters waded into the river and with large squirts and bowls deluged people as they passed over the gangway. Fortunately a man made them stop for us. It is not very pleasant to have all your clothes soaking. Sometimes in the villages one sees people dripping all over.

Thurs. April 18th

I did not go out all day as my cold was troublesome... One of my old girls who lives in Mogok came to see me after tea. We are continually having sellers of precious stones coming to see us with stores of rubies, sapphires, moonstones, peridots, amethysts, aquamarines, topaz etc.

Friday April 19th

Mr Cocks and we went over one of the ruby mines. Loads of sand are dug up and put into the trucks and carried along the rails to the washing station. There a process of washing is done in an engine and the mud and sand is washed away and the stones and gravel are sorted into different sizes. Men with scoops then look through gravel and pick out the precious stones. The natives who sort the stones wear wire caps over their heads to prevent them swallowing the stones and stealing them. A man let us look through one heap of gravel and we found little bits of spinets and moonstones. He told us that a little while ago he found a piece of sapphire worth 30,000 rupees (£2,000). The gravel that is sorted is thrown outside and the right to pick it over is sold to Burmese women. If you pick up a handful of sand from the ground as you walk about you find it full of grains of ruby, spinet etc...

Sat. April 20th

We set out about 8.30 and walked to the top of a mountain about 5 miles off. We were I suppose over 6,000 ft high, but of course Mogok itself is about 3,800. We had taken some food with us, cold chicken and hardboiled eggs and ate it on the top. We could not find any water unfortunately till we were well on our way home, but the wild raspberries were of some use in quenching our thirst. On the way down we climbed into a deep hollow where people had been digging for precious stones. We did not find anything valuable, only little bits...

Mon. April 22nd

We moved on to Kyatpyin, a village about 8½ miles away on the motor road. Our luggage went by bullock cart and Percy and I walked, taking some breakfast with us which we ate on the way.

Kyatpyin is a rich ruby area. We passed a good many Burmese Mines. They dig deep pits and haul up the loads of earth with a sort of crane made of bamboo poles. Then they wash the loads of earth to see if there are any precious stones there.

Tues. April 23rd

Percy wanted to see a Mr Heron, one of the Mines officials, so we walked along to his house to ask where he was, Mrs Heron was very Scotch with four big rosy-cheeked children...

Wed. April 24th

We walked to a village about 2 miles away where Mr Heron had his office and he took us over one of the ruby mines. We saw more than we did at Mogok as he was able to explain it all to us. The handfuls of different coloured stones look very pretty even in the rough. He was saying that the Ruby market fluctuated very much with the state of the war and they can judge how the offensive in France is going by the telegrams they receive from France saying "Buy" or "Not buy" as the case may be. Many of the Burmans deal direct with Paris and send stones worth thousands of pounds to be sold there. The Earl of Warwick is apparently the chief ruby buyer in England. After breakfast did Burmese. After tea we went out and tried to find precious stones in an old digging.

Saturday April 27th

...We left Kyatpyin about 9 o'clock in the motor-car, had breakfast about 11 o'clock at Shwemyaungbin and reached Thabeitkyin about 2 o'clock...

Sunday April 28th

...The steamer from Bhamo arrived 2.15 pm and we got on board to go to Mandalay...

Monday April 29th

The steamer reached Mandalay about 10.30 am. We did some shopping and went to the Club and then caught the train for Maymyo about 1.30. Percy wanted to go there to see his chief, Mr Thompson, to know what to do next. He told me at Kyatpyin that he had written to Mr Thompson to ask if they could spare him to go into the Indian Army Reserve for Officers (I.A.R.O.) and he thinks they will let him go this time as the crisis is so urgent... It is partly to stop the talking at home, as various unfounded rumours have spread. For instance that there were thousands of young Englishmen in the P.W.D. in India who could enlist... In Burma there are only about 500 or 600 Englishmen in all the government services and of these about 150 have already enlisted and of the remainder probably not more than 100 are physically fit... What makes me angry is that the Military Authorities often refuse to accept Eurasians apparently purely through prejudice... Consequently many Eurasians who could afford it have gone to England at their own expense and joined the army there...

We reached Maymyo about 6 pm and went straight up to the Claytons where we were going to stop. We were greeted with the news that Dorothy has a little son. She is in a Nursing Home in Maymyo...

Percy found a letter for him from Mr Thompson saying that he thought it was right for him to apply again for the I.A.R.O. and that he had agreed to spare him. I had been hoping that, as he is in a unique position, they would not let him go. After all there is only one engineering school in the whole of Burma and only one Provincial Art Officer and Percy knows more probably than anyone in the Province both about Technical Education and about the village industries of Burma...

Percy hopes he will get into a Burma regiment and he would like to get into the Sappers & Miners as his engineering training would be of use and he would not probably have so much fighting. It would be natural for him to be put in a Burma regiment as he speaks Burmese, but the Government of India is so stupid that one would never trust it not to put Burmese speaking Englishmen into Indian regiments.

Poor Janie has had a great disappointment. She went to India to meet Gordon and be married and when she got there she found a wire saying that at the last moment all leave was cancelled, as they were moving troops from Mesopotamia to Egypt, so she had to wait there indefinitely... Possibly she will take a post as a governess.

Arthur, Dorothy's husband, was up in Maymyo... he had taken some of the Sappers & Miners up to Maymyo to lay out a Botanical Garden. The late L. G. took it into his head in spite of the war to make a great lake at Maymyo and Lady Cuffe is designing the Botanical Garden which is to be near it to relieve the Forest Officer, who should have undertaken the designing, for war work.

Tuesday April 30th

Percy and I walked to the A.B.M. resthouse to see Miss Patch... However she had moved to a little mud-hut near the hospital so we went there... Miss Elliott has been ill and Miss Patch is looking after her. Miss Patch also has a Burmese baby with her that she bought from an old blind woman, who was not fit to take care of it, for 30 rupees Percy gave as some money to buy Xmas presents for her children and she said she decided to have a Christmas present herself instead, so she bought the baby and is bringing it up...

Wed. May 1st

Mrs Watson, Lady Cuffe's sister, drove us out to the Botanical Garden. It will be perfectly lovely when it and the lake are finished. Lady Cuffe is both an artist and a gardener and she is designing it beautifully...

Friday May 3rd

We left Maymyo by the 9.50 train...

Sat. May 4th

We reached Rangoon about 8.15 am. Percy and I went into the town to do some shopping, then had breakfast at the station and caught the 10.50 train to Insein. We got there about 11.30 and took a gharry to our house. It is exactly eleven weeks since I saw it last.

Tour to Tavoy and Mergui Dec. 1918 - Jan. 1919

Sun. Dec. 22nd

The Fyffes' motor after it had taken Mrs Fyffe to church took us to the wharf. Po Htin and Maung Twe were going with us, also the clerk Ba Gyaw. We did not take Po Khin as he gets very sea-sick if there is the slightest motion. We had to wait outside over an hour before we were admitted to the landing-stage and then a doctor felt our pulses to see that we were all right. Then we got on to a launch and were taken to the "Sir Harvey Adamson"...

There were a great many people on board... There were some American Baptist Missionaries returning to Tavoy after two years' furlough... Most of the other passengers were connected with Wolfram Mines which are the chief industry of Tavoy.

It took us a few hours to go down the river and reach the sea. We were out of sight of land by about 3 o'clock but it was very calm.

Mon. Dec. 23rd

We were in sight of the coast again when we got on deck. It was very pretty as wooded hills came down to the water's edge and the sea was a nice deep green instead of brown and muddy as it is at the mouth of the Rangoon river. We had to leave the Harvey Adamson at the Anchorage, a point at the mouth of the river, and get into a launch, the "Yengyua" which took us to Tavoy. The River Tennaserim is quite broad and has mountains not far from its banks so it is pretty.

We reached Tavoy about 2.15. Bell, the municipal engineer, an old boy of Percy's, met us and took us to the Circuit house which is 2 or 3 miles from the wharf, in a motor belonging, I think, to some friend of his. Tavoy itself is a large place situated in a broad plain near the river, with mountains in the distance. Our luggage took about 2 hours to come up in bullock carts, so we had nothing to do but sit and wait...

Wed. Dec. 25th. Christmas Day

Percy gave me some handkerchiefs, a collar and some violin music. I gave him a fountain-pen, some ties and a pocket book.

About 8.30 am we went down to the A.B.M. Mission and saw the children recite and sing little Burmese pieces, chiefly about the Christian religion. Then the children received gifts from a Christmas tree which stood at one end of the room...

Thurs. Dec. 26th

We went and sketched a pagoda some distance away... After tea we went for a pretty ride in the Government motor-car which Mr Brandon, the deputy Commissioner, lent us... We had a very reckless driver. Tavoy seems full of such drivers who dash along at a great rate right through the town. There are various wolfram mines 10 - 30 miles away, some more, and they have their motors for sending into Tavoy and back and consequently one sees a great many, generally very heavily loaded with people or baggage, racing through the town.

Tavoy is a very expensive place to live in. The mines people are so rich that they don't care what they pay for food and consequently prices are very high.

Friday Dec. 27th

Mr Morgan, the head of one of the mines, said he would send his car to take us out to his mine which was about 12 miles away. The car came about 9.30 and we arrived there soon after 10. The ride between the mountains was beautiful. The shadows on the mountains were of a wonderful deep blue as they very often are here.

...To get the wolfram they bore horizontal tunnels all about the mountain side. It is a black shiny metal and is found embedded in the quartz. The lumps of quartz are crushed in a machine and the wolfram taken out and washed and dried after which it is just a fine powder. Very often there is tin mixed with it and this is extracted by an electrical process as wolfram is attracted by a magnet and tin is not. Wolfram is used for hardening steel and so has been used a good deal during the war for munition-making.

The motor brought us back about 1.30 o'clock, then the Government car came about 2 o'clock to take us to the river as we were going to Maung-Magan, a sea-side place about 10 miles away. Our kit and servants had already gone off. It is about 2½ miles to the river and then we went across in a sampan and hired a pony cart to take us the 8 miles to Maung-Magan. There is just a line of twenty or thirty little bungalows along the shore and a beautiful beach stretching for miles and miles, and lovely sand. The sea does not go out very far and the houses are built really on the sands.

At the far end of the line of houses is a little fishing village, but there is no bazaar, so one has to take most of one's food. Occasionally one can get a chicken or a little fish. We had some tea and then bathed. The sea was a lovely blue-green and very calm. There are one or two islands out in the distance, but it is open sea.

Sat. Dec. 28th

Bathed. We tried to sketch some casuarina trees growing along the sand. They are very soft and fluffy, but it was difficult to do them as there was a strong wind...

Sun. Dec. 29th

Read. We started back for the Tennassarim river about 1.30 as the launch was coming for us to take us across the river to the Tavoy wharf. We had a long time to wait for it till about 5.30... The little Gov. launch... had no furniture and only one cabin and was rather squashed. After dinner we had to put up camp-beds to sleep in...

Mon. Dec. 30th

...We reached "The Anchorage" between 10 & 11 am but the "Harvey Adamson" was not in sight, so we started to go nearer to the mouth of the river. However it was so rough... we came back and waited at the Anchorage. It was very late before the "Harvey Adamson" arrived - nearly 1 o'clock so we were very tired of waiting...

There were 5 or 6 men going on to Mergui, but no ladies besides myself.

Tues. Dec. 31st

We reached Mergui about 11 o'clock. It is rather a picturesque place on the coast with two or three large islands opposite to it. I believe Mergui itself is really on an island though one would not know it. One of Percy's old boys who is Municipal Engineer there came to meet us, a Burman, Po Tun, and we went ashore in a boat as the steamer could not get in. Mergui is built up the sides of a hill and we had quite a steep climb to reach the Circuit House which is a good height up and has a fine view over the water. After tea we went to the Club and found Mrs Stevenson, the deputy Commissioner's wife, and Mr Samuels, the shipping agent, playing tennis, so we joined them... After tennis we looked at papers...

Wed. Jan. 1st

Mrs Stevenson took us round the town to see the mother-of-pearl workers. They make all sorts of things - hair pins, hair-slides, shoe buckles, menu-holders, plates (some people have complete dessert-services of mother-of-pearl. Of course it would be very expensive). We also looked at some blister pearls. We did not see any really valuable pearls. I think this is only the beginning of the season.

I don't care for mother-of-pearl work when it is elaborately carved, but in itself it is extremely beautiful. The green snail shells too are perfectly wonderful in colour. A blister pearl is a little lump in the shell which has had a pearl underneath it. They may take the pearl out or if it is not worth that they leave it in, so a blister is sometimes a solid lump and sometimes it is merely a convex piece of pearl. A real pearl is solid and round on both sides. Of course the pearls that are set in brooches and rings are probably very often just blisters as when it is set you cannot see if the underneath side is as perfect as the other. For a pearl necklace when the pearls are not set, you would have to have real pearls, as you can see the underside.

Corrected exam papers. After tea played tennis again... Mergui is a jolly little club, quite different from Tavoy which was very dull.

Thurs. Jan. 2nd

We went out again with Mrs Stevenson, and she took us to see the silk-weaving. However there was not much going on as raw silk is so expensive, and people can't afford to buy it. We also went to the shed where a rich Indian who trades in pearls etc despatches his goods. We saw dried sea-slugs and sea-snails lying ready to despatch to China as the Chinese eat them. We did not see any birds' nests, though they get them in the caves here. When they take a nest, the little bird builds another and when they take that she builds a third, but the third one is stained with blood and that they are not allowed to take. I suppose the nest is made of a kind of gelatinous saliva from the bird. The Chinese make soup of it.

Fri. Jan. 3rd

...We had a note from a Mr Tennant, the manager of a rubber plantation, saying that he would motor us out to see the plantation. He came about half an hour later and took us to his house about two miles away... and we went to look at the trees.

Rubber is a great industry here. The trees yield rubber from 6 or 7 years old to - they don't know how long as they have not had time yet to experiment. They have trees of 40 still yielding plentifully and showing no signs of decrease. Every morning they peel off a bit of the bark and the white liquid oozes through and is collected in a cup which is fastened underneath. Then in the afternoon they gather in all the cups and empty the liquid into large tubs containing a little acetic acid and water. The acid coagulates it into a huge elastic sort of lump that looks as if it would be delicious to eat, it is so white and creamy. We saw the big tubs and then Mr Tennant motored us out to the mill about 4 miles away. Here the rubber is put into numerous washing-machines which press it out into sheets, each machine making it thinner and thinner. Finally it is just a thin yellow sheet (called crape) perforated with holes. All the strips are then hung up to dry and then packed in boxes to send home. Rubber is a nice clean-looking industry. Of course there is not the least reason why there should be atrocities connected with it as in the Congo and South America. There is nothing in the industry to harm the coolies and nothing to make them dislike the work and be unwilling to take it up provided they are properly treated...

Sun. Jan. 5th

Read... It seems rather sad that in large places like Tavoy and Mergui where there are numbers of Eurasians and a good many English people there should be no English Clergyman except about once in 3 or 4 months...

Mon. Jan. 6th

Mrs Stevenson took us to see a man who makes buffalo horn into combs. We also went into a Chinese shop, but did not see anything very interesting. There are a great many Chinese in Mergui but there was a big fire a little while ago and a whole quarter burnt and many Chinese shops with it...

Tues. Jan. 7th

Percy and I went out to do a little sketch, but the sun was very hot and we had a whole crowd of children watching us which was not very pleasant. Po Tun, Percy's old boy, gave us a basket of large shells - some of them very pretty - on New Year's day. He also gave us a big iced cake and some almonds and oranges. Packed up... had dinner and then we went down to the jetty with the servants and crossed to the steamer which had come in that day. The phosphorescence in the water was wonderful. As the paddle touched the water it seemed to make a great splash of silver over it. Read and went to bed. The steamer set off sometime in the night.

Wed. Jan. 8th

Wrote letters. We reached the Anchorage about 9 o'clock and halted there to pick up the passengers and cargo from Tavoy...

Thurs. Jan. 9th

We got into Rangoon about 1 o'clock. We went in a gharry to the town and did some shopping and then came on to Insein. Inky (the dog) was very pleased to see me. He followed me about for some time and stayed in whatever room I was...

Fri. Jan. 10th

Unpacked - tidied up and talked to Ma Gyi. She was very interested to see all the mother-of-pearl we had got from Mergui. I gave her an ink-stand of mother-of-pearl that Po Tun had given us. It was too much carved to appeal to English taste. Ma Gyi was simply overjoyed with it and said she should give it to a Mandalay pongyi...

Tour in the Shan States, April and May 1920

Sat. April 23rd

Po Khin, Maung San Lun, Percy and I left Taunggyi with our own kit in a motor about 9.15. It was a glorious drive. We halted about 11 o'clock at Htam San for breakfast. A thunderstorm came on, so we sheltered a little while in one of the caves. The country after that was new to me.

We reached Mongpawn about 1.15 and Kawknoi about 2.30. We halted at the bungalow to borrow cups and drink coffee out of the thermos. It is perched right on the top of the mountains about 4,800 ft high and has a wonderful view. After that we crossed the summit about 5,000 and then descended into the Loilem valley, reaching the bungalow about 2.45.

Mon. April 25th

We had breakfast about 9 o'clock and then San Lun, Thein Pe and ourselves with a quantity of luggage were packed into a motor belonging to the Monkung Sawbwa which Mr Kingsley, the assistant superintendent, had asked him to send for us. It was a magnificent ride, but the road was very bad in places and it would not have done for a nervous person to be in the car. About 7 miles from Loilem we arrived at Pinlon and here the hain (headman) came out with about a dozen girls all bearing bouquets of flowers which I had to receive in the car. We were given water to drink out of a silver cup. The hain took us round the bazaar and we bought 2 very nice baskets for tying on one's back and a silver bowl to give as a wedding present to Mr Tew. Before we left, the hain gave us oranges, a pineapple, plantains and some jaggery sweets, (jaggery is raw sugar). The country was sometimes open and bare and sometimes well-wooded, but always beautiful.

The next place we reached was Naungleng and here again the headman came out with water and a few girls bearing flowers, also men beating gongs and drums and cymbals. At both places we had gold umbrellas held over us.

Unfortunately at 1.15 when we were nearing Laikhar, it began to rain heavily and the Ne-Ok (who is officiating Sawbwa as the son is a minor) and people with gold umbrellas who had come a long way out of the town to meet us had a very wet time. The chief had meant to bring all the school children with flowers, but the weather was too bad. We reached Laikhar about 2 o'clock. I was wet through although we had a shade over the motor. Our carts had not arrived but they came about 5 o'clock. We had tea and the chief who was a dear old man came to see us and brought cucumbers etc. It was a very nice little bungalow made of bamboo and wood - very new and clean. No crockery, of course, and only one bed, but we had brought our own things and others were lent us.

P. & I went for a walk after tea as it had cleared up. L. is very pretty, but not so pretty as Loilem. There is a big marsh in the middle of the town and a large pagoda painted red and gold with thitsi. The pagoda has some very fine iron gates from Mandalay. The town was very neat and tidy and what I noticed particularly was how fat and well-favoured the dogs look. I suppose it is because the Shans don't mind killing off the ones they don't want.

In the evening we had some reading, but we only had a lantern and some candles.

Tues. April 26th

After tea we went to call on the chief and his wife. They both speak Burmese, so we were able to get on; she was very nice. She has a dear little girl of 3 and we also saw one of the sons, a very nice-looking bright boy of 12. They presented us with a little basket and a walking-stick made of a root... The chief would not let us pay anything for our food or water or fuel or for the carts from Pinlong to Laikhar or from Laikhar to Möng Kung. All was given free and Thein Pe had 4 Shan girls hanging about fetching water and so on for him nearly all day.

We got off about 11 o'clock and had a lovely ride to Möng Kung tho' it was rather hot and we were going downhill most of the way. Laikhar is lower than Loilem and Möng Kung seems lower still. The road was very bad in places, but we got through all right. We reached Möng Kung about 2 o'clock. Our carts had arrived at 8 am. Po Khin said it was due to him, as he drove the bullocks himself and got them on quicker than the Shans do.

There was a hpongyi-pyan (monk's funeral) going on and everyone was there, so we did not get such a welcome as at Laikhar. The Möng Kung bungalow is very nice - made of wood and quite large and airy - it contained 2 tables and 2 chairs and 2 large green water-pots in the bathroom and that was all. Möng Kung is on a big open plateau surrounded by mountains and there is a fine breeze blowing a good part of the day. It is a lovely country.

The Sawbwa came to call about 3 o'clock with 2 sons and a daughter (about 9 years old)... He sent one of his cars for us and we went to the hpongyi-pyan about 5 o'clock and sat in a bamboo pandal with the Sawbwa. There was a huge ornamental car containing the priest's body and 2 ropes about 4 mile long were attached to each side and hundreds of men held the ropes and had a tug of war. It was really a remarkable sight. One side was the Sawbwa's, one the heir apparent's, tho' they did not pull themselves. Of course the sawbwa always has to win and there were far more men on his side. The car has to be pulled a long way before victory is obtained. There were trees marking the points, but the son seemed to have a longer distance to go than the Sawbwa.

Maung San Lun has heard that some years ago the son won and the Sawbwa was so angry that he kept on firing his gun into the trees and the people were frightened. I suppose he daren't fire at the people because of the British Raj.

Some of the men who were urging on the pulling were very amusing to watch, as they leapt about and threw up their hats and our hain who has escorted us from Pinlong kept taking off his orange gaumbaung (traditional hat) and whirling it about and kicking up his legs. We came away about 6 o'clock...

May 1st

The Sawbwa took us in his motor to Hma, a village about 6 miles out where they make the grey-green pottery. His own motor is a Buick. His sons and San Lun and others came in the other 2 cars.

The old Sawbwa is very kind but it gives one rather a horrid feeling that we are so much in his power. If he turned hostile it would be most difficult to get away as we should not be able to get carts or use his motor. We got home about 9.30...

After tea we went for a long walk round the marsh. It is very pretty down there, with the reflections of trees and mountains in the water. The hills round Möng Kung seem like dream mountains. They are always so blue, sometimes deep ultramarine, sometimes pale and misty. We met the sweetest little foal who let me stroke him, though he was rather nervous.

Mon. May 3rd

...We went to see the Sawbwa in his pandal and thank him for his kindness and offer to pay for the motor. He refused to take anything. We have not paid anything either for food or water or fuel.

He gave us a big roll of very nice Shan paper. The workers came earlier in the morning to show us their apparatus. They make the paper from the bark of a tree and it is strong, practically like cloth.

In the afternoon it began to rain and came down in torrents the rest of the day and night.

Tues. May 4th

The motor driver was very doubtful about the state of the road, but we thought it better to go on. Unfortunately it began to rain again. It was all right at first, as the road was good, but as we climbed up the red road through the pine forest the mud was very thick and we skidded terribly. Sometimes the car was practically sideways on. We were heavily loaded with Thein Pe and San Lun beside the driver and a good deal of luggage with us and it was horrid crossing a plain, where the road was narrow and steep banks on either side. We stuck finally in the mud and had to get out and try to tilt the car over. We got on some distance further to a village, but it was pouring with rain and the driver said he could not go on. He went to see if there were accommodation there and the headman said he would give up his hut. We sent a man back to Möng Kung to ask the Sawbwa to send carts and some food. We were very short as we had expected to reach Laikhar in 3 hours where our servants and stores would be waiting for us.

The driver said he could not get back unless the sun came out. The headman brought us out some cucumbers. Finally we persuaded the driver to try and get on to Khan-Sai-Sei as there was a zayat there. We did not want to turn the headman out and it is awkward staying in a village as there are no conveniences. P. & I walked and the motor went on about another 4 mile and finally stuck on a steep ascent where there were heaps of stones on the good side of the road. We managed to turn it back and decided to put up at the village, but the driver then said he could get back to Möng Kung and we thought it better to go. Percy & I decided to walk as we were very wet and I dreaded the skidding. We had come about 7 miles (from Möng Kung). We left about 10.30 and it was then about 1.30. It was a pouring wet walk and very heavy going in the thick mud and I was getting very tired. We saw a gee[3] and I think 2 wild cats. I was very glad when we met the car coming back to fetch us about 3 miles or so from Möng Kung.

When we got back to the bungalow, everything had been taken out. They had had to find the durwan and get him to unlock. Of course there was no water and no firewood and the Sawbwa's 2 chairs had been taken back to him, so we had to sit on the floor. However we were able to put on dry clothes and later on they got us hot water. There was difficulty about food as we had practically none and the chickens had been specially ordered from a Palaing village in the hills. However, in the end Thein Pe managed to get one, also eggs, so for the next two days we lived on chicken, eggs, rice and cucumber.

Later on the Sawbwa's son came round with 2 chairs, 2 biscuit tins, and a tin of butter and some candles. The Minister of Roads, a funny old man in a big Shan hat, also came round later and said he would see what he could do. He managed to get us some tea and I was very glad as I did not relish the idea of drinking water for every meal.

Wed. May 5th

My under-clothes were deep red with the mud of the roads. Percy tried to wash them, but they were still coffee colour. He had a fire put in the outhouse and spent half the day drying our clothes. It poured all day, so when I went outside I took off my shoes and stockings. We had meant to go off in carts at 4 am the next morning, but P. decided it was too bad, so we had to put off our going. Did painting, fancy-work, reading etc.

Thurs. May 6th

It turned out a beautiful day though still cloudy. We went out sketching by the river. Two men came with us to carry umbrellas

---

[3] A 'gee' is clearly an animal, but I have been unable to identify it.

and when they saw a lady bathing in the river without any clothes were very indignant, and shouted to her. She was a long way off on the other bank and it took some time to make her hear. We could not help being amused.

After breakfast went on with the piano-back. I was getting on fast owing to the rain. The Pinlong hain came back in the afternoon on horseback to see what had happened to us. He brought some of our tinned food. The Sawbwa came to see us about 2.30 and later on he sent for a motor to take us to a village about 1½ miles away where they make black pottery. He did not come with us.

It was very interesting. They had little tiny wheels and a great variety of tools and were very skilful. One old man with a very nice face made a beautiful pot in the shape of a gourd. I was anxious to get one, so they got me a finished one from the village. They said its value was 2 annas.

Fri. May 7th

We got up between 3 & 4 am and got off in the carts soon after 4. We gave 4Rs to the durwan who had been helping Thein Pe and 4Rs to the man who fetched our food and to the woman who fetched our water; our going back had given them all extra trouble and we had given nothing before. We had 3 carts. P. & I were in one with a few of our things and were quite comfortable. It was dark at first but dawn soon came and it was a lovely morning. About 7 o'clock when we had gone about 7 miles P. & I got out and walked. It was beautiful in the pine forests at that early hour. We walked some time and then I got back into the cart. P. walked all the way. We reached Khan-Sai-Su which is about 10 miles away and halted there for the day.

We had some tea about 1.30 and set off again about 2 pm. I rode for some time as it was very hot. All the time we were climbing up and down the wooded hills. I walked the last part of the way with P. and we reached Wankan about 6 pm (distance done in day 19 miles). There was quite a decent little bungalow, but half the roof of the bedroom was off. Fortunately it was a fine night.

We had no chairs and had to manage as we could. We were both very tired and Thein Pe was very stupid and did not try to make us comfortable.

The moon shone down on us in the night and the stars and there was a strong wind but it did not rain.

Sat. May 8th

We got up about 5 am and were off about 6 o'clock. Percy and I walked first of all and the hain came on foot behind us. We walked about 3 or 4 miles and then waited in a zayat for the carts and I got in. My bullocks went very fast as the driver made them trot and P. could not keep up with me. About 2 miles from Laikhar I met the Laikhar chief who had come on a pony, with an old state carriage, to meet us. He is a loveable old man. He told me he had been very anxious when we did not arrive, as he thought we might have got stuck and not been able to go forward or back and that we should be short of food. When Percy came up, we had to get into the carriage and drive into Laikhar. About 1 mile from the town we were met by men carrying gold umbrellas and drums and cymbals and an instrument like an oboe, and we had to process the rest of the way at a snail's pace with the band playing in front of us and men carrying the umbrellas above our heads. We reached the bungalow about 8.30 am and were very glad to see Po Khin again and our kit. We were very tired of having only Thein Pe who does not try to help.

There was a batch of letters waiting us sent by messenger from Loilem. We had been away from all letters for nearly a fortnight. After tea did sewing while Percy read aloud to me. He felt we must go on the next day although a Sunday, because of the time we had been. (Distance covered 10 miles).

Sun. May 9th

We let 3 carts go off early and kept Po Khin and one cart with us. We got off about 6 am. Percy and I walked with the hain behind us. We did not want him but he seemed to think it his duty. We had a climb after we had passed the lovely marsh at the foot of the hills.

Then the walking along the top of the hills was quite easy, so we went about 6 miles and sat under a tree as I wanted to get into the cart. However the hain said it was only 2 miles more to our camping-ground, so we went on. The sun was very hot and the last part was a very stiff climb. However we reached the zayat about 1 o'clock. I tried to draw Po Min, making unleavened cakes for our breakfast and the cart in the background. We have had no bread for ages as the cook does not seem to know how to make it and our potatoes ran out some days ago. However, Mrs Kingsley sent us some cauliflower and beetroot and carrot to Laikhar and we were very glad of it.

We had a very nice breakfast in the open zayat and then I went on with my painting and Percy read aloud to me a book on the Spirit. We set off again before 2 pm and had a very long stiff climb up the mountains. I rode all the way. Then we had a shorter descent and then our road lay through the valley till we got up into the open park country round Nawngleng. Everything is much prettier now as the rain had made the country green.

We reached Nawngleng about 4.30. It was quite a nice little bungalow. We strolled outside and gathered a few raspberries and then we sat in the compound and P. read to me. (Distance travelled 15 miles). It was a beautiful clear evening, but strangely enough it rained hard in the night and some came through onto our beds, so we had to move them.

Mon. May 10th

The 3 carts went off early. We got off soon after 6 am. Percy did not come with me as he was going on a pony to see a pottery village with the hain. I rode in the cart and Po Khin walked the whole way and outstripped us by a lot. We had 11 miles to go and the boy who was driving did not stir up the bullocks so I did not get in till about 10.45. Percy arrived about ½ hour later. Ping Long is very pretty too and there is quite a nice bungalow..

After breakfast did Burmese and writing. It started to rain heavily again. The Laikhar chief gave us a very nice black and gold Kentung bowl. After tea I did some painting while Percy read to me. Then we went out for a walk.

Tues. May 11th

We started sketching a house and then Mr Kingsley arrived from Loilem on horseback so we gave up and went with him to the bazaar where they were going to have an auction and sell the right to collect the stall rents, the beef licence etc. It was quite amusing to watch. It was carried on partly in Burmese, partly in Shan, partly in Hindustani. Mr Kingsley speaks all 3. He seems a very nice man, a Eurasian of the best type, very keen on his work...

We set off in bullock carts and reached Loilem about 4.30. It is only 6 or 7 miles... We had to open up the Forest bungalow. There were only tables and chairs in it, but the Kingsleys lent us furniture. We went round there for tea. They have a delightful garden overlooking the lake. Mrs Kingsley is very nice and kind (also Eurasian)... Mr Kingsley and I went out in the boat... He showed me how to cast and I caught one small fish. It was just glorious on the lake. The light and colours were wonderful... Went back to the Kingsleys for dinner... Mr and Mrs Kingsley sang songs...

Wed. May 12th

Read, wrote letters. Painted. After tea we went out fishing with the Kingsleys... P. & I went to their house again for dinner and had more music...

Fri. May 14th

Wrote letters, did Burmese etc. Went to the Kingsleys again for Breakfast... After tea I tried to finish my sketch but it had rained a good deal and the light was different from the day before. However I got on quite well... We went to the Kingsleys for dinner again and had some more music. They had really been most kind to us all through our visit.

Sat. May 15th

Thein Pe and Po Khin and P. & I went off in a motor about 7 am. The others had gone in bullock carts before. We had a lovely ride to Taung-gyi. We stopped at Htam-San as before to eat our breakfast. We reached the Circuit House about 1 pm...

Mon. May 17th (?)

Percy went to play chess with Mr Lee and I went for a long walk with Mrs Lee... It was quite dark when we got in. Went to dinner at the Thorntons. Mrs Thornton was telling us that one day at Lashio she came out of her bedroom to the drawing room at chota time and saw a Sikh orderly in spotless clothes standing opposite. She went back hastily as she was only lightly clad and then realised she did not know the man and wondered who he could be. She made enquiries all over the house as to whether anyone had seen a strange orderly about, but no one had. At last an old mali (gardener) was asked and he said, "Oh yes, he knew him". He was an old orderly who had served the house many years and when he died had said he would never leave it. He (the mali) often saw him. Mrs T. had never heard the story before, so could not have imagined it...

Fri. May 21st

We had 2 motors for Po Min, Po Khin, the luggage and ourselves. One was the new grey Chevrolet we had had to Loilem. The other servants and kit had gone before.

We had a great fuss over bullock carts. The contractor would not provide them unless we paid R22 cash down. Mg San Lun refused and got 2 other carts not belonging to the contractor and started off. But the contractor came and stopped them near the bazaar and said they were not to go on till they received R22, and he loaded up one which was not full, with his own kit. Mg San Lun had a great trouble, but at last he got them to go on. I don't know what influence the contractor had over them.

We had a glorious breezy ride to Loian. Po Khin and Percy's kit stopped at Aungban and my kit and Po Min came on to Loian. Percy saw us in (to Mrs Browne's guest house) and then went on to Maymyo which he had to visit on business. Only Mrs Warth and a Mrs Jacob are at Loian now. I had a room upstairs inside the house for which I was glad. I did not want to sleep alone in a mud hut...

Mr Ben Browne, the artist, came to tea which we had in the garden. He did not go till about 7 o'clock... After dinner Mrs Warth and I sat talking in the drawing-room... Some of the visitors seem to be very disagreeable and grumble about everything. Mrs Lee said the food was rotten (I suppose from hearsay) but it is really very good and we have very nice mutton and delicious bread and butter.

Mrs Warth is full of her anxieties over Dorothy whom she seems to have put to a little old-fashioned private school where she is not at all happy.

Sat. May 22nd

...Mrs Browne, Mrs Warth, Clayton and I went on the bullock-tonga to Kalaw to see Mr Browne's pictures. We walked up to his house which has a fine situation. We were there about 2 hours and saw about 60 pictures I should think of Taunggyi, the Irrawaddy, the Shwegyin creek, sunsets in the lake and so on. His great feature seems to be colour rather than form. I thought his Taung-gyi cherry trees almost too glorious... After tea I went down to the pond and started a picture of the crag reflected in the water...

Wed. May 26th

After tea went down to the pond and finished my sketch. There was a beautiful light.

One morning Mrs Browne showed us some rough paintings of the hill country where she worked and told us about her life. She was born in the Himalaya and worked as a missionary with the American Mission in the plains. Then she and a lady doctor worked among the Bhotirs (?) hill people. They sometimes crossed mountain passes 19,000 ft high. They were very anxious to go into Tibet and at last went disguised as Bhotir women as far as a trading post. When the officials found out they sent them back, but they were able first to give medical aid and distribute gospels. After the British expedition to Lhasa, as the British behaved so well and paid for everything, the Tibetans were anxious to let the English into the country, but we wanted to keep it closed, so refused. However Mrs Browne was able to go in after that quite easily and even got as far as Monsorova, the sacred lake, which is supposed to be the abode of gods. If the view is clear when you ascend the mountain from which you get a view of the lake, it means there is no sin in your heart. Fortunately they had a very clear view.

The Bhotirs seem a very strange people. All the unmarried girls from about 12 or 13 years upwards collect together at night in a Club-house and stay there all night weaving. Of course the youths sometimes come and see them there and if a youth wants to marry a girl, he and his comrades come and carry her off by force from the Club-house.

Thurs. May 27th

Mrs Warth asked me to go for a walk with her and took me further than I wanted to go, so we did not get in till 9.30... At last about 10.7 I managed to get off and walked very fast down the drive and soon after I heard the train and had to run all the rest of the way to the station. Even then it arrived before me. It came in between 10.15 and 10.20 by Loian time... Po Min had gone with the kit in Miss Browne's bullock cart to Kalaw and met me there. I had a hot journey down to Thazi. I had some tea there and waited for Percy's train. He had been in Maymyo on business. We were fortunate in getting a large compartment to ourselves to Rangoon and had a fairly cool journey.

Fri. May 28th

Reached Rangoon and went to Watson's for the motor car which had been painted green and which they said was ready but we had to wait 2½ hours before they could make it go! Motored to Insein, had breakfast, unpacked etc.

CHAPTER XIII

RETURN TO ENGLAND

My parents left Burma finally in April 1924. My father had enough leave owing to him to be able to add a year's service to the nineteen he had already completed and so qualify for his government pension. Ostensibly he was taking an extended vacation, but he made it plain that he would not be returning. Apart from a brief visit in 1930, when he was spending a year working for British Petroleum in India, he never saw Burma again.

Part of the reason for giving up work which had been deeply satisfying to him to endure all the uncertainty of job-hunting in England in the 1920's was undoubtedly the birth of his children. I was born in January 1922 not in Burma but in Kendal where Theo and Mildred were now well-established. By 1924 Doris was pregnant again. Sooner or later, for health and educational reasons, the children would have to be sent to England to stay with relations and grow up away from their parents. This neither she nor her husband was prepared to accept.

But there were other reasons - disappointment and disillusionment among them. The political climate of Burma was changing: nationalist movements were gathering impetus. It was a long time yet before the Empire on which "the sun never sets" would fade into history, but, looking back, the signs were already there. The diaries do not exhibit any deep political awareness, either because this did not exist or because they are purely a domestic record, but they reflect from 1920 onwards a certain unrest. In March of that year when they returned from furlough in England, Percy and Doris took an acquaintance to the Shwedagon pagoda and walked round, "though we were rather afraid we might be stopped as we were wearing shoes and there has been this political agitation to make Europeans go barefoot to the pagodas." Our sympathies now are with the Burmese. Why should foreigners not respect their customs? But undoubtedly the demand was political, rather than purely religious, crystallizing a change in attitude, a growing resentment of the British Raj.

In December 1920 the Schools' Strike began, part of the nationalist pressure to secure for Burma the same degree of self-government as India had been granted after the Great War. This too earns a comment in the diaries though not much understanding. "Rangoon College Students and many of the boys' schools are on strike, Rangoon College because they don't like the new University Bill, the Baptist High School Buddhist boys because the school was open on a Buddhist holiday. There seems to be a certain amount of intimidation going on. I hope the strike won't affect us, but these things spread so quickly." In February of the same year Doris mentions a strike among the Railway traffic staff and on March 19th she reports, "A Buddhist priest has been arrested for sedition, so the Burmans intend having a hartal (strike) on Monday and preventing people selling in the bazaars and gharries plying etc." Later in the year when she was staying near Loilem she records, "There is a serious railway strike on, manoeuvred by Mr Patal, president of the Insein Municipality. He quarrelled with Mr Robertson and told obvious lies and the European members (chiefly railway officers) resisted him and the municipality are not likely to re-elect him and he wants to have his revenge on the railway officials. Insein is an experimental Municipal Council run by Orientals and non-official Europeans. Mr Patal has always been respected, (except by the Burmans who don't like him) but he showed up his character in the dispute. He is pretending that the railway question is white versus black. Mr Craig is getting the brunt of it, as he is unpopular through want of geniality. He is certainly not anti-black at all and railway wages have been increased a good deal since 1914." These troubles did not immediately affect the Engineering School in Insein or Mr Morris's work but their shadow lay upon it and upon Anglo-Burmese relationships in general. On January 10th, 1921, for instance, there is this comment about the exhibition of art and craft which Mr Morris organised each year. "I don't think the exhibition was as successful as usual. There were certainly fewer Europeans; possibly the strike kept them away and made them disinclined to deal with Burmans." My parents recognised that Burma could not remain under British rule for ever, but, like many well-disposed Europeans, they regarded the Burmese as children to be educated gradually into political adulthood, certainly not as an oppressed nation to be liberated.

I know that my father was completely sincere in his belief that he was working for the good of Burma and its people. But he was, of course, a child of his time. It is ironic that it was his trust in the clerk San Lun, his treating of him as he would have done any junior, Asian or European, that was a factor in ending his easy unselfconscious relationship with the Burmans. San Lun who had accompanied them so often on tours, who had helped his wife with her Burmese, whose grief at his child's death he had shared, whose debts he had paid - Percy, overworked and gullible, never suspected that San Lun was changing figures on the cheques he brought to him. Carelessly, unquestioningly, he signed as required. When the embezzlement was discovered, San Lun at first acknowledged his guilt, but later he retracted, maintaining that Mr Morris, having stolen the money himself, had asked his clerk to carry the blame and, because he was such a kind employer, San Lun had agreed to do so. The case was heard first before a Burmese judge who found against the defendant and sentenced him to five years and six months imprisonment, but, on appeal, the British judge, according to the diary, "let him off the 5 years as he said Percy's evidence was incredible. The 6 months went to a different court and the judge there said there was no doubt about San Lun's guilt."

In 1923, the "New Burma", a militantly nationalist paper, began a series of scurrilous attacks on the Engineering School and its principal. The Morrises thought that, perhaps, San Lun had joined the Staff. Certainly the paper took up his case, arguing that as he was "let off... obviously he did not take the money. Who did? and goes on, of course, to suggest Mr Morris." Another article complained that the boys had been given bad fish to eat and that the Principal had driven them starving to work. In fact, according to the diary, when it was discovered the fish was "off", he had ordered the cook to open tins for them at his own expense. On another occasion a rumour was circulated that the curry contained beef and the students refused, therefore, to eat it. There was no particular reason why Buddhists should not eat beef if they ate meat at all, but it was forbidden to Indian students on religious grounds and the Burmese did not wish to appear less fastidious. Analysis showed that the meat in the curry was mutton or possibly goat, but the harm had been done. It is sadly evident that the principal no longer had the full confidence and cooperation of his Burmese pupils. For example in

December 1923 at the school sports and entertainment, "Except for a song by a Karen master and conjuring tricks by a Karen boy it was all Anglo-Indian talent. The Burmese boys would not join in. I don't think it will be possible to do anything with the Burmese students till Tyaw Tun leaves. He has excited a thoroughly bad spirit among them."

Tyaw Tun was a member of the teaching staff, "thoroughly disloyal and anti-British," who had hoped to be principal of the school when Mr Morris was appointed in 1912. According to Ma Gyi he was "the leader of this conspiracy to damage Percy's reputation... and Kun Gyi is his Lieutenant and about seven other boys are helping. Percy has always thought Kun Gyi to be rather a nice boy and he does not know whether to believe it." On November 4th 1923 the diary has this entry; "the scurrilous articles in the New Burma still continue and I suppose will do until we leave the country. It is a definite attempt to make Percy resign. Tyaw Tun is supposed to have said that he would outlast Percy and he is due to retire in March 1925."

The school sports of 1923 were intended to be particularly splendid as the Governor of Burma, Sir Harcourt Butler, was visiting the school. Burma now, like India, had its own Governor whereas in the past the post had been that of Lieutenant Governor; so far the Schools Strike of 1920 had succeeded. Unfortunately these sports were the occasion of one of those mistakes which have repercussions out of all proportion to their apparent importance. Mr Morris had offered tea at his house to the Governor and his party; his superior, Mr McKenna, Commissioner for Development, had said he would come and bring with him Maung Gyi, one of the three ministers appointed under the Government Reform scheme whereby some higher government posts were to be held by Burmans. Maung Gyi had already met Mr and Mrs Morris and impressed them favourably. Unfortunately Percy foolishly assumed that Mr McKenna would be responsible for the invitation to tea. This was never sent. When Maung Gyi turned up uninvited at the sports ground there was no one to meet him since he was expected at the house. As soon as they realised what had happened, Doris and Percy apologised separately and immediately and followed this up next day by a letter; but in vain. Maung Gyi, perhaps uncertain of his status, felt his dignity had been affronted: he had not been treated with the same respect as that accorded to the British Raj. "He had to walk 40 yards or so unattended when he got out of his motor in order to reach the pandal where Mr Shaw received him." He demanded that the principal of the engineering school should be "severely censured." The affair was finally smoothed over but the bitterness remained. "We thought better things of Maung Gyi, but I suppose he wants to play the oriental despot."

Hard as these misrepresentations and misunderstandings were to bear, the ending of his professional ambitions must have been harder. The Director of Industries post, which in 1917 he had felt so sure he would be offered that he was discussing with Doris whether he should accept it or not, went in 1919 to Basil Holme when the Morrises were on furlough in England. Percy was asked to be sub-director, "I suppose," his wife remarks, "to do all the work and supply all the information." It was therefore Basil Holme who was to organise the Burma section of a big imperial exhibition to be held in London in 1923, a task my father coveted. After the San Lun affair, his honorary post as Provincial Art Officer was removed from him, presumably because it was felt Mr Morris had been too busy and too often absent to supervise his clerk adequately. The post, under a different name, was given to Mr G. E. Harvery, the historian - "with very good pay, of course," is Doris's caustic comment. Even before this he had been disappointed when all his efforts in England to interest British markets in Burmese craft goods had come "to nothing because Government let all his proposals slide." Looking back, that year's leave of 1919-1920 which they had longed for so ardently must have appeared a disastrous water-shed in their Burmese career.

But the "real thing", according to the diary, was the school and there pressures had been mounting for some time as the lack of manpower caused by the war was not repaired. "For about four years he has been writing saying he must have staff and since we got back from leave (about a year ago) he has written most urgent letters saying there would be a crisis, but still nothing done... Mr Gibson came during six months leave from his ship and wanted to stay if the post was made permanent. Percy wrote and wrote and then the leave was up and nothing sanctioned." In this year (1921) the position was made more desperate by the loss even of such staff as he had. "Mr Pilley had been offered a post in Madras, Mr Nayagum has to have a year's medical leave, Tyaw Tun chooses to take leave." By July 30th the situation was such that "Percy has had to send the senior boys away for three months as there is no one to teach them. They will try to do practical work and come back from January to March instead."

Arthur Percy Morris was appointed as principal of the Insein Engineering institute in 1912 as a young man of 32. He had then been working in Burma for seven years, first attached to the Irrigation circle and, in 1911, to the Rangoon Construction Division in charge of construction work at the General hospital. When he took over the school there were only twenty-six students and, of those, only three were Burmese. In fact the Government was considering closing the place down. The new principal laboured hard and successfully to increase the recruitment among Burmans: he gave time, energy and imagination to fostering the school and convincing the authorities that it had a future. It must have been bitter indeed when his work there seemed to be crumbling.

Not surprisingly the strain told on his health. The climax came in June 1921. "Percy came home at breakfast and said he could not go on any longer and went to bed. It is really mental and physical exhaustion, but he has also had diarrhoea hanging about him 2 or 3 months. He has really been working up for this since we came back from leave and it is partly due to disappointment and partly to overwork." Dr Taylor, who was also advising his wife in her pregnancy, put him on a diet of milk and plantains. He reported a month later "that Percy really ought to go home as he is not fit. He has cured his diarrhoea and he can cure his malaria, but beyond that he can do nothing. He is afraid if he goes to a hill station, he will go on worrying about his work."

In September 1921, Doris left her husband behind in Burma because it was thought advisable for her to go to England for the birth of her first child. From her return in April 1922, the diaries tend to focus on the baby, worries about her health, delight in her development and behaviour. Yet, even apart from the record of her husband's misfortunes, a sour note is discernible. She mentions a lecture which Mr Harvey gave in September 1923 dealing with the events leading up to the Anglo-Burmese war of 1823 and comments, "The extraordinary conceit and arrogance of the Burmese was very apparent in their letters." Mr Harvey was later to come under attack as a partial and pro-British historian: already both sides were showing a hypersensitivity, betrayed, as far as the imperialists were concerned, by their anxious self-justifications. Mrs Morris had no sympathy with the nationalists and regarded Sir Harcourt Butler as weak in dealing with their demands. In December 1923 she writes: "There is a movement of the Nationalist party to put the new university under popular control instead of letting the course of study etc be directed by experts. Sir Harcourt Butler, the Governor, is giving in. He is supposed not to care about what happens in Burma as he wanted to be made Governor of Madras." Even Ma Gyi comes under criticism. She is idle. "We had to send for Dr Taylor as Ma Gyi had a swollen knee and could not walk. He said it was only-housemaid's knee and nothing serious. He says people sometimes get it who do nothing and Ma Gyi certainly does nothing. She sits practically all day except for just taking Sylvia little walks." It is perhaps a little inconsistent with this comment that when Ma Gyi went off to Mandalay for Aung Houet's initiation ceremony the inconvenience of being left alone with a small child is mentioned! And when the parting came in April 1924 the affectionate emotionalism of the two servants does not entirely escape censure. "Po Khin and Ma Gyi have been feeling the separation intensely for some time and been inclined to sit and mope all the time instead of trying to help us (so different from a faithful English servant)..."

All this seems sadly far from the "Mr Morris" of the Taunggyi holiday who "is so nice with the Burmans and has great faith in their possibilities and believes that there is a future before the Burmese craftsman instead of thinking him quite useless as many people do." But it falsifies the picture to over-emphasise the bitterness. Although Percy Morris had little patience with this "foolish nationalism", he retained his affection for Burma and the Burmese, and by some, at least, this affection was returned. Perhaps, in view of all the friction, it may not have been possible to accept the farewell celebrations and the flowery address printed in gold lettering with which the Principal and his wife were presented without a twinge of wry suspicion. But there could be no doubt of the sincerity of the four Burmese craftsman who, when he visited Burma six years later as a private person and without any possible influence on their careers, gave him a fine silver vase, "with the request that you will be pleased to accept this in memory of your kindness to us while you were in charge of Arts and Handicrafts of Burma. We beg further to state that we are always remembering your kindness and sympathy towards us in your capacity as a Provincial Art Officer and that this humble present from us will always remind your goodselves of the master-craftsmen of Rangoon."

Letters passed, too, for some years between Ma Gyi and Mrs Morris. Three of these survive, the last handwritten though whether by Ma Gyi or a letter-writer is impossible to tell. In September 1926 her letter, which still expresses a hope that Mr and Mrs Morris will return to Burma, congratulates her old mistress on the birth of her third child; "It is with the feelings of happiness accompanied by joy that I am to convey you the receipt of your letter, bringing the welcome news of your birth of a boy. Since you left us in Burma we have been engaged in constant prayers for God to fulfil your long felt want for a boy. Now we are greatly please at heart to learn from your letter that you are blessed with a boy and I think, your long felt wish has now been fulfilled by our prayers."

Early in 1926 my father at last found employment under the London County Council on the Downham housing-estate, the construction of which was likely to take some years. The family moved to Beckenham in Kent. Here in 1928 their last child was born. And here, from time to time, ex-pupils or colleagues, Burmese and Indian, visited us and were comforted by my mother's curry, with its reminder of home, a reminder reinforced by the many Burmese artefacts which the house held. Most of the visitors came once only, perhaps for an overnight stay, perhaps for a meal. I can just remember a bearded Sikh whose turban is imprinted on my mind. But there is only one I recall as an individual, a young man known to us as Maung Maung (roughly the equivalent of Mr Mister in English) who was a student of architecture at Liverpool University. He came frequently, sometimes with little warning, between 1930 and 1933. At some point he must have acquired a motorbike for on one exciting Sunday afternoon he gave us children and the girl-next-door rides in a side-car round the quiet suburban streets where the slumbrous after-dinner peace was disturbed by our progress. A complaint to the police ended that particular entertainment. I cannot help wondering now whether my parents knew of his intention or were they too grateful to have their brood taken off their hands to enquire what he meant to do with them? I have a dim memory of meal-time discussions and polite arguments in which host and guest took opposite sides. My impression is that it was politics and the future of

Burma which was under debate, though I was too young to understand and not much interested. But one last glimpse remains vivid and will serve as an endpiece for this book.

I suppose it must have been at the conclusion of Maung Maung's final visit to our house. I know I was standing in the hall with the door open into our dining-room, where the black lacquered table and side-board my father had had made demonstrated his belief in the virtues of "thitsi" as a heat-resistant anti-corrosive material and his faith in Burmese craftsmen. I saw Maung Maung, the sophisticated young man in his western dress, get down on his knees before my father and make a profound shiko, putting his forehead to the floor. My father, much moved, said to him, "You know I like you to keep you own customs."

In the Burma of today there is much that my father would not approve. He must have been saddened when, in 1942, the nationalists fought with the Japanese to drive out the British: he died before they changed sides and joined the allies. He would, I think, have been doubtful about the wisdom of independence in 1947, and feared - events show with some justice - for the future of minority groups, Shans, Karens, Chins. Almost certainly he would have been horrified by the coup of 1962 and the establishment of a communist regime. But there is one aspect of modern Burma in which he would have delighted: the determination, against all the flood of Westernisation with its commerce and culture and technology, to keep their own customs.